9780405115356

D1712745

THE STOIC CREED

THE STOIC CREED

WILLIAM L. DAVIDSON

ARNO PRESS
A New York Times Company
New York • 1979

Editorial Supervision: MARIE STARECK

———

Reprint Edition 1979 by Arno Press Inc.

Reprinted by arrangement with T. & T. Clark Limited,
    Publishers
Reprinted from a copy in The University of Illinois
    Library

MORALS AND LAW IN ANCIENT GREECE
ISBN for complete set: 0-405-11529-6
See last pages of this volume for titles.

Manufactured in the United States of America

———

Library of Congress Cataloging in Publication Data

Davidson, William Leslie, 1848-1929.
    The Stoic creed.

    (Morals and law in ancient Greece)
    Reprint of the 1907 ed. published by T. & T. Clark,
Edbinburgh in series: Religion in literature and life.
    1. Stoics. I. Title. II. Series. III. Series:
Religion in literature and life.
B528.D3   1979   188   78-19341
ISBN 0-405-11535-0

THE STOIC CREED

Printed by

MORRISON & GIBB LIMITED

FOR

T. & T. CLARK, EDINBURGH

LONDON : SIMPKIN, MARSHALL, HAMILTON, KENT, AND CO. LIMITED
NEW YORK : CHARLES SCRIBNER'S SONS

THE STOIC CREED

BY

WILLIAM L. DAVIDSON, M.A., LL.D.

PROFESSOR OF LOGIC AND METAPHYSICS IN THE UNIVERSITY OF ABERDEEN
AUTHOR OF "THE LOGIC OF DEFINITION"
"THEISM AS GROUNDED IN HUMAN NATURE" "CHRISTIAN ETHICS"
ETC. ETC.

EDINBURGH : T. & T. CLARK, 38 GEORGE STREET

1907

"Our individual natures are all parts of universal nature. Wherefore, the chief good is to live in accordance with nature, which is the same thing as in accordance with one's own nature and with the universal nature."

CHRYSIPPUS (in Diogenes Laërtius).

"Be like the headland, on which the billows dash themselves continually; but it stands fast, till about its base the boiling breakers are lulled to rest."

MARCUS AURELIUS.

PREFACE

——◆——

THESE chapters are a contribution towards the exposition and just appreciation of Stoicism—which, whatever its defects, was a system of lofty principles, illustrated in the lives of many noble men. The subject has perennial fascination ; and there are not wanting signs that it appeals with special attractiveness to cultured minds at the present day. It has both speculative and practical value ; its analysis of human nature and its theory of knowledge, no less than its ethical teaching, giving insight into the problems of the universe and the right mode of guiding life. As an important stage in the march of philosophical thought, and as a luminous chapter in the history of natural theology, it solicits our attention, and will repay our study.

Ample quotations are designedly made from the Stoic writers themselves and from ancient Greek and Latin expositions. Responsibility for the translation of most of the passages must be accepted by myself. One exception, however, has to be made. The passages from the *Meditations* of Marcus Aurelius are reproduced from the fine rendering of Dr. Rendall in his *Marcus Aurelius To Himself*.

Hearty acknowledgments are made of the friendly services of Mr. R. S. Rait, Fellow, Tutor, and Dean of New College, Oxford, in going over the work in proof.

WILLIAM L. DAVIDSON.

THE UNIVERSITY, ABERDEEN,
March 1907.

TABLE OF CONTENTS

Section A.—MOULDING INFLUENCES, AND LEADERS OF THE SCHOOL

CHAPTER I

THE SOCRATIC IMPULSE

CHAPTER II

THE STOIC MASTERS AND THEIR WRITINGS

II

SECTION B.—STOIC SCIENCE AND SPECULATION

CHAPTER III

CONCEPTION OF PHILOSOPHY

I

II

FROM π TO θ

LEADING CHARACTERISTICS

THE CONSTITUENT SCIENCES

CHAPTER IV

LOGIC: THEORY OF KNOWLEDGE

I

CHAPTER V

PHYSICS : NATURE, GOD, SOUL

I

II

III

IV

CHAPTER VI

THE EPICUREAN CONTRAST

I

II

III

IV

Section C.—MORALITY AND RELIGION

CHAPTER VII

PREDECESSORS OF THE STOICS IN ETHICS

I

CHAPTER VIII

ETHICS: EXPOSITION

CHAPTER X

ETHICS: DEFECTS

I

II

III

CHAPTER XI

THEOLOGY AND RELIGION

I

THE WORLD ONE AND PERFECT

PROVIDENCE : OPTIMISM

IS GOD PERSONAL OR IMPERSONAL ?

CHAPTER XII

PRESENT-DAY VALUE OF STOICISM

I

II

III

THE STOIC CREED

——◆——

Section A.—MOULDING INFLUENCES, AND LEADERS OF THE SCHOOL

CHAPTER I

THE SOCRATIC IMPULSE

> " First Socrates,
> Who, firmly good in a corrupted state,
> Against the rage of tyrants single stood,
> Invincible ! calm Reason's holy law,
> That voice of God within th' attentive mind,
> Obeying, fearless, or in life or death :
> Great moral teacher ! wisest of mankind ! "
>
> Thomson.

I

ALL the Greek philosophies that have permanently influenced the world attach themselves ultimately to Socrates—not least that of the Stoics,[1] whose founder was first drawn to philosophy by the *Memorabilia* of Xenophon (see Diogenes Laërtius, vii. 3), and which reproduced as its fundamental features the leading

---

[1] The name " Stoic " comes from Stoa Poecile or Painted Porch at Athens, in which Zeno, the founder, lectured.

characteristics of Socrates, namely, his ethical spirit, his religious reverence, his psychological standpoint, his regard for experience and concrete fact, and his distinctively practical cast of mind. There are differences, of course, and very marked ones too—seen most in the speculative tendencies of the Stoics and their interest in the science of nature ; but the inspiration is undoubted. And so the subject of Stoicism is best introduced by some consideration of Socrates and the Socratic impulse.

This consideration may very well, for the purpose in hand, concern itself with the four points of (1) the relation of Socrates to the pre-Socratic philosophers, (2) his distinctive position, (3) his relation to the Sophists, and (4) his personal character.

II

The study of mind may, in a general sense and with necessary qualifications, chiefly with the qualification that Socrates was in part anticipated by the Sophists, be said to date from Socrates (B.C. 469 to 399). Previously to his time, no doubt, there was much speculation and eager questioning of a philosophical kind among the Greeks, but for the most part it centred in external nature or the material universe— its structure and constitution, the phenomena of change or flux exhibited by it, its being or reality ; and man himself was interpreted from the side of the universe, as a part of nature. The Ionic or Physical philosophers (Thales, Anaximander, etc.) occupied themselves with the examination and investigation of the world, and regarded it as the end and aim of philosophy to achieve a cosmogony or physical explanation of the cosmos. In this way, they were all naturally materialists, and took simply a mechanical view of things. Their great quest was for the material ἀρχή or first principle of existence—the primitive stuff or matter out of which the world was formed ; Thales (B.C. 640 to 550) finding it in water, Anaximenes in air, Heracleitus in fire. But if the first principle of things was material, so too must be all that is dependent on it: so too must be the human soul, which was variously conceived as fire, air, breath. Mental facts and processes, accordingly,— consciousness itself, sensation, intellection, volition,— were interpreted materially. Parmenides, the Eleatic, laid down the doctrine that like acting upon like is the cause of sensation. This doctrine Empedocles (born about 500 B.C.) accepted, and, combining it with his own special teaching that man, like the universe, consists of the four elements fire, air, earth, water, proceeded to explain thereby sense-perception in all its forms. Effluvia or emanations (ἀπόρροιαι) from the different external bodies enter man through pores (πόροι), and, like being recognized by like (fire by fire, water by water, etc.), give rise to what we know respectively as the sensations of sight, hearing, taste, smell. All is explained by material effluxes and pores, and the recognition of like by like (ἡ γνῶσις τοῦ ὁμοίου τῷ ὁμοίῳ). This dominance of materialism is specially obvious in the Atomic philosophy, represented by Democritus (born about 460 B.C.), the doctrines of which we shall see, later on, in their full development, when we come to the psychology of Epicurus. Even Anaxagoras (born about 500 B.C.), who was probably

the first of the Greek philosophers to attain to the
conception of mind or νοῦς as the explanatory term
of existence, did not put this conception to any very
effective use. Striking, indeed, was his utterance,
"All things were together ; then mind came and set
them in order (πάντα χρήματα ἦν ὁμοῦ· εἶτα νοῦς ἐλθὼν
αὐτὰ διεκόσμησε)," [1] but its efficiency depended on the
application of it ; and, unfortunately, Anaxagoras put
it forth only in a tentative way, as a shy, philosophical
suggestion of design in the universe, rather than as
a firmly-grasped all-explanatory principle. Aristotle
tells us (*Met.* i. 4) that "Anaxagoras uses his Intelligence simply as a device to create the world where-
withal ; or when he is hard pressed to say why it must
be necessarily as it is, then again he drags it in : in all
other cases he would credit anything and everything
rather than Intelligence with being the cause of phenomena." And it is the bitter complaint of Socrates in
the *Phædo*, in a passage that may very well have been
autobiographical, that when he (Socrates) went to the
writings of Anaxagoras to be instructed in his teleological principles, he was put off with a discourse on
the secondary and physical causes of things,—indeed,
on "the conditions" of things instead of "the causes,"
—and gives as a concrete example his own present case
of calmly sitting awaiting his fate in prison in place of
making his escape, as his friends counselled him to do.
"I might compare him," he says, "to a person who
began by maintaining generally that mind is the cause
of the actions of Socrates, but who, when he endeavoured to explain the causes of my several actions in

[1] See Diogenes Laërtius, ii. 6.

detail, went on to show that I sit here because my body is made up of bones and muscles ; and the bones, as he would say, are hard, and have joints which divide them, and the muscles are elastic, and they cover the bones, which have also a covering or environment of flesh and skin which contains them ; and as the bones are lifted at their joints by the contraction or relaxation of the muscles, I am able to bend my limbs, and this is why I am sitting here in a curved posture—that is what he would say ; and he would have a similar explanation of my talking to you, which he would attribute to sound, and air, and hearing, and he would assign ten thousand other causes of the same sort, forgetting to mention the true cause, which is, that the Athenians have thought fit to condemn me, and accordingly I have thought it better and more right to remain here and undergo my sentence. . . . There is surely a strange confusion of causes and conditions in all this." [1]

III

It was the characteristic of Socrates that he turned men's thoughts from the study of matter and mechanical causes to self-reflection or the study of mind : as Cicero puts it rhetorically, in the *Tusculan Disputations* (v. 4), " Socrates was the first to call down philosophy from heaven, and to place it in cities, and to introduce it into the houses of men, compelling men to examine into life and morals, and good and evil." This he regarded as a divine vocation, as a work imposed upon him by the Deity, in discharging which he made prominent the position that self-knowledge, " know thyself" (γνῶθι

[1] Jowett's trans.

σεαυτόν [1]), is man's first duty and chief concern. This
meant, on its negative side, that attention must be with-
drawn from physics and physical speculations—from
natural science and cosmology; and, on its positive
side, that it must be concentrated on the mind—"the
proper study of mankind is man." But this is, in part
at least, psychology. Not, however, that Socrates, like
Aristotle, worked out a psychology, or did much
towards the scientific exposition of the province and
functions of mind generally. His interest lay mainly
in Ethics and Politics, not in mental science; and what
we owe to him is, (1) the impulse to the determinate
and exact consideration of ethical and social phenomena,
and (2) the clear presentation and systematic application of the true method of psychological investigation,—namely, the inductive method—comparison and
generalization—leading to clear concepts and precise
definitions. In this second particular, he is the father
of the Logic of Consistency, and, in especial, of that
province of Logic known to moderns as Definition
and Classification. It was in direct contact, however,
with living minds, not by the dogmatic enunciation of
abstract formulæ, that he exercised his art; and how
he proceeded was thus :—

Through dexterity and skill in Dialectic, by persistent
oral cross-questioning of his fellow-citizens in the
market-place, in the workshops, in the schools, under
pretence of his own ignorance (εἰρωνεία), thereby
bringing ideas to the birth (ἡ μαιευτικὴ τέχνη), he
elicited and enforced two things, — (a) men's in-

---

[1] In the *Memorabilia* of Xenophon (iii. 9), he puts this from the
obverse side, "Be not ignorant of thyself" (μὴ ἀγνόει σεαυτόν).

veterate ignorance, or conceit of knowledge that they
did not possess ; and (*b*) the true way of one's attaining
knowledge, namely, by becoming explicitly conscious of
one's ignorance and of the cause of it (that is, *confused*
ideas), and so by directing one's effort to get rid of
confused ideas and to acquire clear ones.[1] In all this,
he never questioned the existence of truth or the possibility of man's attaining it ; but he saw that it had
to be strenuously pursued and carefully articulated.
Consequently, he made it his business to subject prevailing notions, generally accepted opinions, as held in
concrete instances, in all departments of human interest,
to a strict criticism and review. It was not enough
to him that they should rest upon " use and wont " or
long-established custom : they must stand the test of
reason, or else be rejected. This meant, of course, a
revolt against tradition and against the lazy servile
acceptance of truth on mere authority. In which
attitude, there was unquestionably something unsettling,
even although his ultimate object was, like that of
Descartes, later on,[2] through doubt and searching to
attain Certainty—to establish both truth and morality
on a sure foundation (see Diogenes Laërtius, I. v. 7) ;
and, on the face of it, there seemed to be the same
dangerous tendency that characterized the scepticism
of the Sophists. Hence, we do not wonder that
Socrates should have been represented, as by Aristophanes in the *Clouds*, as a Sophist ; nor is it matter for
surprise that he should ultimately have been condemned
to death on the charges of atheism and impiety and

[1] See, *e.g.*, *Apologia* and *Theætetus*.
[2] See his *Discourse on Method* and *Meditations*.

corrupting the youth.[1] Not religious, any more than social or other, belief was safe, if it rested merely on popular prejudice or on unreasoned (much more, irrational) adherence to antiquated usage; and well might elderly people, thus shaken rudely out of their lethargy, look askance at a teacher who habituated his hearers, especially young men, to demand a reason for every proffered truth and every cherished conviction. Free thinking like this was certainly disconcerting.

Nevertheless, in the Socratic procedure there was, beyond dispute, supreme psychological insight and just appreciation of the power of human reason; and here we find the beginnings of psychology as a science and of rational metaphysics, even though Socrates himself may not have explicitly said so. In point of positive doctrine, we get little from Socrates, even in his favourite sphere of Ethics—no enumeration of fundamentals, no elaborated system. He had no architectonic, such as we find in Plato or in Aristotle or in any of the modern epoch-making thinkers—Spinoza, Kant, Hegel. No doubt, we have the difficulty of ascertaining precisely what it was that the historical Socrates really taught. The Socrates of Plato and the Socrates of Xenophon are not identical.[2] Yet we can distinctly see that his teaching centred in a prominent ethical dictum, based in psychology,—namely, that no man sins willingly, or, as he also expresses it, that vice

---

[1] See Plato, *Apologia*, etc.; also, Xenophon, *Memorabilia*, i.

[2] See Zeller, *Socrates and the Socratic Schools* (Eng. tr.), p. 181 ff.; also, Gomperz, *Greek Thinkers* (Eng. tr.), vol. ii.; and Benn, *The Greek Philosophers*, vol. i. chap. iii.

is ignorance and virtue knowledge.[1] Again, we can scarcely be wrong in ascribing to him the emphatic assertion of the supreme importance for character of the virtue of abstemiousness or self-control. His own life was one in which this virtue played a prominent part;[2] and his laudation of moderation in Xenophon,[3] and his insistence on the necessity of reducing the number of our desires and wants, and of strictly subordinating the lower pleasures of our nature to the higher, if we would not be slaves, showed that he made this the foundation of morality. We can see, further, that it was the tendency of Socrates to ground virtue on utility, to estimate it by its consequences : that alone is good which is good for someone or which serves some end—"a dung-basket that serves its purpose is more beautiful than an unserviceable shield of gold."[4] In this respect, he anticipated the modern pragmatist (Professor James, for instance, or Mr. F. C. S. Schiller), who maintains that truth, in order to be true, must have practical results, must *work*—yea more, in the wider doctrine of "humanism," it *consists* in consequences, more especially if those be good.[5] Then, lastly, we can hardly question that the historical Socrates reasoned on Theistic lines, basing his conception of God and God's providence on teleology or the marks of design manifest in the universe;[6] and that his views on the Soul are accurately represented,

---

[1] See the *Protagoras* of Plato.
[2] See Xenophon, *Memorabilia*, i. 2.
[3] See *Memorabilia*, i. 5, 6; also ii. 1.
[4] See Xenophon, *Memorabilia*, iv. 6.
[5] See Appendix.
[6] See Xenophon, *Memorabilia*, i. 4; iv. 3.

in all essentials, by Plato in the *Apologia* and the *Phædo*. The real Socrates was characterized by religious reverence and personal piety (Xenophon and Plato alike—*e.g.*, in *Euthyphro*—being witnesses), and his teleology is strict and definite—so much so that it commended itself as a model to natural theologians in Christendom for many centuries. Nor are his views on Immortality less striking (Xenophon and Plato, again, being at one here); although it is not often observed that the ultimate conclusion that Socrates reaches is a guarded one. Of the immortality of the soul, he affirms, he is personally convinced, but he does not profess that he can prove it by irrefragable argument—absolute demonstration is impossible in the matter. "It came to me," he says, "apart from demonstration, with a sort of natural likelihood and fitness." That is all; but it is much.

Apart, however, from positive doctrine, Socrates was practically the founder of mental and moral science, and the great stimulator to philosophic thought because of his firm grasp of the inductive method applied to mental and moral subjects and carried systematically out in his peculiar dialectic of cross-examination, and because of the variety and many-sidedness of his ideas, leading to great developments in the hands of his pupils. Although gruff and even repulsive in his outward person, he had the extraordinary magnetic power of attracting and stimulating thinking men of all temperaments, and of sowing seeds that should germinate and grow in many different soils. That he should have laid hold on the heart and the imagination of Plato, and become the hero and the sage of the Platonic Dialogues, is itself sufficiently remarkable. Remarkable is it also that he should have so captivated Xenophon as to impel him, like another Boswell, to write a treatise of recollections of the master's conversations, and this, too, with a view to defend him against the accusations that had brought about his condemnation and death,—a treatise charged with the reverence and affection of the whole-hearted admirer and devoted disciple. But it is no less remarkable that he should have thrown out so many fruitful and suggestive thoughts as to be virtually the founder of all the leading post-Socratic schools— Platonic, Peripatetic, Cynic, Cyrenaic, Megaric, Stoic, Epicurean alike. All derived their impulse, directly or indirectly, from him ; and each claimed for its own tenets a basis in the Socratic teaching.

IV

But the position of Socrates cannot be fully understood unless we take it in connexion with the Sophists. The Sophists were pre-eminently educationists, active teachers of the liberal arts, but more particularly of the arts that bear upon the business and duties of life. They were, therefore, necessarily rhetoricians and logicians (in so far, at any rate, as logic has to do with disputation), and theoretical politicians as well. They claimed in special to teach the art of discussion and address, so as to guide public opinion and to train young aspirants for political honours, fitting them for civic life, and enabling them to be a power in the senate or in the law-courts. "If Hippocrates comes to me," says Protagoras, in the Platonic dialogue of that name, "he will learn . . . prudence in affairs private as well as public ; he will learn to order his own house in the best manner, and he will be able to speak and act for the best in the affairs of the State. Do I understand you, I said ; and is your meaning that you teach the art of politics, and that you promise to make men good citizens? That, Socrates, is exactly the profession which I make." In this respect they may be designated professors of intellectual fencing, with a distinct and definite practical end in view. But they were philosophers also; and, although they had no fixed philosophical system of their own, although they founded no school, philosophical principles lay at the root of their dialectical procedure, for there can be no true education, there can be no true rhetoric (even if we understand rhetoric simply as *oratory*, forensic or political), that does not implicate psychology. It was in his treatise on *Rhetoric*, not in his *Psychology*, that Aristotle gave his completest analysis of the Emotions ; and modern writers on Rhetoric have equally laid psychology under contribution—witness, for example, Campbell in his *Philosophy of Rhetoric* and Bain in his *Rhetoric and Composition*.

What, then, was peculiar to the Sophists as philosophical educationists was this. In philosophy, they made the first great start towards amended thinking under the leading of Protagoras by departing from the old physical speculation and directing man's attention specially to man himself. In doing so, they raised some of the perennial problems of thought and will (such as, the nature and power of reason, the value of sense-perception, the basis of morality, the dependence of virtue on education), giving explicit utterance to them and offering a solution of them from the standpoint of individual consciousness and of practical experience; and although their philosophy was in many ways unsatisfactory and inadequate, it was a distinct advance in the march of human thinking. No doubt, the disputation by which it was operated was of a peculiar kind—it was what is known as Eristic or wrangling, or the art of " popular and approximate debate "; but that is not to be condemned without discrimination, even though, in the hands of degenerate teachers (say, during the latter part of Plato's life and in the days of Aristotle), it became what we nowadays know by the disparaging name of *sophistry*—of cavilling, of captious criticism and quibbling, of arguing for the sake of victory, or attempting against all comers to "make the worse appear the better reason." For that simply means that it shared the fate of many other good things, which have been brought into disrepute by being unworthily handled, and cannot reasonably be held responsible for men's abuse of it.

On the side of politics, on the other hand, the effort of the professional Sophists about the time of Socrates was to get men to think and act in an independent fashion, to feel dissatisfied with inherited custom and mere authority, and to subject common opinion and popular belief to a thorough sifting. For this purpose, they did, in the spirit of free inquiry, treat of such things as government and positive institutions and law, and they handled the political virtues (justice and the like), not forgetting, however, the training of the individual in character. And if here again degeneracy set in, and the rhetor made a base use of his opportunities, disregarding high principle and contracting a mercenary spirit, prizing his art only in the light of how much money it could bring him, we must not condemn the ideal because the real fell so far short of it. The day for passing a wholesale condemnation on the Sophists is gone—thanks mainly to Hegel in Germany and to Grote in England, and Gomperz has nobly followed up the lead at the present day.[1]

The situation was as follows : Given an age far back, long before the invention of printing (such as we conceive printing) and the influence of the Press—an age, therefore, when spoken address was all-powerful ; given a highly intellectual, an eagerly inquisitive, a naturally disputational, an eminently artistic, and a politically enthusiastic people, democratic in their leanings ; and given the desire of the patriotic and the ambitious to be able to sway this people, and the circumstance that it was only by ability to sway them that high place and influence could be achieved in the State ; given, further, the keenness of the ancient Greek for culture and for the artistic expression of it in speech,—and there we have, in brief form, the circumstances that determined the nature and marked off the limits of the sophistic art.

Yet, it must be emphasized—*the basis of the sophistic*

[1] See Grote, *History of Greece*, vol. viii. ; Zeller, *Presocratic Philosophy* (Eng. tr.), vol. ii. ; Schwegler, *History of Philosophy*, especially Dr. Hutchison Stirling's Essay in the Annotations of his English translation ; Gomperz, *Greek Thinkers* (Eng. tr.), vol. i. bk. iii. chap. 5.

art was psychology,—a distinct view of human thought
and human volition, implying a knowledge of men's
passions, interests, and motives, and a familiarity with
the various springs of human action. Even the phi-
lological researches of the Sophists, in which they
excelled, point in this direction. More still, the Sophists
had their own view of the nature of thought. They
held that Reason was a powerful instrument for criticism
and destruction, but was not competent to reach
absolute truth. It is limited in its extent, and deals
necessarily with the impressions of sense, which are
different to different individuals and relative to the
percipient ; so that knowledge, in the strict sense of the
term, is impossible, and there is no greater justification
for the opinion that one may hold than there is for its
opposite ; or, to put it in express sophistic phraseology,
an assertion and its contradictory are equally defensible.
But if there is no such thing as absolute truth, neither
is there any such thing as absolute morality. Here as
there, all may be questioned, and belief may be im-
pugned. The logical result, therefore, is universal
scepticism—scepticism in cognition and in morals alike.
Gorgias of Leontini (date about B.C. 483 to 375) put
it bluntly, on the intellectual side, when he said :
"Nothing *is* ; if anything *is*, it cannot be known ; if it
be known, it cannot be communicated." Thus being,
cognition, and articulate speech fell at a stroke, each
and all came under the ban of nescience. But the
formula of sophistic negation that most deeply affected
subsequent thought, and is prominent in the history of
philosophy, is that of Protagoras (born about 490 B.C.).
"Man," said he, "is the measure of all things (πάντων

χρημάτων μέτρον ἄνθρωπον εἶναι) ; of things that are, that
they are ; of things that are not, that they are not."

Now, this sophistic view of the relativity of human
knowledge and of human morality, this Protagorean
doctrine of *homo mensura* (μέτρον ἄνθρωπος), individualistically interpreted,[1] was met by Socrates—met, not
after the manner of the modern critic of philosophical
positions, but according to his own dialectic, in the
critical clash of intellect personally confronting intellect ;
and the contrary doctrine, though not in so many words,
was championed by him, namely, that human reason,
though limited in its range, can give us truth, and that
morality has a stable basis in reason and is universally
valid. In this way, while agreeing with the Sophists in
upholding the rights of the individual to think and to
act, he separated from them wholly in his appreciation
of the dignity of the individual and his ability to effect
great things as participating in universal reason.

If "man is the measure of all things," then the
logical conclusion seemed to be that truth is merely

---

[1] It has been argued (*e.g.*, by Gomperz) that this individualistic
interpretation is not the correct one ; for, however it may have
been in the days (say) of Aristotle or even at the end of Plato's
life, neither Protagoras nor the Sophists of Socrates's time did interpret it individualistically. In this there probably is some truth ; but
the point is that the Sophists did actually degenerate, on the line
of this interpretation, and that both Plato and Aristotle (the one in
the *Theœtetus* and the other in the *Metaphysics*) did interpret the
Protagorean formula individualistically, which seems to show that
relativity to the individual was at any rate implicit in the formula.
It is never well to forget that Plato and Aristotle were themselves
Greeks and lived near to the Socratic moment, and so were able
to appreciate movements of their time and to gauge tendencies
in a way that is scarcely open to modern non-Hellenic thinkers.

relative, and things are as they appear to each to be : there is no universally valid knowledge. That conclusion was drawn by Plato and by Aristotle alike.[1] Whence it follows logically, also, that Ethics has no unimpeachable groundwork, but varies with the individual and the age, according to circumstances, and expediency or self-interest becomes the supreme virtue : that is right or wrong to each man as it seems to each to be. That Protagoras himself drew these conclusions is very far from obvious ; but they were implicit in the ordinary rendering of his formula. Here the historic Socrates, in his principles and method, stood forth as the defender of Reason. In discussion, he demanded as the criterion of truth clear concepts, and enforced the dictum that, given clear concepts, consistent and coherent thinking becomes possible, and high-principled and coherent action too; and this just means unconditional knowledge and absolute or objective moral law. He did not, any more than Protagoras, desert the subjective standpoint—the standpoint of the conscious self or ego : he had simply a more just idea of what the self or ego meant. He fully admitted that error is possible, and that the senses may deceive us and convention mislead ; but, at the same time, he insisted that Reason has in itself the power of detecting and correcting error, and so of reaching certainty. Subjective conviction, he practically maintained, rests on objective grounds — what is true for me is true for you and for other intelligent beings (intelligence itself secures that, for intelligence is not a mere individual or private possession, but is shared by others and

[1] See Plato, *Theætetus* ; and Aristotle, *Metaphysics*, bk. x. 6.

2

designates our common nature, thereby giving "truth for all ") ; and absolute nescience or universal scepticism is suicidal—even in proclaiming that truth is unattainable, the sceptic assumes the truth of reason, *its trustworthiness as destructive of itself*,—which is absurd.[1]

Thus Socrates virtually enunciated the principle that lies at the root of epistemology, and may claim to have placed metaphysics on a stable foundation.

V

That, then, was what gave Socrates his position and marked him off from the Sophists (strictly so called), separating him from them in spirit and in aim alike, as also in the conclusions reached, and what gives him his distinctive importance in the history of human thought. His influence on the Stoic teaching, more especially on its ethical side, will be apparent as we proceed. Meanwhile, as the personal character of Socrates counts for much, owing not only to the nobility of his death but also to the energy and nobility of his life, this chapter may fitly end with a passage from Xenophon's *Memorabilia*, characterizing the Socrates whom he knew so well. For if it be so that the *Memorabilia* was the book that first drew Zeno to the study of philosophy, the picture of Socrates that we there find may very well be credited with having aroused, to some extent at least, his regard for the master, and may serve to suggest to us how the Stoics

[1] For modern presentations of the doctrine of the relativity of knowledge, see Hume (*A Treatise of Human Nature*), Hamilton (*Metaphysics* and *Discussions*), J. S. Mill (*An Examination of Sir William Hamilton's Philosophy*), Herbert Spencer (*First Principles*).

should have come to venerate Socrates and to accept him as one of their Ideal sages. If Plato, at one in his estimate of Socrates with Xenophon, could conclude the *Phædo* with the sentence, "Such was the end, Echecrates, of our friend; concerning whom I may truly say, that of all the men of his time whom I have known, he was the wisest and justest and best," Xenophon could conclude his *Memorabilia* thus:

"To me personally he was what I have already endeavoured to describe: so pious and devoutly religious that he would take no step apart from the will of heaven; so just and upright that he never did even a trifling injury to any living soul; so self-controlled, so temperate, that he never at any time chose the sweeter in place of the better; so sensible, and wise, and prudent, that in distinguishing the better from the worse he never erred; nor had he need of any helper, but for the knowledge of these matters, his judgment was at once infallible and self-sufficing. Capable of reasonably setting forth and defining moral questions, he was also able to test others, and where they erred, to cross-examine and convict them, and so to impel and guide them in the path of virtue and noble manhood (ἐπ' ἀρετὴν καὶ καλοκἀγαθίαν). With these characteristics, he seemed to be the very impersonation of human perfection and happiness. Such is our estimate. If the verdict fail to satisfy, I would ask those who disagree with it to place the character of any other side by side with this delineation, and then pass sentence" (*Mem.* iv. 8, trs. by H. G. Dakyns).

Perfection embodied in an individual — such did Socrates appear to his immediate disciples to be; and that explains how he should have become the object of special regard and devotion even to the Stoics, whose test of greatness was life and character, not mere power of abstract speculation.

CHAPTER II

THE STOIC MASTERS AND THEIR WRITINGS

"Those budge doctors of the Stoic fur."—MILTON.

I

ASSUMING, then, that the Stoic philosophy shared in the Socratic impulse, and, consequently, has thus far its general character determined, it next becomes necessary to consider the determining factors of its special form.[1] This will best be done if we take a brief preliminary survey of the circumstances under which it arose and the situation it was designed to meet, as well as of the difficulties that beset us in our interpretation of it.

Although destined to be a philosophy wielding a deep and widespread influence in Athens and by and by in Rome, and thence outward throughout the civilized world, it had neither Athenian nor Roman for its founder, but Zeno, a native of Citium, in Cyprus, in whose veins is said to have run Phœnician blood.[2] Nevertheless, its teaching was originally formulated at

[1] More will be said, later on, regarding the Cynic influence and the contrast of the Epicurean Physics and Ethics.

[2] The strength of the case for the Semitic origin of Stoicism may be seen by a reference to Sir Alexander Grant's *The Ethics of Aristotle*, vol. i., Essay vi., and to Bishop Lightfoot's *Epistle to the Philippians*, Diss. ii., "St. Paul and Seneca."

Athens, was addressed to Greeks, was cast in Hellenic moulds and nurtured under Hellenic patronage. When first it saw the light, at the end of the fourth century B.C., it came to a declining people—a people past the heyday of their political freedom, with their intellectual interest in truth narrowed, and the disintegrating touch of social corruption and moral turpitude visibly laid upon them. The greatness of the days of Pericles was gone, and the distance between the age of Plato and the age of Zeno was enormous. It may be illustrated by the character of the comic plays that found favour.

"The comedy of Aristophanes has for its scene the main resorts of the public political life of its time. It is a caricature of public men and public measures. Athens, with its foreign relations and its domestic politics, is the topic which reappears in a hundred shapes, and drags into its compass even the inmates of the women's chamber and the character and ideas of the public thinkers. In the new comedy of Menander and Philemon, public life is unknown. It is the family and the social aspects of life which are the perpetual theme. Instead of generals and statesmen, demagogues and revolutionaries, the new comedy presents a recurring story of young men's love affairs, and old men's economies, cf swaggering captains and wily valets-de-chambre, hangers-on at rich men's tables, and young women working mischief by their charms. The whole comedy turns on one aspect of domestic life—it is full of embroiling engagements between lovers, and brings the cook and the dinner-table prominently on the stage." [1]

To stem the tide of deterioration, and, if possible, to produce in men a healthy robust moral nature, which would be able to resist the temptations to degeneracy that on every hand presented themselves,

[1] W. Wallace, *Epicureanism*, p. 10.

and which would yield inward and abiding peace in the midst of the exceptional difficulties and trials that were inseparable from the exigencies of the times,—was one great object that Stoicism served, and for the accomplishment of which it was consciously called into existence. This so far explains some of its distinctive positions—particularly, its doctrines of Providence and the true nature and source of human happiness. It explains also, in part, how Ethics became to it the supreme and all-important science; speculation, physical and metaphysical, being subordinated thereto. Ariston of Chios even went the length of saying that "dialectical arguments are like cobwebs, which, although they seem to weave something artistic, are useless" (Diog. Laërt. vi. 2). That might stand as a motto for Bacon and for Locke.

But the personal character, natural temperament, and intellectual training of its great founders had also their marked influence.

We can clearly discern, throughout the whole term of the existence of Stoicism as a separate philosophical school, traces of the austerity and simplicity of life that characterized the Semitic Zeno; of the deep religious spirit, anchored on physical speculation, that distinguished Cleanthes; of the hard logical reasoning and subtle dialectic that was conspicuous in the self-confident and redoubtable Chrysippus. Moreover, the period of years, whether twenty or ten (the number is disputed), spent by Zeno, in preparation for his work of teaching, in the various Greek schools—Cynic, Megaric, Academic, Peripatetic—was not without its effect in shaping the form that Stoicism took. Even though ultimately opposed to one and all of these schools, Zeno learned and assimilated something from each, and reproduced it in his teaching. Although repelled by the slovenly and sometimes offensive habits and not less by the intellectual narrowness of the Cynics, he, nevertheless, caught their spirit of a high ethical ideal and a contempt for mere pleasure, and based his own ethical system on the conception of the Ideal wise man. Hence, Diogenes the Cynic could be accepted by the Stoics as a pattern sage (along with Socrates and Hercules and a few others); but it was Diogenes *without the tub*.[1] From the Megarics, and more especially from Stilpo, whose pupil he was, he would at least acquire an interest in Logic, and would be sharpened by them in the practice of Eristic, for which they were famous. He would learn from Stilpo, further, the doctrine of Passionlessness or ἀπάθεια, which that great Megaric shared with the Cynic school. By the Academics he would be introduced, among other things, to certain Platonic ethical notions, and to the teaching of Heracleitus — a teaching which, as we know, he highly prized, accepting it as the groundwork of his own physical theorizing. He would learn from the Aristotelians formal logic and metaphysics, no less than natural science. Indeed, so fully did the various Greek schools affect Zeno, that even in his own day he was roundly accused of being a plagiarist or a mere eclectic, devoid of originality.[2] But this may simply have meant that he had an open and receptive mind,

[1] The Cynic influence is further considered in Chapter VII.
[2] See Diogenes Laërtius, vii. 20.

and that he was less under the sway of the spirit of sect than many of his contemporaries. It is no easy matter, in any age, for a partisan to see that a thinker's first duty is to be sympathetic towards other thinkers, and ready to believe that there is truth even in systems from which he himself dissents. If Zeno was comparatively tolerant, that surely was a virtue, not a vice. When he listened to and learned from the different teachers of the diverse tenets, he only showed that he had in him the genuine spirit of the earnest seeker after truth ; and when he broke off from this teacher and from that at particular points, and essayed to occupy an independent position, he simply acted on the proper philosophic maxim, "Dear to me is Plato, but dearer still is Truth (*amicus Plato, magis amica veritas*)."

Nevertheless, the founders of Stoicism were—perhaps by nature, at all events from the pressure of circumstances—eager controversialists ; and controversialists were all their successors. It was the fate of the school to be constantly engaged in philosophical warfare.

One ground of polemic lay with Epicurus and the Epicureans on the physical explanation of the nature and constitution of the universe. Zeno possibly, and Cleanthes certainly, entered the lists here ; but Chrysippus was the combatant that stood forth pre-eminent. To those protagonists it seemed impossible that the world should have arisen, as the Epicureans maintained it did, by a fortuitous concourse of atoms. That doctrine appeared to give an erroneous idea of Providence, and left the world an inexplicable riddle. Therefore, it had to be strenuously resisted. "Either an ordered

universe," urged Marcus Aurelius (*Meditations*, iv. 27),
"or else a welter of confusion. Assuredly then a
world-order. Or think you that order subsisting
within yourself is compatible with disorder in the All?"
"Recall to mind the alternative (iv. 3)—either a fore-
seeing providence, or blind atoms—and all the abound-
ing proofs that the world is as it were a city." In like
manner, Balbus, in Cicero's *De Naturâ Deorum* (ii. 37),
maintains that it is as easy to believe that, by throwing
a large quantity of the letters of the alphabet at random
on the ground, there would emerge, legible and clear,
the *Annals* of Ennius, as to believe that the world, so
obviously showing marks of wisdom and design, could
have been produced by the fortuitous concourse of atoms.[1]

To the Epicurean Ethics a no less strenuous opposition had to be made. If "pleasure" were man's
highest good, then, it seemed, egoism and selfishness
ruled, virtue was stripped of its absolute value, and
morality had no sure foundation. "In the constitution
of the reasoning being I perceive no virtue in mutiny
against justice ; in mutiny against pleasure I see self-
control" (Aurel. viii. 39). Hence the Stoical treatment of the emotions and desires. Complete repression
of these was the counsel, if peace were to be secured :
"Banish joys, banish fear, put hope also to flight, and
let not grief be present" (Boëthius, *De Consol. Phil.*
Lib. i. metrum 7). No one carried on this antagonism
to Hedonistic Ethics more persistently than Epictetus.[2]

---

[1] The Epicurean Cosmogony will be considered in Chapter VI.

[2] See, for example, *Dissertations*, i. 23 and ii. 5. The arguments
against Epicurean Hedonism will be adduced in Chapters VIII.
and X.

In the same way, a merciless war had to be waged, over the Theory of Knowledge, with Pyrrho and other sceptics. If there were no such thing as Truth, or if Truth were not attainable by man, if man's wisest motto were *nihil scire* ("to know nothing"), then human reason was rendered impotent and human action paralyzed. In this connexion, a prominent place must be assigned to Chrysippus.

These oppositions were inveterate and permanent; and they explain much of what might not at first sight be obvious in the Stoic philosophy.

But "the Stoic philosophy" is a wide word; and we must not forget that it covers teaching that grew and developed from the fourth century B.C. to, at any rate, the second century A.D., and that, while the home of its first activity was Greece, the city of its later development was Rome. We must remember, moreover, that the materials for our knowledge of the first period of it are very meagre—only fragments of the voluminous writings of Zeno, Cleanthes, and Chrysippus (for they all wrote voluminously[1]) have come down to us, and the Stoicism with which we are most familiar is that of the second or Roman period—associated specially with the names of Seneca, Epictetus, and Marcus Aurelius; *i.e.*, the Stoicism which has been modified by the lapse of time, by change of country (from Greece to Italy, from Athens to Rome), and by assimilation of elements from other and competing philosophies. No

---

[1] See, for instance, the list of writings given by Diogenes Laërtius in his *Lives, Doctrines, and Sayings of Eminent Philosophers.*

doubt, through the labours of recent scholars—particularly Zeller, Stein, Hirzel, von Arnim—we are able, to a not inconsiderable extent, to reproduce the leading teaching of the earliest Stoics, and to apportion to each his distinctive doctrines, and thereby to trace advance in the first or Greek period. Yet not without a certain danger. It is proverbially difficult to prove a negative ; and if we were left solely to deep-sea dredging for our evidence, we should inevitably infer that no human body was ever buried in the sea, for human bones have not been dredged from the depths of the ocean. It needs great care and discrimination before we can, with any plausibility even, demonstrate from mere fragments of the writings of an author that this or that doctrine was not held by him. But with care and discrimination much may be done ; and, at any rate, we can now, more specifically, appraise the works of Cleanthes and appreciate his originality. So long as "the Hymn to Zeus" was the solitary specimen of his productions known to students, or taken notice of by them, his place could only be that of a religiously-minded man, bent on giving a theological interpretation of the universe, and breathing a pious submission to the world-order which it was refreshing to feel and to come in contact with. But now that his fragments and the references to him and criticisms of him in Greek and in Latin writers have been fully brought together,[1] he is seen to stand forth a most important figure in Stoicism, stamping his personality on the physical speculations of the school (just as Chrysippus stamped his personality on its logic) ; and by his Materialism carried through-

[1] See, *e.g.*, Pearson's *Fragments of Zeno and Cleanthes*.

out all the spheres of philosophical inquiry he gives a remarkable unity to the system. But, for all this, our knowledge of early Stoicism is fragmentary, and, for the most part, at second hand,[1] and the Stoicism in which we are most at home is that of the Roman period —matured developed Stoicism, old yet fresh and vigorous, and destined to leave a permanent mark on the civilized world.

The respective contributions of the first three great Stoics have been succinctly expressed by Mr. Pearson (*The Fragments of Zeno and Cleanthes*, p. 48) thus: "To Zeno belong the establishment of the logical criterion, the adaptation of Heraclitean physics, and the introduction of all the leading ethical tenets. Cleanthes revolutionised the study of physics by the theory of tension and the development of pantheism, and by applying his materialistic views to logic and ethics brought into strong light the mutual inter-dependence of the three branches. The task of Chrysippus was to preserve rather than to originate, to reconcile inconsistencies, to remove superfluous outgrowths, and to maintain an unbroken line of defence against his adversaries."

A further difficulty confronts us in the fact that the Stoic writings possessed by us are not methodical expositions of the system, but either notes of lectures delivered on promiscuous subjects, or treatises on separate portions of the Stoic doctrine, or jottings of random thoughts (resembling Pascal's *Pensées* or Cole-

---

[1] Our chief authority is Diogenes Laërtius, who lived probably in the second century after Christ.

ridge's *Aids to Reflection*) made for private use and as helps to personal conduct—one might almost say, to personal piety and devotion.

To the first class belong the *Dissertations* or *Discourses* of Epictetus (originally eight books, now only four), which were simply Arrian's memoranda of his master's prelections—unpruned, unassorted, and unsifted,[1] a mixture of the gold and the dross, yet charged with human interest and enlivened by anecdote and humour ; and even Arrian's selections of the master's dicta, known as the *Encheiridion* or *Handbook*, while it removes the dross, does not present a homogeneous system, or give more than glimpses which the reader must develop for himself. It is, moreover, rather lopsided, presenting in excess the more unbending side of Stoicism and subordinating too much the "amiable" virtues.

Seneca's prose writings exemplify the second class. They are either books on isolated Stoical themes ("On Anger," "On Benefits," "On the Blessed Life," etc.), or casual expositions contained in Letters (one hundred and twenty-four in number, addressed to Lucilius)—letters, no doubt, that are practically lectures of the moral philosopher, hortatory, edifying, full of sage counsel clothed in graceful language, with a tendency to prolixity, and a proneness on the part of the moralist to become the moralizer (to be classed, as to style and spirit, along with the philosophical group of Addison's papers in *The Spectator*, or with Dugald Stewart's moral philosophy lectures), but not systematic treatises,

[1] According to modern notions, Arrian would not be regarded as a good editor.

unfolding in a continuous coherent fashion the various branches of Stoical investigation. Indeed, Seneca was distinctly averse to system-building. He. had neither the inclination nor the ability for methodical speculation ; and, even in Ethics, he is more of the preacher than of the philosopher. He ever and anon seems to long for the wisdom of the ancients, which was concerned merely with precepts about what to do and what to avoid, when men, being less learned, were far better morally ; and it is a real pain to him that " plain and open virtue should now be turned into an obscure and ingenious science, and that men should be taught to dispute and not to live " (*Epistles*, 95). Moreover, the conditions under which he wrote were unfavourable to system. He had to address himself to specific points as opportunity required, and he meant his counsel for edification — he was always ready to "improve the occasion." The nearest, perhaps, that we come to a systematic Stoic treatise is in Cicero's *De Officiis* ("On Duties") ; two books of which are avowedly reproductions of Panætius's teaching—clearly tinged, however, with the shrewd common sense of the Roman statesman and politician himself.

The third class is represented by Marcus Aurelius's *Meditations* (τὰ εἰς ἑαυτόν),—a supremely precious volume, as giving us the artless picture of a great Emperor drawn by himself, yet a picture, in all probability, never intended for public gaze,—precious as revealing to us the upright nature of an amiable, pure, magnanimous soul, full of high thoughts and generous sentiments, and inspiring us by its whole-hearted resignation to destiny, but not in any way a rounded whole or an articulated dissertation. In a word, we have here simply the guileless earnest presentation of a limited number of great ethical notions in the shape of self-musings, and the stimulating example of a lovable man in the highest social rank, the idolized "philosopher-pontiff," moulding his life consistently on his own principle—"Whatever any one else does or says, my duty is to be good ; just as gold or emerald or purple for ever says, Whatever any one else does or says, my duty is to be an emerald and keep my proper hue" (*Med.* vii. 15).

This lack of system all along the line is unfortunate and tantalizing,—all the more so as it was in great measure intentional. One can quite well understand the position of Epictetus, who was a teacher by pro-fession and a man with a mission, and who naturally conceived it to be his duty to lecture rather than to write, and, in lecturing, to stir his hearers by ardent words uttered straight from the heart in conversational style, rather than to perplex and possibly to repel them by sterile logomachies and mere intellectual conceits. Arrian's characterization of him insists on his intensity and his infectious enthusiasm.[1] But the position of others, not thus situated, is more difficult to understand. Marcus Aurelius, however, near the opening of his *Meditations* (i. 7), lets us into the secret. When acknowledging his debt to the Stoic Rusticus, who was the first to arouse in him the desire to live rightly, he expresses his gratitude that he was kept back by him from "sophistic ambitions and essays on philosophy, discourses provocative to virtue, or fancy portraitures

[1] See Arrian's dedicatory letter to Lucius Gellius.

of the sage or the philanthropist," while he "learned to eschew rhetoric and poetry and fine language." This is significant. As it was the aim of the Stoics to form *men*, and not merely to train reasoners or to produce orators, that determined their mode of procedure. To them, character was the great thing ; and so it seemed better to stimulate the heart to morality and to attend to conduct than to pose as learned pedants, or even to delight the intellect with legitimate logic and speculation.

Hence, the later Stoics have done themselves an injustice. When what we have to judge them by is simply a collection of partially disjointed reflections, frequently reiterated, and of practical moral counsels—wise, searching, and direct, yet not systematized,—it cannot but be that they should often appear to us inconsistent, and that we should sometimes find it extremely difficult to see how different utterances of the same man are to be reconciled.

Lastly, we have the difficulty of teaching as tested by practice.

We shall do the Stoics a grievous wrong if we be not on our guard against allowing our knowledge of the aberrations of individual Stoics, or traditional stories regarding them, or, perhaps, unworthy and false charges of opponents against them, to prejudice us in our estimate of the intrinsic value of the system. If, on the one hand, there were Stoics who drew antinomian conclusions from Stoical premises, especially from the "apathy" of the wise man and the doctrine of things "indifferent," and lived accordingly (just as there were early Christians who defended antinomianism by St. Paul's doctrine of God's free grace), there were, on the other hand, Stoics (and many of them) who lived noble lives ; and, in particular, we have Epictetus and Marcus Aurelius, who are brilliant examples to all ages of practice conforming to precept. Earlier, we have Zeno, the founder, of whom it is recorded by Diogenes Laërtius (vii. 9), that the assembly decreed him a golden crown and a tomb in the Ceramicus at the public expense, on the ground that " he had spent many years in the city in the pursuit of philosophy, and was in all respects a good man, and had exhorted the young men who sought his intercourse to the practice of virtue and temperance, setting up his own life to all as a model in the things that are best, being in conformity with the doctrines on which he discoursed." So that noble lives there were among the Stoics, of which any creed might be proud ; and, for the rest, we may ask, What philosophy, or what religion, can stand the rigorous test of absolutely consistent lives on the part of all its adherents ? It is *principles* that we must gauge—principles in their legitimate, and not merely in their actual, effect in practice ; and on an unprejudiced examination of these principles and their legitimate outcome, must our estimate be formed.

II

There is no need here to offer biographies of " those budge doctors of the Stoic fur." That has been done with sufficient fulness by Zeller and others ; and, in particular, the three great Roman Stoics—Seneca, Epictetus, and Marcus Aurelius—have been limned in

his wonted picturesque manner by Dean Farrar in his
Seekers after God.   But a table, embodying the leading
names, with dates, may here be appended.   It will
show at a glance the Presidents of the Greek School,
as well as the masters of the Latin period.

TABLE

I. Greek Period

Presidents of the School

Founders[1]
Zeno (who founded the school about 308
   B.C.).
Cleanthes (born 331 B.C. ; died 232 B.C.).
Chrysippus (282–209 B.C.).

Zeno of Tarsus (about 206 B.C.).
Diogenes of Seleucia (about 150 B.C.).
Antipater of Tarsus (about 144 B.C.).

Transitional
Panætius of Rhodes (about 180–111 B.C.—
   a friend of Scipio Africanus the younger,
   and greatly instrumental in introducing
   Stoicism into Rome).
Posidonius of Apamea in Syria (born about
   135 B.C.—teacher of Cicero, when he
   visited Rhodes).

II. Roman Period

L. Annæus Seneca (3–65 A.D.).
Epictetus (left Rome in 94 A.D. — on
   the expulsion of the philosophers by
   Domitian — for Nicopolis in Epirus,
   where he taught and died).
M. Aurelius Antoninus (born 121 A.D. ;
   Emperor, 161–180 A.D.).

---

[1] Chrysippus is usually designated "the second founder of the
School," according to the saying, "Had there been no Chrysippus,
there would have been no Stoa."   But the independent work of
Cleanthes seems to entitle him also to the name of founder.

According to the usual division, the first three names constitute the Older Stoa ; the other names of the Greek period designate the Middle Stoa ; and the Later Stoa is covered by the names of the Roman period

How far this grouping seems to mark advance in teaching, or to exhibit the development of doctrine in the school, will be shown at the close of next chapter.

CHAPTER III

CONCEPTION OF PHILOSOPHY

" To every impression apply, if possible, the tests of objective
character, of subjective effect, and of logical relation (φυσιολογεῖν,
παθολογεῖν, διαλεκτικεύεσθαι)."—AURELIUS.

" He who neglects education walks lame to the end of his life,
and returns imperfect and good for nothing to the world below."
PLATO.

" Philosophiæ servias oportet, ut tibi contingat vera libertas."
SENECA.

I

WHEN Philosophy, in the early part of the sixth century
of the Christian era, disclosed herself in vision to
Boëthius, as he lay in the prison of Ticinum waiting
his tragic end, she appeared as a Woman of a very
reverent countenance, with glowing eyes, penetrating
with a power beyond that of human eyes, of vivid
complexion and inexhaustible strength, although so full
of years that she could not be deemed to belong to the
present age. Her stature was difficult to define. For,
at one time, she would confine herself within the
common human measure ; at another time, she seemed
to raise her head so high as to penetrate the heavens,

36

and be lost to the gaze of the beholder.   Her garments, woven by her own hands, were wrought of the slenderest threads, with exquisite art and of imperishable material. Yet withal the mist of antiquity and even of neglect had overspread them.   On the lower edge was inscribed the letter π; and, on the upper, the letter θ.   And between these two letters there was a series of others, by which you could ascend, as by the steps of a ladder, from the lower to the higher.   The vesture itself, however, had been torn by violent hands, and fragments of it borne away.   In her right hand she carried books; and, in her left hand, a sceptre.[1]

Now, all this was allegorical, and was intended to indicate, as in a picture, the nature and pretensions of Philosophy, as conceived by one who may not unfairly be designated the last of the Stoics, if also "the last of the Romans."

The majestic Lady, with reverent countenance and glowing eyes and exhaustless vigour and lively complexion, typifies Philosophy, and emphasizes its perennial interest and worth.   The exquisite apparel, woven of indestructible material, points to the value, durability, and excellence of philosophic thought.   The changing figure of Philosophy—now human, now divine—indicates the twofold subject-matter,—things of earth and things of heaven.   The lower letter π represents Philosophy in its practical and more mundane aspect; while θ is the region of theory — of theology and speculation.   And the way from the one to the other is unbroken; the ascent is made by a continuous gradation.   Alas! that men should have rent the garment,

[1] See *De Consolatione Philosophiæ*, Lib. i. Prosa 1 and 3.

and carried off the fragments ; prizing the parts more
highly than the whole.   Philosophical sects, like all
others, have much to answer for.   Yet, take Philosophy
in its entirety, and what, according to Boëthius, have
we ?   We have an instructress and a consoler : light
and comfort come from thence—the deepest intellectual
insight and sovereign regulative power.   We have both
the " books " and the " sceptre " : on the one side,
illumination of the mind ; on the other side, guidance
of the will.   Philosophy, when rightly interpreted,
is of studies supreme ;   for unity is given to human
nature and   harmony to life, when principles and
practice meet.

II

What then, let us ask more   particularly, is Philosophy ?

From π to θ

The Stoics defined it in a single phrase as " striving
after wisdom," and wisdom they defined as " knowledge
of things divine and human," so that these things determine the scope of philosophy.[1]   To modern thinkers,
this definition may seem inadequate and even naïve.
But there is more in it, especially when taken in connexion with the Stoics' application of it, than at first
sight appears.   There is this, at least, in it :—first,
that no speculation is philosophy that does not run up
into consideration of the divine or all-comprehending
principle of existence ; and, secondly, that no philosophic speculation on things divine can rightly claim to
be legitimate that does not start from, and guide itself

[1] See, *e.g.*, Epictetus, *Diss.* i. 14 ; Seneca, *Ep.* 88.

by, a knowledge of things human. The ascent from π to θ is continuous, unbroken. Two errors, therefore, are here excluded—errors into which students of the mind have frequently fallen, and which are still pitfalls : —first, the error of supposing that psychology or study of psychical states alone is philosophy ; secondly, the reverse error of ignoring psychology and dealing with metaphysics as though it had for us a wholly independent footing—were entirely unrelated to, and independent of, the facts and principles of human nature. Philosophy, in order to be correctly understood, must neither be separated from an experiential basis nor be identified with the bare scientific investigation of experience.

In another sense, also, study of the divine, as well as of the human, is necessary—namely, when we come to deal with the practical applications of philosophy. The two classes of interest, theoretical and practical, are so intimately connected as to be interdependent ; and any neglect of the one necessarily tells adversely on the other. The Stoics were very insistent on this point ; and earnest ethical teachers ever since have been equally emphatic. Take a single example from Marcus Aurelius. In the third book of his *Meditations* (iii. 13) occur these sentences : " As surgeons keep their instruments and knives at hand for sudden calls upon their skill, keep you your principles ever ready to test things divine and human, in every act however trifling remembering the mutual bond between the two. No human act can be right without co-reference to the divine, and conversely."

Philosophy, then, has for its subject-matter things

human and divine : it must rise from π to θ, and determine the principle of union between the two. *That* is the first step in the definition.

Leading Characteristics

But now, if there is a principle of union to be determined, that means : (1) That philosophy is the unifying science : it is the effort of the mind to reach the rational interpretation of the universe, by viewing the parts in the light of the whole and grasping the underlying principle. Consequently, it must deal with the deepest problems of human life—those connected with God or the Absolute ; with Self, the Ego, or the Soul ; and with the World or Nature. (2) Hence, it rises beyond the mere study of isolated occurrences or existences in their fragmentary aspects and the formulating of their laws,—in other words, beyond the mere scientific study of them,—and seeks to determine their *reason* or their *why*: as Aristotle puts it (*Met.* v. 1), "Philosophy is the knowledge of things by their causes." (3) Nevertheless, it presupposes that knowledge of existences in their laws and modes of existence has first been obtained. The secondary unities of knowledge must be established before the great all-comprehending unity can be reached.

Whence it follows that there is no real opposition between philosophy and science,—not even between philosophy and the physical sciences. For, though the procedure of physical science is analytic, it is not that alone. All analysis leads up to synthesis ; and every one of the physical sciences aims at unifying its material. Indeed, the material itself, when brought under science (*scientia*) — that is, when it is really *known*,—is a subject for philosophy ; and the deeper conceptions of science (such as " force," " space ") are seen to have full meaning only in a philosophical setting. But if so, then philosophy differs from physical science mainly in the circumstance that it lays bare the intellectual presuppositions of such science, and is, therefore, more general.

But if there is no opposition between philosophy and physical science, much less is there opposition between philosophy and mental science.   On the contrary, the mental sciences are philosophy's handmaids ; and philosophy, from one point of view, may quite correctly be conceived as a genus, having the mental disciplines under it as species, for a knowledge of the *that* and the *how* is inseparable from a knowledge of the *wherefore* and the *why*.

The Constituent Sciences

Let us then, next, view the various mental disciplines and sciences as branches of philosophy—as the parts of the three - barbed arrow with which Hercules wounded Here and vanquished Hades—that is, being interpreted, dispelled ignorance and penetrated into things secret.

In an inquiry of this kind, modern philosophers naturally look first to psychology, and ask, What, in any proffered scheme of the sciences, is the place assigned to psychology, and why?   But this was not how the Stoics proceeded—at least, not explicitly. With them there is no definite and specific treatment of psychology.   Their classification of the sciences (one that, in all likelihood, originated with them) was simply threefold—namely, into Logic, Physics, and Ethics. In explication of this grouping, they " compared philosophy to an animal, likening logic to the bones and sinews, physics to the fleshy parts, and ethics to the soul ; or, again, to an egg, logic being the shell, and ethics the white, and physics the yolk ; or to an all-productive field, logic being the surrounding fence, ethics the fruit, and physics the soil or the trees ; or to a city well fortified and governed by reason " (Diogenes Laërtius, vii. 33). From this threefold grouping, psychology is apparently excluded. And even when, as with Cleanthes, we duplicate each science and extend the division to six members—namely, Logic and Rhetoric, Physics and Theology, Ethics and Politics, we seem to be no nearer effecting an independent place for psychology than we were before. Yet there can be no question that the Stoics were supremely psychological. Their whole philosophy, indeed, may be said to repose on psychology, for the study of human nature, on its individual and on its social side, is for them paramount and fundamental, and even physical speculation and metaphysical inquiries have their basis in man's mental constitution, and repose on his conscious experience. Hence the Stoics (more especially, those of the earlier times) were conspicuous among the philosophers of antiquity in insisting on a philosophical vocabulary (which was very much the same thing as a psychological vocabulary)—on the discrimination of synonyms and the precise and scientific use of mental terms ; thereby anticipating the demands of the present day. Indeed, so strict were they in their requirements here, that Cicero, unable duly to appreciate the need for exact terminology (which is only another way of expressing the need for exact thinking), criticizes them for introducing and coining new terms, or for giving new meanings to old terms, and designates Zeno *ignobilis verborum opifex* ("a vile coiner of words"). But, clearly, the Stoics were right. There can be no true mental science without an abundance of properly defined and accurately applied terms ; and though we may allow that a newly-coined word ought not to be barbarously formed (an admission that contains a rebuke to many modern men of science, as much as to any of the ancient Stoics), we must insist that the attempt to introduce technical exactness into philosophical speech bespoke a psychological interest on the part of the Stoics that is remarkable, and that augured well for their future.

Then, further, psychological insight and psychological analysis run through all the Stoical sciences. Their Logic, when it comes to Theory of Knowledge or Epistemology, is markedly psychological. Pyschological, again, is their Physics, in so far as the universe is conceived as a macrocosm, with man as its counterpart microcosm, and in so far as the substance of the universe is regarded as identical with that of man's soul. Psychological, too, and supremely so, is their Ethics. Here, they essayed a psychological analysis and classification of the Emotions ; from the standpoint of psychology, they handled moral science, emphasizng the mind's *assent* ($\sigma\upsilon\gamma\kappa\alpha\tau\dot{\alpha}\theta\epsilon\sigma\iota\varsigma$) as the basis of responsibility and laying the essence of morality in its *inwardness*—in the agent's motive and intention ; and both their doctrine of human Happiness and their

doctrine of Habit are eminently psychological. They
had, also, a distinct psychology of Pleasure ; maintaining that pleasure indicates, not the fulness and vigour,
but the decline of vital energy,—the point where the
climax has been reached, and where descent and decay
begin,—while, in the interests of virtue, they confined
pleasure to the lower psychical energies, chiefly the
sensuous, and refused to allow it any application to
the higher energies of the soul at all. Psychological,
furthermore, is the basis of Religion with them, and
their main argument for the existence of God—that
which grounds it in human nature. So that, paradoxical though it may appear, the Stoics must be
pronounced to be in the first instance psychologists,
even though they have no separate place for psychology
in their scheme of the sciences.[1]

This being understood, let us proceed to the first of
the Stoical sciences—namely, Logic. It is rightly called
the first, because Zeno himself so regarded it : his
arrangement, rising in the order of importance, was—
Logic, Physics, Ethics.[2] But it is first also, because
the Stoics, with rare insight, looked upon it as the

---

[1] Hence, a work of Stein's on the Stoics is entitled *Die Psycho-
logie der Stoa.*

[2] This order, however, was not always followed, for, as Diogenes
Laërtius tells us (vii. 33), some Stoics maintain that " no part is to
be preferred to another, but they are all mingled together and so
are handled ind scriminately (τὴν παράδοσιν μικτὴν ἐποίουν) ; while
others place logic first, and physics second, and ethics third, as
Zeno in his treatise *On Reason*, and Chrysippus and Archedemus
and Endromus. For Diogenes of Ptolemais begins with ethics,
but Apollodorus puts ethics second, and Panætius and Posidonius
begin with physics."

necessary introduction or propædeutic to philosophy.
" For this reason," says Epictetus (*Diss.* i. 17), "I
think the logical arts are placed first, just as in the
measuring of corn we place first the examination of the
measure.   But if we do not first determine what is a
modius, nor first determine what is a balance, how shall
we still be able to measure or to weigh anything ?   In
this case, then, if we have not learned thoroughly and
investigated accurately the criterion of all other things,
and that through which they are understood, shall we
be able to accurately investigate and thoroughly understand anything else ? . . . It is enough that Logic has
the power of distinguishing and examining other things,
and, as one may say, of measuring and weighing them."

Now, Logic, in the view of the Stoics, consisted of
three parts—not, however, of co-ordinate value.   As
they did, in all probability, themselves coin the name
" logic," they had quite a right to give it whatever
meaning they chose ; and they used it to designate a
wide area.   Not only did it cover to them what has
been regarded by many as alone Logic, namely, " the
science and art of reasoning " or of " thought," but it
included also Rhetoric (or the art of style) and Epistemology (or Theory of Knowledge).

In the sphere of Rhetoric there is no great Stoical
accomplishment to record.   Although there were Stoics
—for example, Panætius and Seneca—who were profici-
ents in literary composition, and could express themselves with elegance, and although there were among
the Stoics rhetoricians of the ornate stamp,—such as
Posidonius of Apamea in Syria,[1]—the whole tendency

---

[1] " Inspired with hyperboles," as Strabo puts it.

of the school was to sit loose to the mere linguistic clothing of thought. Substance, not form, was to them the main thing ; and it little mattered should the grammar be defective or the expression faulty, if the meaning were intelligible. Take Marcus Aurelius's writing, and you find that it is bald and unimpassioned ; and we have already seen that Rusticus, his teacher, encouraged him to that. This lack of sympathy with style, however, did not prevent Epictetus from rising occasionally to heights of real eloquence ; but that, perhaps, was owing more to the fire and energy of his nature and to the intensity of his convictions than to any conscious effort at effect. For though in his most generous mood he can admit that the man who denies that there is a faculty of expression or an art of literary form is both impious and cowardly,—*impious*, "for he holds in disesteem the gifts that come from God" ; *cowardly*, "for such a one seems to me to be afraid lest, if there be any faculty of this kind, we shall not be able to despise it" (*Diss.* ii. 23),—nevertheless he utters, at other times, a note of warning, lest eloquence puff up the uninstructed and feeble, and sophistry lead them astray. "For by what means now could any one persuade a young man who excels in these matters that he ought not to become an appendage to them, but should make them an appendage to himself? Does he not trample all such reasons under foot, and strut before us elated and inflated, not suffering that any man should reprove him and remind him of what he has neglected and from what he has turned aside?" (*Diss.* i. 8). Under any circumstances, rhetoric was always to be taken as a subsidiary study, useful only as subservient to higher disciplines. "There is a certain value in the power of speaking, but it is not so great as that of the will. When, then, I say these things, let no one think that I require you to neglect speaking any more than I require you to neglect eyes or ears, or hands or feet, or clothing or sandals. But if you ask me, What then is the best of all things? what shall I say? The faculty of speaking (τὴν φραστικήν)? I cannot say that; but the faculty of the will, when it is right,—for this it is which uses that and all other powers both small and great" (*Diss.* ii. 23).

It was different with Formal Logic and with Epistemology. Owing to polemical exigencies, Formal Logic, especially as ratiocination and intellectual fencing, became a necessity to the Stoics; and, in the hands of Chrysippus, it did effective work both of an offensive and of a defensive kind.

But of the three intellectual disciplines, Epistemology was the most important; for here the canon or criterion of truth was established, and Academic scepticism and Epicurean hedonism were alike rebutted. Hence Epictetus can say (*Diss.* ii. 11): "This is the beginning of philosophy, a perception of the contention of men with one another, and an inquiry into the cause of the contention, and a condemnation and distrust of that which merely seems, and some inquiry concerning that which seems, whether it seems rightly, and a discovery of some rule (κανόνος), as we have discovered a balance for weights, and a carpenter's rule for straight and crooked things. This is the beginning of philosophy. . . . And to philosophize is this, to examine and confirm the rules; and, then, to use them when they are known is the act of an upright and good man."

Next comes Physics. By this, however, is not meant merely observation of natural phenomena and scientific investigation of nature and nature's laws after the manner of the modern physicist, but, more still, the metaphysical interpretation of the universe—philosophy, indeed, in its higher speculative reaches. That the ancient Stoics did investigate nature in a scientific way, up to the full light of the science of their day, is quite true. But this was a minor part of their business. Their great achievement was their Cosmogony or Theory of the world, and their Theology or philosophical conception of God. Their physics, therefore, was pre-eminently Ontology : it was Science of Being—occupied with the three great entities, God, the World, and the Human Soul.

Lastly comes Ethics.
This was the crown and glory of the Stoical sciences. As philosophy was to them a substitute for religion, it was, above all things, their aim to make it a rule of life, " a way of living "—not merely, as now, a necessary part of a University curriculum, but a power operative for good in daily action. If, then, men were to be guided in their conduct, it was not enough to teach them to reason, or to harangue, or to speculate. You may feed the imagination on cosmogony, you may sharpen the intellect by logic, you may train literary faculty through rhetoric, but you cannot nourish the soul, or produce a robust, manly character, unless you

bring your cosmogony into a definite immediate relation
with living, and utilize your logic and your eloquence
for the defence and establishment of life-directing
truth.[1] "What does it matter to me," said Epictetus
(*Frag.*), "whether things are composed of atoms or
of similar parts, or of earth and fire? For, is it not
sufficient to know the nature of good and evil, and the
measures of the desires and the aversions, and also of
the inclinations and the disinclinations, using these as
rules to manage the affairs of life, but leaving alone
the things that are above us?" And of Logic he said,
"The handling of sophistical and hypothetical arguments, and of those that reach conclusions by means
of questioning, and, in a word, of all arguments such
as these, relates to duty ($\pi\epsilon\rho\grave{\iota}$ $\kappa\alpha\theta\acute{\eta}\kappa\omega\nu\tau\omega\varsigma$), though this
is not known to the many" (*Diss.* i. 7). So that even
Dialectic is subordinated by him to an ethical end,
and is valued as an aid to right living.

Hence Ethics to the Stoic becomes specifically and
par excellence "philosophy";[2] and Epictetus lays down
three topics with which it is concerned—namely, (1)
the desires and the aversions; (2) impulses and acts,
including, of course, duty and its various forms; (3) the
assents ($\sigma\nu\gamma\kappa\alpha\tau\alpha\theta\acute{\epsilon}\sigma\epsilon\iota\varsigma$), or the relation of the will to
truth and falsehood, "freedom from deception and
rashness of judgment." Earlier, Ethics had been defined as including the following subjects: "appetite,
good and evil, the affects, virtue, the chief good,

---

[1] See Seneca on the Liberal Sciences, *Ep.* 88.
[2] See Seneca, *Ep.* 89; also 88. But some of the earlier Stoics
were even more pronounced, such as Ariston of Chios, the pupil
of Zeno, who despised speculation, and made Ethics everything.

4

primary value (*honestum*), actions, duties, exhortations and dissuasions." "This is the division," says Diogenes Laërtius (vii. 51), "made by Chrysippus, and Archedemus, and Zeno of Tarsus, and Apollodorus, and Diogenes, and Antipater, and Posidonius; for Zeno of Citium, and Cleanthes, belonging to an earlier date, treat of these things more simply."

Hence, also, the Stoical Ethics, although not in any systematic fashion, traversed the whole range of Practical Philosophy—this, at any rate, in the Roman period. Not only did it occupy itself with character and conduct (which is the province of Ethics, strictly conceived), but it took in hand also the investigation of the Emotions, Politics or the science of human beings formed into societies (the equivalent of the modern Sociology and Economics), and Natural Theology, or the Knowledge of God, and determination of the relations between Him and man—over and above the theological speculations of the physics.

It did, further, as seen pre-eminently in Epictetus, show its intensely practical character by laying down rules for the guidance of the individual in the discharge of his duties and social relations,[1] and as a means of testing his progress (προκοπὴ) in the higher life. For the same purpose, it counselled systematic self-examination—review, every night or evening, of one's conduct during the day, so as to ascertain precisely what one had done well, and thereby find encouragement, or done ill, and thereby be stimulated to amendment.[2] It even discoursed on the ethics of reading books

[1] See, *e.g.*, Epictetus, *Diss.* iii. 16; and Seneca, *Ep.* 94.
[2] See also Seneca, *De Irâ*, iii. 36.

(Epictetus, *Diss.* iv. 4). One branch only of practical ethics does it seem not to have found very congenial— namely, Casuistry, or consideration of cases of conscience, when different duties conflict, and instances in experience when the *utile* is opposed to the *honestum*. This subject came distinctly into view in the Middle Stoa, but not even Panætius gave it a thorough handling; and Cicero developed it, as a branch of moral philosophy, in addition to the formulated teaching of Panætius, in the third book of the *De Officiis*.

How thoroughly practical the Stoical ethics was, or became, may be seen, further, from Epictetus's mode of lecturing. He delights in similes and concrete examples, dealing with the incidents and situations of daily life; his discourses are full of homely illustrations, so that thereby he may be helpful to the man of the work-a-day world.

III

Such, then, was the Stoic conception of Philosophy and of its various branches. It is obvious that all the fundamental subjects that occupy the philosopher's attention to-day, were here, in one shape or other, included. Greater precision, of course, has been given to the definitions, and fuller and deeper handling has been accorded to many of the problems discussed. A vast advance has been made, all along the line, in knowledge and in insight, since the days when Stoicism was an independent philosophic power in the world. Much has come with lengthened experience and a deeper life; but the main conceptions and the leading themes continue the same.

IV

A further point must now be noted. As the Stoic philosophy was pre-eminently and essentially a rule of living, as its aim was to help men in the formation of character and the discharge of daily duty, its demands on the personal character of the philosopher were extremely high. "The residue of life is short. Live as on a mountain. It matters not whether here or there; everywhere you are a citizen of the city of the world. Let men see and witness a true man, a life conformed to nature. If they cannot hear him, let them make away with him. Better that, than life on their terms" (Aurelius, *Med.* x. 15). This is best seen in the *Dissertations* of Epictetus.

In the first place, Stoicism required that the philosopher be himself a man of simplicity of aim and a person thoroughly convinced of his doctrines—convinced, not merely upon bare authority, but upon rational grounds.[1] Indeed, Epictetus held that firm conviction is the one thing that is practically irresistible in the world; and by this he explained the fact that senseless opinions so often gain a hold on mankind when sensible teaching fails. "Why is it," he asks his disciples, "that the vulgar are stronger than you?" "Because," he answers, "they utter these stale words from their real opinions (ἀπὸ δογμάτων), but you utter your elegant words from the lips. For this reason they (your words) are feeble and dead; and it is sickening to listen to your exhortations and your miserable virtue, which

[1] See Epictetus, *Diss.* ii. 19.

is prated up and down. Thus the vulgar have the advantage over you ; for everywhere opinion is strong, opinion is invincible" (*Diss.* iii. 16).

Next, the philosopher must show his principles in his life: he must be a man of noble character and consistent walk and conversation. "Practice before precept" is the test. Not the distinctive cloak and beard make the philosopher, but the life. "Above all things, the Cynic's ruling faculty must be purer than the sun ; and if it is not, he must of necessity be a gambler and a rogue, inasmuch as, while he himself is entangled in some vice, he will censure others" (Epictetus, *Diss.* iii. 22).[1] "Such will I show myself to you —faithful, modest, noble, unperturbed. Not also then deathless, unageing? not also diseaseless? No, but dying as a god, sickening as a god. This is within my power ; this I can do. But the other things are not within my power ; I cannot do. I will show the sinews of a philosopher. What sinews are these? Desire never failing of its object, aversion not liable to chances, proper impulse, diligent purpose, assent that is not precipitate. These you shall see" (*Diss.* ii. 8). Surely a man of that stamp might very well command, as the greatest of the Stoics did command, the confidence and the esteem of his fellow-men.

But, thirdly, the philosopher must have wide human sympathies, and must not despise the plain man—he has a clear duty towards his illiterate and unsophisticated brother. The opprobrium of contempt for the

[1] See also *Diss.* iv. 8.

unlearned (which is only, indeed, the revelation of the contemner's own inefficiency as a philosophic teacher) is well exposed by Epictetus in the words (*Diss.* ii. 12): "Yes, indeed, give to any one of us whom you please a plain man to converse with, and he cannot find out how to deal with him; but, when he has moved the man a little, if he meets him inopportunely, he can no longer handle him, but henceforth either reviles or ridicules him, and says, 'He is a plain man; it is not possible to deal with him.' But a guide, when he finds a man wandering about, leads him into the desired way, and does not ridicule or abuse him and then leave him. Do you also show him the truth, and you will see that he follows. But so long as you do not show him, do not ridicule him, but rather realize your own incapacity."

Again, the philosopher must know his business, and have a high idea of his vocation. Hence, he must not aim at praise, but at benefiting his hearers. "Rufus was wont to say, 'If you have leisure to praise me, I am speaking to no purpose.' Consequently, he used to speak in such a way that each of us sitting there supposed that some one had accused him individually— he so touched on what was doing, he so placed before the eyes the faults of each. The philosopher's school, ye men, is a surgery: you ought not to go out of it pleased, but pained. For you are not in sound health when you enter; but one has dislocated his shoulder, another has an abscess, another a fistula, another is suffering from a headache. Do I then sit and utter to you small thoughts and witty sayings that you may praise me and go away, one with his shoulder just as it was when he entered, another with his head still aching, another with his fistula, and another with his abscess? Is it for this, then, that young men shall quit home, and leave their parents and their friends, and relatives and property, that they may say to you, 'Wonderful!' as you utter your witty sayings? Did Socrates do this, did Zeno, did Cleanthes?" (Epictetus, *Diss.* iii. 23).

Lastly, the philosopher must be careful not to offend by careless neglect of his body: he must guard against repelling people from philosophy by his own personal habits and appearance.[1]

Fine dress, indeed, is not the desidératum. Once there came to Epictetus a young rhetorician with elaborately dressed hair, and in ornamental attire.[2] Epictetus must needs chaff this fashionable youth on his dandyism, but with a serious purpose under it. Through a process of Socratic cross-questioning, not without a touch of humour, he tried to get him to understand that he was expending his exertions in the wrong direction. Not the body but the will, not the outward form but the inward being, is the fit subject for care and decoration. But though that was suitable treatment of the young rhetorician under the circumstances, Epictetus saw, with deepest insight, the hopeful sign even in the love of outward adornment, still more did he estimate aright the value of personal cleanliness, and so, on occasion, he could say (*Diss.* iv. 11): "I, indeed, had rather, by the gods, that a young man in

---

[1] This against the Cynics.   [2] See *Diss.* iii. 1.

his first movement toward philosophy came to me with his hair dressed than dishevelled and dirty. For there is discernible in him a certain impression of the beautiful, and a desire for what is becoming (εὐσχήμονος); and where it appears to him to be, there also he practises his art." For the rest, it is only necessary to show him and to say, "Young man, you are seeking the beautiful, and you do well. Know, then, that it grows there where your reason is; there seek it where are your inclinations and disinclinations, your desires and aversions, for this is what you have in yourself as a special honour, but the poor body (τὸ σωμάτιον) is by nature clay. Why do you spend labour upon it heedlessly? If you learn nothing else, you will learn from time, that it (the body) is nothing? But if one came to me besmeared with filth, and with a moustache down to the knees, what have I to say to him? By what likeness can I draw him on? For with what that is like beauty has he ever busied himself, so that I might change his course, and say, 'Not here is beauty, but there'? Will you have me say to him, 'Beauty consists, not in being besmeared with filth, but in the reason'? For, does he desire reason? has he any impression of it in his mind? Go, and talk to a pig, that he wallow not in the mire."

V

In this exposition, it has not been possible, except incidentally, to bring out the fact that, although the conception of Philosophy remained the same throughout all the ages of Stoicism and little alteration was made upon the constituent sciences, nevertheless the subject-matter underwent change as time passed. Hence it may be proper here, although anticipating what is to follow, to note briefly the steps or stages in the development of Stoicism, following the list of founders and leaders as given at the end of Chapter II.

The general form of the system was fixed and determined once for all by the three great founders, each of whom, however, had his own way of enunciating and emphasizing the doctrines. To Zeno the school is indebted for its general physical theory, for the value attached to logic as propædeutic, and for the uncompromising purity of its ethics and the demand for "plain living and high thinking." Cleanthes stands conspicuous as the religious interpreter of its physics, poetically expressed, and, consequently, touched by emotion—yet of the calm contemplative kind, deeply reverential and devoutly submissive to the world-order ; and for his unqualified materialism and the stress he laid on the principle of "strain" or "tension." The logician *par excellence* is Chrysippus—systematizing, safeguarding, and controverting. This, however, is specially to be observed, that, while, by one and all, ethics was regarded as supreme, the other two disciplines (logic and physics) were enthusiastically cultivated. The founders were essentially dialecticians as well as ethicists, and their moral theory rested on metaphysical principles drawn from a reasoned study of the universe.

By the presidents of the Middle Stoa the fundamental doctrines were accepted and tenaciously held, but they were carried forward, and, in the process, modified or transformed. Two names, in particular, have importance here—namely, Panætius and his learned successor Posidonius. These two leaders mark the transition to the Roman period, for both were greatly instrumental in the propagation of Stoicism in the Roman world. They were both eclectics, and both directly influenced distinguished Romans, such as Cicero. To Panætius, in especial, may roundly be ascribed the merit of having rendered Stoicism a potent working system. He devoted his energies to its ethics and shaped its teaching on "Duties," so as to give a really helpful place to "indifferent" things in the formation of character; he endeavoured to rid the system of the incubus of Divination; and he expressed advanced views on the existence of the gods and the theology of the day. Less marked in their immediate influence were his disbelief in the doctrine of the final conflagation and the recurring world-cycles; and, conformably with this, his refusal to allow any personal existence to the individual human soul after death.

The eclectic movement thus typified in Panætius certainly transformed the system, but without discarding its basal principles.

Hence issued the Stoicism of the Roman period —which was largely eclectic.

For one thing, Ethics was now pursued with unflagging energy, and both logic and physics were thrown into the background. This is seen conspicuously in Epictetus and in Seneca. Not, however, that physics and logic were absolutely disowned

by these masters; on the contrary, Seneca wrote
a treatise on *Natural Questions*, and often speaks of
physics elsewhere in the terminology and from the
view-point of an Older Stoic ; and both Epictetus and
Aurelius reproduce sympathetically, although not always
consistently, the physics of the Earlier Stoa, and the
former can, when he thinks fit, utilize its logic.   But
ethics was to them the supreme interest, and that which
rendered philosophy the noble and purifying study that
it seemed to be.   Hence, the severity of the older ethics
was toned down by them ; and the sharp-cut distinction
between the wise man and the fool (though still regarded as ideally valid) ceased to be an absolute contrast,
marking off two mutually exclusive classes, and the
fact of moral progress in the individual and the need
for acquiring character now got due recognition.[1]   In
like manner, full acknowledgment was made of degrees
in virtue and in vice ;[2] thereby taking off the edge of
the older teaching and giving hope to struggling aspiring humanity.   Moreover, the warm breath of emotion
was now breathed upon the ideal wise man, so that he
became far more human than the original hard and
harsh portraiture of the passionless and indifferent sage
would have led us to anticipate.   Force of circumstances
had driven men to the intuitions of the heart, and the
result was an accession of winsomeness to the ethical
creed, which thereby became more generally effective.

In the next place, we have now the pantheism of the
Older Stoics tending steadily to theism.   The Universe
is constantly personalized, and the Deity is spoken of
as Creator, Father, Guardian, and men are viewed as

[1] See Seneca, *Ep.* 75.   [2] *Ibid.* 72.

His sons.[1] Thus the goodness, as well as the majesty
and might, of the supreme cause is recognized, and this
goodness is seen to operate through love. Moreover,
sin is set forth as disloyalty to an unseen Master, whose
eye is ever upon us, who knows our every thought, and
to whom we are in very truth responsible. The God
"with whom we have to do" becomes to the later
Stoics a living actuating presence, in many ways resembling the God of Hebrew and of New Testament
Scripture. The motto that Seneca gives to Lucilius for
a rule of life is this,—"So live among men, as if the eye
of God were upon you; and so address yourself to God,
as if men heard your prayer" (*Ep.* 10).

In the last place, the Cosmopolitanism of the Stoics
now attains a warmth and intensity that it did not
before possess. This arose from various causes—(*a*)
from the spectacle before men's eyes of many diverse
nationalities and creeds united in one great Commonwealth, in the vast Roman Empire, thereby suggesting
to the imagination an Empire vaster still, and one more
homogeneous and complete, only needing to be interpreted in the light of Christianity to yield the *Civitas
Dei* of St. Augustine; (*b*) from the growth of the
theistic conception and, along with this, the vision of a
future life beyond the grave, enforcing the conviction
that, if there is a God, He must care for His children
and provide for their everlasting security, and if all
men are His children, thus precious to Him, none of
them should be despised by us here; (*c*) from the
corruption of the times, which sent forth the Stoics as
missionaries and moral preachers—aglow, therefore,

[1] See Epictetus, *Diss.* i. 9.

with the enthusiasm of humanity and the desire to reclaim and to reform mankind.

It was thus a real change that was effected when the philosopher was transformed into the preacher, and the attempt was made to win men to righteousness by "sweet reasonableness" rather than by hard intellectual disputation, and when ethics became dominated by a religious motive and made it its chief aim to arouse the conscience. The elements of the original system were all there ; but the combination of them was different, and the use to which the whole was put was insistently curative. The note was sounded clear and significant —"The philosopher's school, ye men, is a surgery : you ought not to go out of it pleased, but pained."

CHAPTER IV

LOGIC: THEORY OF KNOWLEDGE

"There be but two causes from which can spring an error in the demonstration of any conclusion in any Science whatsoever. And those are Ignorance or want of Understanding, and Negligence. For as in the adding together of many and great Numbers, he cannot fail, that knoweth the Rules of Addition, and is also all the way so carefull as not to mistake one number, or one place for another; so in any other Science, he that is perfect in the Rules of Logick, and is so watchfull over his Pen, as not to put one word for another, can never fail of making a true, though not perhaps the shortest and easiest demonstration."
—HOBBES.

I

IT has already been stated that Logic has a wide meaning in the mouth of the Stoic; including Rhetoric, as well as Logic in the narrower sense or "dialectic," and Theory of Knowledge.

Of the Stoical Rhetoric nothing further need be said. It was cultivated in a watchful spirit, although encouraged in so far as it aided the appreciation of the niceties attaching to the handling of words and the proper use of them in discourse. Elegant expression of thought was not discountenanced, but it was condemned when it exerted, as it tended to do, an undue power over the will, persuading through the emotions and not convincing through the reason.

II

For Logic in its stricter signification, the earlier
Stoics, like most of the other early Greek sects, had a
distinct enthusiasm ; and, under the lead of Chrysippus,
they devoted much attention to it. They cherished it,
however, not so much because of the positive results it
yielded, as because it was a powerful instrument for
testing theories and exposing fallacies and preparing
the way for truth. In one of the various similes which
Diogenes Laërtius (vii. 40) tells us they applied to
philosophy,—namely, that of "an all-productive field,"
—they likened Logic to the fence that surrounds the
field, while ethics is the fruit, and physics is the soil
or the trees. As a fence, it was greatly used by them.
Nevertheless, they did not contribute much of any
permanent value towards perfecting it. They did,
indeed, make some alterations on the doctrine of
Aristotle and additions to it, but these were not of
high importance. Their fame as dialecticians is
associated chiefly with their zeal for definition, with
a certain treatment of the categories, and with a
special and original handling of hypothetical inferences,
—still more, perhaps, with a love for trivial intellectual
puzzles and an inordinate use of the syllogism,[1] and
of Sorites, and a tendency to defiant argumentation.
Their spirit in this respect is typified by Chrysippus,
who is said to have requested of his master Cleanthes,
"Give me the principles, and the proofs I will find for
myself" (Diog. Laërt. vii. 7).

[1] Hence the point in Lucian's caricature of Chrysippus in *The
Auction of Lives* or *The Sale of Philosophers* (Βίων πρᾶσις).

The later Stoics must be, so far, separated from the earlier in this matter, that they were much less enthusiastic for logical studies. Practical interests engrossed their attention, and the clamant corruption of the Roman Empire naturally left them with little inclination to pursue abstract subjects that had only a distant reference to conduct. Hence, Epictetus often speaks disparagingly of the power of resolving syllogisms, and of dealing with hypothetical arguments, as compared with the power over oneself and the right use of appearances ;[1] and in Marcus Aurelius there is scarcely a reference to formal logic at all.

Two points, however, deserve to be specially noted on the side of the Stoic Logic. One is the view of Logic, *in its negative aspect*, as a safeguard against error. This, no doubt, is but the reverse side of the positive characteristic that logic deals with truth and is an aid to correct thinking ; but the prominence that the Stoics gave to it is testimony to their appreciation of the power of falsehood over men and the tendency of human nature to fall into error. If correct reasoning did not imply the possibility of reasoning incorrectly, logic would be a useless science ; but if men may err in their thinking, then it becomes of the utmost importance that they be equipped against such error, for the consequences of mistake are frequently disastrous. Hence, while quite alive to the fact that logical training sharpens the intellect and gives nimbleness to thought, the Stoics laid the stress upon its negative function— upon its power to expose and refute fallacies. They accepted it as furthering truth ; but they valued it

[1] See, *e.g.*, *Diss.* iii. 24.

specially as a detector of error—"as a prophylactic against the deceitfulness of arguments and the plausibility of language." This is a point of view of very great importance ; and logicians have again awakened, though only recently, to the full significance of it. "When one of those who were present said [to Epictetus], 'Persuade me that logic is necessary,' he answered, 'Do you wish me to prove this to you?'— 'Yes.' 'Then, must I needs prove it dialectically?'—He admitted. 'How, then, will you know if I am imposing on you by sophistic arguments (ἄν σε σοφίσωμαι)?'— The man was silent. 'You see, then,' he said, 'that you are yourself admitting that logic is necessary, if without it you cannot know even as much as this, whether logic is necessary or not necessary'" (*Diss.* ii. 25).

The other point is the doctrine that words and thoughts are the same thing, only looked at from different sides—a second note of modernity that is extremely striking, anticipative of Max Müller and his followers. This led the Stoics to their famous distinction of "inward reason" and "embodied reason" or "speech" (λόγος ἐνδιάθετος and λόγος προφορικός),— a distinction that played a great part in the Judæo-Hellenistic thought of Alexandria in the first century B.C., as seen in Philo Judæus ; one, too, that seems to have influenced the Christian conception of the Divine *Logos*, as given in the prologue of the Gospel of St. John ("in the beginning was the Logos . . . and the Logos was made flesh "),[1] and that was re-

---

[1] The Stoics, however, in their doctrine of *logos* were influenced by Heracleitus, who belonged to Ephesus, where also (according to tradition) St. John wrote his Gospel.

iterated and emphasized by the Church Fathers of the early Christian centuries (Justin Martyr, for instance), and, through them, became the property of the schools of Christendom in later times.

III

But the most important part of the Stoic Logic is their Epistemology or Theory of Knowledge (*Erkenntnistheorie*), to which we now turn.

Here, the object is to determine the nature of the human mind and the criterion of truth—partly, indeed, to trace the genesis of knowledge and to analyze the concept of it, but still more, to ascertain its import, its validity, and its limits. So far as genesis and analysis of concept are concerned, the operation belongs in strictness to psychology; yet such psychology is a necessary prelude to the right understanding of cognition in its metaphysical and deeper meaning.

(1) *Exposition*

The points of particular interest in it are these :—

First, the Stoic conceived the human mind as in substance material, and he regarded it as at birth, a *tabula rasa*—a blank page or sheet of clean paper. As such, it has its knowledge to acquire from experience. The senses are the primary source, whence it derives impressions. These impressions (φαντασίαι) are of two kinds : they may be either true or false. False impressions may arise from one of two sources—from the mind itself, and so be mere subjective delusions ; or from hasty or excited inference or from careless perception, thereby leading us to mistake one object for another. We have the first case exemplified in the visions or hallucinations of madmen; Orestes mistaking his sister for a fury exemplifies the second. It is characteristic of true impressions that they come from objects and conform to them; they lay hold on the mind, and are the means whereby the mind lays hold on reality. Hence, the Stoics denominated them "grasping impressions" or "apprehending representations" (φαντασίαι καταληπτικαί). In a definition which very probably emanated from Zeno, they are set down by Sextus Empiricus (*Adv. Math.* vii. 248) as "representations proceeding from the object and agreeing with it (κατ' αὐτὸ τὸ ὑπάρχον), stamped and sealed upon the soul, such as could have no existence but for the existence of the object." A similar definition is given in Diogenes Laërtius (vii. 35), where "apprehending representation" is distinguished from what is "non-apprehensible" (ἀκατάληπτον) by the circumstance that the former proceeds from a real object and conforms to it; not so the latter, which either has no relation to the object at all, or, if it has a relation, it does not conform to it, "inasmuch as a clear impression is wanting." These apprehending representations are, according to an image of Zeno, the closed hand or fist, only needing the determinate and strenuous grasp of the other hand (*i.e.*, only needing to be connected and systematized) to make them absolutely complete and sure knowledge (Cicero, *Acad.* ii. 47). Their distinguishing feature is, that they are clear, distinct, perspicuous (ἐναργεῖς); thereby revealing both themselves and the object that produced them, just as light shows both itself and other things besides. Consequently, they are irresistible (πληκτικαί), and carry complete conviction along with them. In the crass materialism of Cleanthes, they are actual dints made upon the soul by outward things—the impressions of a seal upon wax ; and the strength or clearness that characterizes them is due to the physical property of tightening, strain, or tension (τόνος). This was modified by Chrysippus, who maintained that they are simply alterations or changes in the soul.[1]

Nevertheless, next, the mind, although material and at birth a clean slate, is not a purely inert thing—susceptible of impressions, without responding. On the contrary, it is active and responsive, and is capable of manipulating the material that is supplied to it, and of giving its free assent (συγκατάθεσις) in the conviction that impressions produce. The conception that underlies this seems to be, that the minds of men are formed according to one definite plan—a plan that unfolds itself as the individual's experience grows. Hence, the genesis of knowledge is this:—Starting with sense-impressions, these produce memory, and repeated acts of memory generate experience, and from experience the mind, through its native power, forms concepts and turns sensation into knowledge. These concepts are of two classes. Some of them are produced by the mind spontaneously ; others of them reflectively. Those of them that are spontaneously produced are common to men, inasmuch as mind is

[1] See Diogenes Laërtius, vii. 36.

generically the same in all human beings and develops in the same way, under the practically identical experiences of life all the world over. They are, accordingly, distinguished as "natural concepts," "primary concepts," "pre-conceptions," "common notions" (προλήψεις, κοιναὶ ἔννοιαι). These form the criterion of our fundamental beliefs; and as they take a wide range, they refer to intellectual, to moral, and to religious truth alike. Hence, among them we find the notion of God,[1] and the leading ethical notions —such as the Good, and the supremacy of the higher over the lower nature. "Implanted in us," says Seneca, "are the seeds of all ages and of all arts; and out of the hidden the master, God, produces our faculties" (*De Beneficiis*, iv. 6). Hence, the practical test of pre-conceptions is *consensus gentium* or the general consent of mankind: "for we are wont to lay much stress on the conception (*præsumptioni*) of all men, and among us it is regarded as an index of its truth, that a thing seems so to all: as, for example, that there are gods we infer, among other things, from this, that a belief in God is implanted in all men; nor is there any people so far outside the range of laws and morals as not to believe in some gods" (*Ep.* 117).

We must not, however, regard these common notions as (in the vulgar sense) innate, notwithstanding the ambiguous epithet "implanted." There was no such thing as an "innate idea," according to the teaching of the Stoic, if by that term be meant an idea born with us, brought with us full-grown at our birth, and

[1] See Seneca, *Ep.* 117.

wrapped also in an appropriate pre-natal name.[1]
Knowledge is not reminiscence, as Plato taught, basing
his doctrine on the belief of the pre-existence of the
soul—a belief that the Stoics did not share. All (so
the Stoic maintained) has to be learned by the individual
from experience, sense supplying the raw material:
even the notion of God is dependent upon our experience
of the external world. But what is innate is the
spontaneous power of concept forming, on the basis of
man's common experience, and so the power of reaching higher truths than mere sense-impressions could
alone afford—a power that is distinct from the deliberate,
methodical, or consciously logical concept-forming of
philosophical reflection, which gives us the other or
second class of concepts.[2]

But surely it may be asked, in connexion with the
common notions, May not men err? Yes, replied the
Stoic; but not in the natural concepts themselves,

[1] This, notwithstanding occasional unguarded expressions, as
by Epictetus in *Diss.* ii. 11.

[2] When answering Thomas Burnet's criticism of Locke's
critique of innate moral ideas as given in the *Essay concerning
Human Understanding*, and the question whether Locke "allows
any powers to be innate to mankind," Locke wrote on the margin
of his copy of Burnet's tract—"I think noe body but this author
who ever read my book could doubt that I spoke of innate *ideas*;
for my subject was the understanding, and not of innate *powers*."
That is precisely what a Stoic might have written: the mind has
innate *powers*, not innate *ideas*. So it is interesting to recall that
Descartes, in reply to objections, defined innate idea, not as an
actual existence in the mind antecedent to, and independent of,
experience, but simply as a *potentiality*—"a faculty in ourselves
of *eliciting* it (nos habere in nobis ipsis facultatem illam eliciendi)."
This gives the key to the interpretation of his real doctrine, notwithstanding many passages and phrases in his writings to the
contrary.

only in the application of them: "for this is the cause to men of all their evils, their not being able to adapt the common notions to particular cases" (Epictetus, *Diss.* iv. 1). For example, all are agreed that the Good is desirable, and is to be followed in all circumstances; but some men place the good in things not in our own power (wealth, prosperity, etc.), whereas it is to be found only in things that are within our own power—namely, in the will and its acts. "When one man says, 'He has done well; he is a brave man,' and another says, 'Not so; but he is obstinate,' then the disputes arise among men one with another. This is the dispute among the Jews and the Syrians, and the Egyptians and the Romans—not whether holiness should be preferred to all things, and in all cases should be pursued, but whether it is holy to eat pig's flesh or not holy" (Epictetus, *Diss.* i. 22).

In this way, it will be seen that the Stoic Epistemology struck direct at the root of scepticism; and, indeed, it was consciously aimed at Pyrrho and his brother sceptics. According to the sceptics, Truth is unattainable, all is uncertainty and doubt; and the best thing that one can do is to assent to nothing, to suspend one's judgment.[1] To this the Stoic replied, that Reason itself can conquer doubt, that, through its spontaneous working, it shines by its own light and discloses truth; and he maintained further that absolute scepticism is suicidal. "Propositions that are sound and perspicuous," says Epictetus (*Diss.* ii. 20), "are of necessity used even by those who contradict them; and, perhaps, a man might consider it to be the

[1] This is cleverly caricatured in Lucian's *Auction of Lives.*

greatest proof of a thing's being perspicuous that it is found to be necessary even for him who denies it to make use of it at the same time. For instance, if a man should deny that there is anything universally true, it is evident that he must make the contrary negation, that nothing is universally true. Slave! not even this. For what else is this than to affirm that if there is anything universal it is false?" He also bursts forth indignantly against the Academics who have failed "to cast away or blind their own senses, though they have tried with all their might to do it." "What! is there not a miscarriage?" he exclaims. "A man, when he has received from nature measures and rules for knowing the truth, does not further strive to add to these and to make up what is lacking, but, quite the contrary, tries to take away and to destroy whatever is fitted to give us a knowledge of the truth" (*Diss.* ii. 20). So Antipater in reply to Carneades, in Cicero's *Academica* (ii. 9): "Whoever asserts that nothing can be known with certainty must, at any rate, believe that he can with certainty know this." The Stoics saw with clearness that, on the assumption of absolute nescience, fixed principles and consistent action were alike impossible, intellect and will both became paralyzed, the ban was laid on thought and on conduct too.

(2) *Analysis and Estimate*

Now, with regard to this teaching, it may be remarked :—

First, in laying the origin of knowledge in sense-

experience, the Stoics only did what the Cynics before
them and the Epicureans contemporaneously with them
did, and what modern psychologists are practically
unanimous in doing, and what is necessary to be done
if the growth of the human mind, as disclosed to our
observation, is to be correctly represented.   It is
through sense - impressions that the individual first
becomes aware of himself, and not otherwise does he
gain a knowledge of the external world and of his
fellow-men.   But, in order to a full presentation of
the case, the " object " in sense-perception must be
analyzed far more carefully than it was by the Stoics,
and many things must be taken account of by the
genetic psychologist that did not come within the
Stoic's ken.   In the first place, Heredity, as psychologists have now come to see, is a potent factor in
the determination and development of the individual
mind ; and it forbids our regarding the mind in the
strict Stoical sense, as a clean tablet, a sheet of white
paper.   Palimpsest would be a better figure, though
not perfect.   The mind, at birth, brings with it the
impress of the past experience of ancestors of the
race.   The individual has transmitted to him, not only
nervous, but also mental predispositions, which count
for much.   They are the *a priori* element in the mind,
which explains in part the rapidity with which he
progresses in knowledge and acquires such complex
conceptions as those of space and time.   In the second
place, account must be taken of another social fact,
namely this, that the individual is born into a formed
language.   No doubt, through his own experience,
the child learns a vast number of things that are

indispensable to knowledge. As he is carried to and
fro in the nursery, and is brought into contact with
this object and with that, he is laying in a store of
impressions that will stand him in good stead some
day. But by means of Language, into which he is
born, he is introduced to knowledge far beyond his
own experience. When he is taught, as he is at the
earliest moment, to call this a dog, that a cat, this
a tree, that a house, and when he hears these animals
and things so denominated in all kinds of circumstances
and with many specific differences (dogs of all sizes
and colours and in many different attitudes are still
"dogs"), he is thereby taught to assimilate and to
discriminate in a most effective, albeit unconscious,
fashion, and has, moreover, imparted to him, through
the word-symbol, the idea of an object, whose complex
presentation (form, size, colour, solidity, etc.) could be
reduced to unity only after long and laborious effort.
Otherwise put, words are bottled-up knowledge ; and
thereby the process of acquiring knowledge is vastly
hastened and the possibility of further progress
secured.

These, then, are two great advantages that the individual gets from being a *social* creature—the member
of a family and of a race, and not a simple isolated
unit. As he develops in society, heredity and formed
language tell powerfully upon him, and show us that
his mind must be viewed as more than a *tabula
rasa*.

Next, objection may be taken to the doctrine of
"apprehending representations." Yet perhaps it is

more to the form or wording of it than to the actual
matter or substance. True, the phrase is an ambiguous
one, and is of doubtful interpretation. There is, first,
the difficulty of correctly rendering the term "apprehending" (καταληπτική). Are we to take it as active,
or as passive, or as both? And what is it that the
mind apprehends? Is it the impression or representation; or is it the object, the reality? Some view it one
way, others another.[1] But, supposing these points
settled, there next comes the difficulty of the term
"representation" (φαντασία). If this be regarded as
designating an intervening "idea" or *tertium quid*
between the percipient and the object perceived, then
all the objections that the Scottish philosophers, headed
by Thomas Reid, and nobly aided by Sir William
Hamilton, have brought against representationism or
"the ideal system" would apply here. In particular,
it may be urged that if we know only the representation
or intervening idea and yet maintain, as Zeno did, that
it "comes from the object and agrees with it,"—still
more, if we assert that it "resembles" the object, as
the impression stamped on wax resembles the figure
on the seal,—we must know both things. If we are
ignorant of either, then the assertion that the one
comes from and "agrees with" or "resembles" the
other is a mere assumption, a begging of the question.[2]
Yea more, if we lay stress upon the point that the
perceiving mind, as well as the object perceived, was

[1] Zeller takes one view here, Hirzel another, Ueberweg another,
and Stein another.

[2] Compare Case's criticism of selected representational theories,
mutatis mutandis, in his *Physical Realism*; also, S. Bailey's *Letters
on the Philosophy of the Human Mind*, 1st and 2nd series.

looked upon by the Stoics as itself material, if we press home the doctrine of Cleanthes that the impressions themselves are actual dints or prints upon the soul, further objections, as specially directed against crude materialism, will not be wanting. But if, on the other hand, we neglect for the moment the Stoic machinery or mechanism of perception, and fix our attention on the fact of certitude connected with perception that was intended to be expressed, then perhaps we may find here, not an inane conception, but a point of real significance. Not only are the Stoics explaining the mode of perception (in which they are necessarily crude), they are also aiming at supplying a Criterion of Truth ; and that criterion they declare to be the power that the mind has of laying hold of reality through the strength and clearness of consentient impressions, as proved by the undoubting conviction of the percipient—at least, if the percipient be a wise man. It is quite true that this last qualification, "if the percipient be a wise man," leaves a margin of difficulty, and opens the door to the objection (urged, as a matter of fact, in olden times against the Stoics) that you have only to claim to be yourself the wise man and to dub the man who disagrees with you a fool, and the matter is ended. But this objection is inconclusive and superficial. For we must not forget that we do all of us, whether Stoics or not, consciously or unconsciously, guide ourselves, in the matter of sense-perception, by an ideal or absolutely normal standard : we suppose healthy perfectly-working sense organs (eyes, for instance, uninjured and free from visual defect) and a healthy mind, free from aberration ;

and we make carefully planned experiments to test our perceptive powers, and bring our scientific knowledge to bear, so as to correct for the personal equation. Our methods are far more exact, and our knowledge of the fallacies of sense-perception far more precise and fuller,[1] but the principle that underlies this procedure is precisely that of the Stoics, who, from the time of Zeno, clearly laid down the nature of false or unfounded sense-impressions, and, in doing so, implicitly defined the foolish man as the hasty, the careless, the prejudiced percipient, or as a man suffering from mental disorder; while the wise man is he of unclouded mind, calm, careful, deliberate, unprejudiced. Impressions equally affect the wise and the unwise; but, while the latter may give an occasional or accidental assent to them, the former has the characteristic of yielding a free, consistent, and unerring assent, and of stamping them with his approval. "For as in a balance the scale must needs fall down if weights are placed in it, so the mind must yield to things perspicuous; for just as no animal can resist seeking for what appears suited to its nature (the Greeks call it οἰκεῖον), so it is not possible to refuse assent to an object that is perspicuous" (Cicero, *Acad.* ii. 37). Moreover, as Epictetus said (*Diss.* ii. 20), it is the greatest proof of a thing's being perspicuous, "that it is found to be necessary even for him who denies it to make use of it at the same time." And if even a wise man may sometimes seem to be mistaken, the story of Sphærus may show us how the Stoic surmounted this difficulty. It is recorded of Sphærus, a disciple of Cleanthes, that,

[1] See Professor Sully, *Illusions.*

after he had gone to Alexandria, to the court of Ptolemy
Philopator, the king on one occasion, when the question
was raised whether a wise man would allow himself to
be guided by opinion, and Sphærus had affirmed that
he would not, desiring to confute him, caused some
wax pomegranates to be set before him, and when
Sphærus was deceived by them, exclaimed in triumph
that he had given his assent to a false perception.   To
this Sphærus cleverly replied that he had not assented
to their being pomegranates, but only to the probability
of their being so ; for "an apprehending representation," he said, "is a different thing from what is probable" (Diogenes Laërtius, vii. 6).

Now, to put the matter in more modern phraseology,
the point is that, given the normal percipient, vividness
and warmth of impression do create conviction ; and,
through concentration of the mind upon it, we come
to take in the character of the impressing object, and
to feel its power.   Moreover, we can verify and test
our experience of it ; and as itself is found to be part
of a general system and to have a place in an ordered
scheme of things, that very fact adds strength to it,
and gives it a cogency that is irresistible.   We have
now, according to the figure of Zeno, the clenched
hand in the grasp of reality.   Reality reveals itself to
us, and we give our voluntary assent to it.

In a similar way, the wise man in Ethics (for, as
virtue is knowledge to the Stoic, Epistemology has
a necessary connexion with morality) can penetrate
appearances (φαντασίαι), and refuse to give assent to
those that are false, while no one can prevent his
assenting to such as are true : he affirms the good and

denies the evil.[1]   Hence, Marcus Aurelius declares that
objects of aversion and desire do not press upon us,
it is we that make up to them ; if we let our judgment
about them lie still, they too will keep still.[2]   And a
celebrated simile of Epictetus is also in place here.
"As is a dish of water, such is the soul.   As is the
ray of light that falls on the water, such are the appearances.   When, then, the water is moved, the ray seems
to be moved, yet it is not moved " (*Diss.* iii. 3).   Here,
too (in Ethics), assent is voluntary and is determined
by the reason ; for—

> " He that complies against his will
> Is of his own opinion still " ;[3]

and not the least important ground of ethical conviction resides in perception of the fact that this or that
ethical notion works into a system of moral thought
and attaches itself to consistent moral practice.   Vividness of moral principles and, therefore, strength of
conviction, is gained by constant application of the
principles : life reacts upon thought, and truth becomes
all the clearer when it is assimilated by the individual
and acted on in conduct.

Thirdly, objection may be taken to the form of the
Stoic doctrine of " pre-conceptions " or " common
notions "—a doctrine rife in the school from Cleanthes
downwards.   But there is truth in the substance of it.
Reason is, indeed, generically identical in men, and acts

[1] See Epictetus, *Dissertations*, i. 8 and ii. 23.
[2] *Meditations*, xii. 11 and vi. 52.
[3] Butler, *Hudibras*, Pt. iii. Canto 3.

both spontaneously and reflectively ; and human experience is, in fundamental points, very much the same in every land and in every century. There is a natural untaught logic, instinctive and effective, as well as a highly organized logic of the trained disputant. Even on the plain man life's experiences enforce truth ; and it counts for much that every human being has uniform natural surroundings and is born into society. Wherefore, there is such a thing as common convictions among mankind, irresistible beliefs ; and these come with an authority that is altogether their own. Given man and given the world in which he lives, and certain notions will inevitably emerge, accredited by his reason or satisfying his natural wants. He lays hold of them and trusts them, and frames his life accordingly. They are, therefore, in a special sense secure, and need not the *ad captandum* argument of Epictetus : " Let the Pyrrhics and the Academics come and make their defence. For I, as to my part, have no leisure for these things, nor am I able to join with them and advocate common usage. If I had a petty lawsuit about a small field, would I call in another to advocate my cause ? With what, then, am I satisfied ? With that which belongs to the matter in hand. How, indeed, perception is effected, whether through the whole or the part, perhaps I am unable to explain ; and both opinions perplex me. But that you and I are not the same, I know with perfect certainty. How do you know it ? Never, when I wish to swallow anything, do I carry the bit there [to your mouth], but here [to mine]. Never, when I wish to take bread, do I take a broom, but I always go to the bread as to a mark. And do you

yourselves who confute the senses act otherwise?
Which of you, wishing to enter a bath, ever went into
a mill?" (*Diss.* i. 27).

Some have asserted that there is an incompatibility
between the Stoic doctrine of pre-conceptions or natural
notions and that of the sense origin of knowledge.
But, in reality, there is no such incompatibility, unless
we interpret pre-conceptions as literal innate ideas—
which was not what the Stoics intended.   It might be
a valid objection to say that this natural power of
forming concepts is incompatible with thoroughgoing
materialism, but that is a different affair.   If mind
is essentially active, there is no inconsistency in holding that its activity is first elicited by and exercised
upon material supplied by the senses, and yet that
itself has the power of reading the hidden meaning
of this material—of apprehending truth, as well as
reality.

Objection has also been taken to the Stoic test of a
pre-conception.   That test is *consensus gentium*, the
general or universal consent of mankind.   This, it has
been said, is to appeal to mere vulgar or uncriticized
opinion ; and it is, moreover, inconsistent with the
Stoic's contempt for the plain man, whom he regarded
as other than a wise man.

But by " universal consent " the Stoics did not mean
the consent of everybody throughout the world and
throughout the ages, without exception.   They quite
well knew that there were people who will deny anything ; and of such people they had ample experience in

6

their own day. What they meant was that pre-
conceptions are everywhere accepted when the mind is
calm, clear, and unprejudiced—when, therefore, it is in
the state that characterizes the wise man. On the
other hand, they quite readily admitted that the plain
man might be a wise man. In order to a sound judgment, learning was not indispensable : it was enough
if a man were intelligent, and, above all, were of
upright character. What distinguished the wise man
was not so much intellectual acumen as moral excellence ; and so far were the Stoics from despising the
plain man, that they drew no marked distinction between
him and the cultured man, but laid the emphasis on the
distinction between the good man and the bad man.

(3) *Summary*

Viewing their Epistemology as a whole, then, we can
very well see that the Stoics set themselves strenuously
to grapple with the problem of the nature and validity
of knowledge, and not without success. They were,
indeed, handicapped by their materialism ; but, apart
from that, they proceeded on suggestive lines, and in
measure anticipated thoughts that were to be fully
productive only many centuries later. In the criterion of truth, for instance, Descartes and Spinoza
were foreshadowed ; and it would not be difficult to
find Stoic parallels to the Epistemological teaching of
Thomas Reid and Lotze. Though they erred in con-
ceiving the mind as originally a sheet of clean paper,
they rectified this, in great part, when they allowed
the mind's native activity to count for much in knowledge ; and they had implicit faith in reason. They

thoroughly understood that to criticize reason itself is impossible ; for that would imply possession of a reason above reason, and another reason above that, and so on *ad infinitum*,[1] whereas absolute distrust of reason is both intellectual and volitional imbecility. Naturally, their doctrine of sense-perception was, in many ways, immature ; but their clear recognition of the fact that reality is given in perception, and their distinction between hasty inference and calm unprejudiced assent,—assent, too, that is not forced upon the mind by compulsion, but is voluntarily rendered,—are points of the greatest importance for theory of knowledge, significant for all time.[2]

[1] See Epictetus, *Diss.* i. 17.

[2] In a wider sense, it is interesting to compare this doctrine of assent with Cardinal Newman's position in *The Grammar of Assent*, and with Professor James's *Will to Believe*.

CHAPTER V

PHYSICS: NATURE, GOD, THE SOUL

" Both Stoics and Platonics held the world to be alive. . . . But in this, notwithstanding what hath been surmised by some learned men, there seems to be no Atheism. For, so long as the world is supposed to be quickened by elementary fire or spirit, which is itself animated by soul and directed by understanding, it follows that all parts thereof originally depend upon, and may be reduced unto the same indivisible stem or principle, to wit, a Supreme Mind ; which is the concurrent doctrine of Pythagoreans, Platonics, and Stoics."—BERKELEY.

I

BY Physics, as already said, the Stoics did not alone understand what in modern science is designated by that name, but rather the metaphysical explanation of the world, comprising Cosmogony, Rational Psychology, and Theology. The mixed nature of it may in part be judged from the enumeration of topics with which, according to Diogenes Laërtius (vii. 67), it dealt—namely, " bodies, first principles, elements, the gods, limits, place, and the void " ; or, again, dividing according to genera, "the world, the elements, and the investigation of causes ($\tau\grave{o}$ $a\grave{i}\tau\iota o\lambda o\gamma\iota\kappa\acute{o}\nu$)." It was, in great measure, philosophy interpreting nature to the reason ; endeavouring to satisfy the intellect by giving a coherent view of the cosmic system, and determining man's place, lot, and destiny therein.

The problem was, Given the universe, with our multifarious experiences of it and our relations to it, how are we to interpret it? Clearly, the interpreting term must be the principle of unity. But this unity must not be incompatible with plurality and diversity; otherwise, we have not explained the world that we know, but have merely ignored a prominent factor in it. In our experience, things change. But, in order to change, there must be presupposed something changeless,—law, or process, or substance. There are differences on all hands in nature; and if these are to be gathered up in a unity, that unity must be one from which they are also seen to emerge. In the solution, God, the World, and the human Soul must all find a place; and there must also be an Eschatology, or doctrine of last things.

The problem was not new to thinking minds—how could it, as curiosity is natural to man? It had been bravely faced by the pre-Socratic philosophers, and solutions on two distinct lines had been offered of it. The Eleatics had fixed exclusively on the unity, and had denied the possibility of change, regarding it simply as a delusion of the senses. Heracleitus of Ephesus, "the obscure," started with plurality and change, with the perpetual motion and transmutation that are discernible alike in human consciousness and in outward nature, and explained them in the light of the world-ruling reason, the cosmic *logos*, the permanent "antiphonal rhythm," "which, proceeding uniformly from movement to movement, as in some intricate musical theme, might link together in one those contending, infinitely diverse impulses."[1] To him, "the many are the moving realisation of the Eternal One. 'Being' was always 'becoming'—not a state but a process, not rest but motion—and its true image was the flame which in kindling extinguishes, and in extinguishing kindles that which is its fuel. . . . His two cardinal contributions to physics were, his resolution of mechanical change into continuous dynamical progress, and, as its consequent, the idea of an unbroken sequence of successions, constituting an invariable cosmic march or rhythm of events, which might be personified as an unalterable cosmic will or destiny (δίκη, λόγος, εἱμαρμένη), or generalised into an abstract uniformity of natural law. He himself persistently interpreted it as the expression of an *ethical* order ; and his followers, the school of Ephesus, continued to be the avowed and scornful antagonists of all who remained content with base materialistic Sensationalism."[2]

The primitive matter, according to Heracleitus, was Fire, rationally determined : from this all things orderly proceed, and by it they are all consumed. "This one order of all things," he says, "was created by none of the gods, nor yet by any of mankind, but it ever was, and is, and shall be—eternal fire—ignited by measure, and extinguished by measure."[3] Thus, in the midst of all diversity and change, there is rational order, universal causality ; and man's wisdom lies in recogni-

[1] Walter Pater, *Plato and Platonism*, p. 12.

[2] Principal Rendall, *Marcus Aurelius Antoninus To Himself*, pp. xviii and xx. See also Gomperz, *Greek Thinkers*, i. 73–79 ; and Windelband, *A History of Philosophy*, part i. chap. i. sec. 4.

[3] Quoted by Gomperz, *Greek Thinkers*, i. 64.

tion of this and in submission: "Therefore, we ought to follow the universal; but, though the logos is universal, the majority of men live as though they had an intelligence of their own (ὡς ἰδίαν ἔχοντες φρόνησιν, Sextus Empiricus, vii. 133):" "they do not understand how that which is discordant is concordant with itself: as with the bow and the lyre, so with the world—it is the tension of opposing forces that makes the structure one." Such universal order, harmonizing opposites, is designated by Heracleitus *logos* — to which are ascribed, besides unity and rationality, eternity, omnipresence, and divinity. It is the eternal divine reason immanent in the world, and finding its highest interpretation in ethical order.

II

It was to Heracleitus that the Stoics attached themselves in Physics, although they did not by any means follow him slavishly. On the contrary, their deep religious sentiment and their leanings towards a theistic interpretation of the world (seen conspicuously in the Later Stoa) led them to part from him at many points.

They began, in true monistic fashion, by positing a primitive substance. This primitive substance, or original source of all things, is Fire—fire, however, not in its grosser earthly form, but as a sublimated all-pervasive essence or ether, denominated (though not by the Stoics themselves) "ethereal fire" (πῦρ αἰθερῶδες), called by Cleanthes "fiery breath" (πνεῦμα). This primordial fire, which is also the Deity, is eternal; and

from all eternity, it is possessed of activity—of thought
and of will. Endowed thus with inherent productive
power or creative activity, it is the " seminal reason "
(λόγος σπερματικὸς) of the world, manifesting itself in the
various phenomena of the universe as " seminal reasons "
(λόγοι σπερματικοί) — termed by Aurelius (*Med.* ix. 1)
"certain germs of future existences, [endowed with]
productive capacities of realisation, change, and pheno-
menal succession."[1] This thinking volitional Ether—
known technically as "artificial fire" (πῦρ τεχνικόν)—
produces from itself the world that now is, all pheno-
menal existence ; giving birth to solid and fluid, to earth
and air, etc., by means of the two principles of condensa-
tion and expansion, the solidity of matter being due to
the former, and its various qualities or attributes being
got from the latter (τόνος, strain or tension). First, in the
order of evolution, came a fiery vapour yielding moisture
(τὸ ὑγρόν),—which, by and by, condensed, and, in con-
densing formed the four elements, becoming respectively

---

[1] This conception of "the seminal reason" was a chief point
that early Christian writers (especially those who had themselves
been philosophers) laid hold of, so as to connect Greek thought
with Christian teaching. Thus, Justin Martyr, maintaining that
every man at birth shares in the universal reason and so has in
him a λόγος σπερματικὸς (which, of course, he associated with Christ
as the Logos), holds that, on this account, men such as Socrates
who lived noble lives before the coming of Christ could be saved :
he even claimed them as Christians. "Those," he says (*Apology*,
41), "who have lived with reason (μετὰ λόγου), even though they
were reckoned atheists, are Christians, such as, among the Greeks,
Socrates, Heraclitus, and those like them." And well may
Heracleitus be included here, for the doctrine of the *logos* may be
said to have originally emanated from him ; and he enunciated it
more in the spirit of a prophet making a revelation, than of a
philosopher maintaining an intellectual position—hence, perhaps,
his designation "the obscure."

fire, water, air, earth;[1] so that the four elements are but tension in different degrees or grades. By the intermingling of its elements the individual thing is produced.[2] This is the celebrated theory of mixture, or κρᾶσις δι' ὅλου, "which is in effect a denial of the axiom that two bodies cannot occupy the same space."[3] All things that exist in the world thus partake of the divine substance, but in different degrees. What appears in inorganic matter as cohesion or "hold" (ἕξις), becomes in plants "vital force" (φύσις), manifesting living growth; in animals, "soul irrational" (ψυχὴ ἄλογος), endowed, perhaps, with the power of inference (which Chrysippus, for instance, allowed to dogs), but devoid of self-consciousness and ignorant of the meaning of existence; in man, as "soul rational," possessed of self-consciousness and the higher thought (ψυχὴ λόγον ἔχουσα).[4] The heavenly bodies,—sun, moon, stars, and planets,—inasmuch as they are made of very pure fire, stand specially near to God, and may be themselves regarded as divinities: their unsurpassed brilliancy and heat and the regularity of their movements seemed to sanction that conception. Man shows in himself the divine—especially, in his soul; and, indeed, according Zeno, he was originally formed out of the divine substance—is con-substantial with the divine. Under any circumstances, his Reason (λόγος, τὸ ἡγεμονικὸν) is a ray of the celestial fire, a spark from the primal ether —"that particle of Zeus, which Zeus gives to every

---

[1] See Diog. Laërt. vii. 135. [2] *Ibid.* vii. 151.
[3] Pearson, *The Fragments of Zeno and Cleanthes*, p. 11.
[4] See Sextus Empiricus, ix. 81 and viii. 2; also, Marcus Aurelius, *Meditations*, vi. 14.

man for his controller and governor."[1] "And from Him [God] have descended the seeds, not only to my father and my grandfather, but to all things that have been begotten and are nourished on the earth, but chiefly to those that possess reason, for these alone are privileged by nature to hold communion with God, being united with Him in intercourse through reason : why may not a man then call himself a citizen of the world? why not a son of God?" (Epictetus, *Diss.* i. 9). This reason is essentially "the ruling faculty" in man ; and hence to it are subordinated the other seven parts of the soul, namely, the five senses, speech, and reproduction. It is significantly (so the later Stoics were fond of regarding it) the dæmon or genius (ὁ δαίμων), in each individual man, his guardian angel, given him by Zeus to direct his life, as Aurelius had expressed it in the passage just quoted (*Med.* v. 27)—as Menander designates it, μυσταγωγὸς τοῦ βίου. Into the Universal Reason, whence he came, man is resolved again : "You exist but as a part inherent in a greater whole. You will vanish into that which gave you being ; or rather, you will be transmuted into the seminal and universal reason" (Aurelius, iv. 14).[2] The world is a macrocosm (at least, so taught Cleanthes), to which man is exactly correspondent as microcosm. The Deity, therefore, is the soul of the world,[3] and inhabits it as Divine Reason— possessed of "infinite power and transcendent wisdom," as well as, according to later views, of "absolute goodness" ; and whereas in man the seat of the reason is the

---

[1] Aurelius, *Med.* v. 27. See also Epictetus, *Diss.* i. 3.
[2] See also Epictetus, *Diss.* i. 9.
[3] See Seneca, *Quæstiones Naturales*, ii. 45.

breast, the seat of the world's reason (so taught Cleanthes) is the sun.[1] All things that are undergo perpetual flux or change, and are ever passing into something which they are not now; as Heracleitus put it, "all things are in flow" (πάντα ῥεῖ), or "change is the path upwards and downwards, and the world exists according to it."[2] "Watch how all things continually change, and accustom yourself to realise that Nature's prime delight is in changing things that are, and making new things in their likeness. All that is, is as it were the seed of that which shall issue from it" (Aurelius, *Med.* iv. 36). Hence, the world itself has only a temporary existence. It comes from God, the primal ether, completes its course, and then is absorbed in God again. This takes place according to an infinite and unvarying series of cycles. At the end of each cycle comes a great conflagration (ἐκπύρωσις); and then, as the Pythagoreans too had taught, things begin to run their course (there is a "regeneration," or παλιγγενεσία), in the exact same way as before: the exact same incidents and events come round in one cycle as had happened in the previous cycles; the same people, the same experience, the same history and achievements, the same failures are reproduced—inexorable fate and dire necessity rule all.[3] From God and to God—issuing, becoming, and reabsorption—is the invariable order; to be repeated times without end. In the midst of all, what remains steadfast is the divine primal

---

[1] Different Stoics, however, located it differently.

[2] Diog. Laërt. ix. 1.

[3] This doctrine of World-cycles had an immense fascination for, and was elaborated by, Cleanthes; but many eminent Stoics (*e.g.*, Panætius) rejected it.

fire,[1] consuming all, yet itself consumed by none. Universal law, too, or fixed course of things, continues ; so that Destiny or Fate rules the Deity, as well as mundane affairs. Yea, this Fate or Destiny is, from one point of view, itself the Deity ; although, from another point of view, the Deity is the Reason of the World and divine Forethought or Providence (πρόνοια). " In the God's work there is providence everywhere. For, the action of chance is the course of nature, or the web and woof of the dispositions of providence. From providence flows all ; and side by side with it is necessity and the advantage of the Universe, of which you are a part " (Aurelius, *Med.* ii. 3).

III

This cosmic theory is, in many ways, a striking one, although it does not possess for modern thought the interest and significance of the rival Epicurean theory —which, with a difference, was that of Democritus and the Atomists. In view of the nebular hypothesis and of several more recent physical conceptions, a certain scientific interest attaches to the teaching that the universe originated in a fiery vapour ; and if it be so, as physicists have maintained, that the earth is destined to be absorbed in the sun, the doctrine of the final conflagration ceases to be an absolutely wild unbridled fancy, and the early Christian writers were justified in bringing it into comparison with the Scripture presentation of the end of the world.[2] Perhaps, too, the conception of recurrent cycles and of the return of all

---

[1] Personified as Zeus or Jupiter. See, *e.g.*, Seneca, *Ep.* 9.
[2] See, *e.g.*, Marcus Minucius Felix, *Octavius*, 33.

created things to the bosom of the primal substance is but a far-off and dimly conscious recognition of the doctrine of the conservation of energy. But the real interest in the theory for the present day is not scientific but philosophical. In the face of modern materialism and of pantheism, it is instructive to see how these same doctrines were maintained and held together by the most materialistic, and yet the most fervently religious, of the ancient Greek sects. Points, therefore, to be specially noted are the following :—

First, as the world, with all that it contains, is the product of divine power, and, when viewed pantheistically in strict Stoic fashion, is itself the Deity, it is necessarily perfect. It is an organic unity, with its parts adapted to each other, and each necessary to the perfection of the whole. "There is nothing existent," says Balbus, in the *De Naturâ Deorum* (ii. 13), "that is not defective, except the universe, which is well provided and fully complete and perfect in all its parts and members."

Next, the Deity is in essence material ; yet, this materialism is dynamic and not mechanical—it includes all mental and spiritual characteristics, summed up in Thought and Will, or in the single term Active Reason.

This fact that the primitive matter is characterized by reason and activity deprives the Stoic materialism of what would otherwise be a baneful influence, and explains how the Stoical ethics and also the Stoical theology should be so highly spiritualistic as they

unquestionably are.[1] Matter is simply one aspect of
the first cause, and expresses the passive principle
(with nothing derogatory thereby connoted); while
the other aspect is the active principle, as reason and
will, and this active principle is supreme.[2] If, in this,
spiritualism and materialism seem blended in a confusing fashion, one can only ask whether there is
anything more confusing here than is to be found in
many modern forms of materialism—*e.g.*, in Clifford's
doctrine of matter as "mind-stuff," or in Tyndall's
conception of it as "the promise and potency of every
form and quality of life," or in Haeckel's ascription to
it of an "atomic soul" possessed of "will and
sensation."[3]

Thirdly, if the Deity is material, so also is everything
that proceeds therefrom: so is the human soul, which
is simply a fiery current diffused throughout the body,
and grows along with the body, developing gradually
under sense-experiences, and reaching the full power of
reason only when the individual attains the age of
fourteen. Moreover, it holds the body together. And
not only is the human soul material, but material are
all its qualities and properties as well—emotions and
intellections, truth and knowledge, virtue and morality.
"Whatever acts is corporeal ($\sigma\hat{\omega}\mu\alpha$)."[4] "It is a dictum

[1] See, for instance, Cleanthes, *Hymn to Zeus*, and Epictetus,
passim.

[2] See Diog. Laërt. vii. 139.

[3] Thoroughgoing materialism was carried out in early Christian
times by Tertullian, whose leading principle was, "What is not
body is nothing at all (*nihil enim, si non corpus est*)."

[4] Diog. Laërt. vii. 38.

of ours that the good is corporeal (*corpus*), because
what is good acts, and whatever acts is corporeal."[1]

Here, again, nothing derogatory is implied in
designating the soul material. Man's mind has a
passive and an active side. But, as ethics and
knowledge both repose on the mind's activity, the
Stoical materialism is practically innocuous.

It is worth remarking, however, that although
the soul's materiality follows deductively from the
materiality of the primal fire, nevertheless the Stoics,
true to their experiential tendencies, based it also on
certain observed facts. Thus, Cleanthes argued that
it was proved (*a*) by the circumstance that not only
bodily qualities, but also mental capacity, are transmitted by ordinary generation from parent to child;
and (*b*) by the sympathy of the soul with the body—
seen in the fact that, when the body is struck or cut,
the soul is pained; and when the soul is torn by anxiety
or depressed by care, the body is correspondingly
affected.[2]

Further, the Stoic eschatology calls for remark.
According to the doctrine of reabsorption into the
primal fire, everything is indestructible: though a
thing may change its form, itself persists. The human
soul, therefore, is in this sense immortal. But about
this reabsorption of the soul, there are several unex-
plained difficulties in Stoicism:—

---

[1] Seneca, *Ep.* 117.

[2] These arguments were reproduced afterwards among early
Christians by Tertullian, in support of his doctrine of the
traducianist origin of the soul.

First, whether the absorption takes place immediately on the death of the individual ; or whether the individual continues to exist as an individual till the great conflagration ; or whether he falls by degrees into the Deity, through a process of gradual purification,—was not dogmatically determined. For each of these positions high Stoical authority could be quoted ; and high authority could be quoted also for suspense of judgment on the point. All that even Aurelius can say is : "Thou hast embarked, thou hast made the voyage, thou hast come to shore ; get out. If, indeed, to another life, there is no want of gods, not even there. But if to a state without sensation, thou wilt cease to be held by pains and pleasures."[1] And even among those who maintained that the individual soul lived on till the conflagration (which was the earlier opinion), there was doubt as to whether this held of all souls or only of the souls, of the wise ; Cleanthes upholding the first of these opinions, and Chrysippus the second. [2]

Next, whether, when the individual is absorbed, the past experience of his life on earth has any effect, by way of unconscious influence or impulse, in urging on or causing his return to individual existence, is not plain. It is in itself quite conceivable that desire of individual life might remain, or, at any rate (to put it more exactly), that the fact of a man's having existed individually here might leave a permanent effect, which would tell, though unconsciously to the man himself, in procuring his future reissuing from the divine source.

[1] *Med.* iii. 3. See also Epictetus, *Diss.* iii. 13, 24.
[2] See Diog. Laërt. vii. 157.

This point, however, seems not to have occurred to the Stoics. The doctrine of Unconscious Will had to await Schopenhauer.

Nor, thirdly, did the Stoics settle whether any recollection of former states of existence remains to the individual when he does return again to the earth, and the new cycle runs. Had they accepted the Platonic doctrine of Ideas and Reminiscence, their answer would, presumably, have been in the affirmative. But that doctrine was disowned by them. They maintained, however, that the Socrates of a future period would not be numerically one with the Socrates of the present —the two would simply be alike. And if, as some Stoics held, this similarity between the two Socrateses was accompanied by marked differences, then, perhaps, an answer in the negative would be necessitated.

But, all this apart, the noteworthy point is, that (from the time of Cleanthes, at any rate) Immortality, as continued, though not endless, existence after death, was a doctrine of the Stoics; and this not merely "subjective" immortality, such as the Comtists or Positivists of to-day promise us as our sole consolation —namely, posthumous fame, or the continuance of a man's name and influence among posterity, the abiding effect of his life and work upon succeeding generations. This kind of immortality they admitted, and they even regarded it as a "good" (at least the later Stoics did); but, with moments of inconsistency and vacillation, they demanded something more. While, on occasion, Seneca could say, as he contemplated the possibility of a young man's death, "he lived, and passed away to posterity, and gave himself to be a memory," he was

7

too well aware, like Marcus Aurelius, that the most lasting fame is but of brief duration, to rest satisfied with this. Speaking of death, he says, "The day that you dread as though it were your last is the birthday of eternity,"[1] and so he advocates a personal or "objective" immortality, and supports it by characteristic reasoning. To him, as to other later Stoics, the immortality of the soul was not only a logical consequence from the Stoical physics; it was also corroborated by the fact of men's general belief in it, and thus came with particular authority. And the object of the belief is to Seneca, in his highest apocalyptic moments, no vague colourless hereafter, no mere abstraction of the intellect, but a vivid, definite future life of bliss, a state in which we shall revel in ineffable light, and have the mysteries of nature revealed to us, and in which we shall hold intercourse with the gods and with the spirits of the blessed. His delineation in such a mood almost approaches to the warm glowing picture of the Christian teaching in the New Testament.[2] Thus did the later Stoicism try to meet the claims of the human heart, which the earlier Stoicism had to a large extent ignored, and to adjust its pantheism to the deeper personal needs of human nature, which were more and more making themselves felt. Had the views of Plato regarding immortality (as disclosed, say, in the *Phædo*) affected the older Stoics, their treatment of the future state would have been different; but it is one of the peculiarities of the case that the earlier Stoics, though conversant

[1] *Ep.* 102 : "Dies iste quem tanquam extremum reformidas æterni natalis est."
[2] See *Epp.* 26, 55, 63, 102, 120.

with Plato, left it to Seneca to appreciate Plato's teaching in this connexion, and to advance upon it.[1]

IV

But now comes the inevitable criticism.

First, the Cosmology of the Stoics, although in many ways remarkable, is not in its ultimate principle philosophically satisfactory. The origin of the world is not really explained by the doctrine of Matter, even when the materialism is not mechanical but dynamic.

As to the conception of Matter, in relation to Active Reason or the Supreme Mind, one of four conceivable views may be maintained :—(1) First, we may posit two distinct entities—God on the one side, and matter on the other ; each of them independent, and each eternal. (2) Secondly, we may posit two distinct entities—God and matter ; but the latter, though eternal, not independent of the other, but eternally derived from it. (3) Thirdly, we may posit God as the alone independent and eternal, and matter as the product of His creative power, brought into existence through His efficiency. (4) Fourthly, we may posit one sole existence, eternal and self-contained ; and, if we favour Idealism, this sole existence will be God as Mind or Spirit, if Materialism, it will be matter or the world (*mundus*).

Now, as to the first of these, two independent and eternal existences, though the words seem to have sense before we consider them, yield a contradiction in terms. For, by the supposition, matter is exclusively

[1] See S. Dill, *Roman Society from Nero to Marcus Aurelius*, bk. iv. chap. ii.

shut out from mind: there are no bonds of causation between them, and they have no points of community. But, if so, there is no means whereby the two can be brought together: they must for ever remain apart, and by no possibility could the world, as we know it, have come into being at all.   Dualism of this stamp is utterly unworkable.

As to the second, we have not here, as in the previous case, a self-contradiction; for the eternity of matter is quite a tenable notion, if matter be not from the beginning rigidly shut out from intelligence, but, on the contrary, be conceived as something harmonized from the first—ordered, with its parts in rational relationship. This was Aristotle's idea, which he claims to have been first thrown out by himself—namely, not the eternity of matter *per se*, but the eternity of matter *as a cosmos*. The strong point about it is, that it clearly recognizes that an eternal Deity must have an eternal manifestation, and that matter absolutely unordered is an impotent conception.   But it is liable to objection on the score that it seems not to perceive that the modes of Divine manifestation—actual, possible, or conceivable— are countless. We can dogmatically affirm ordered matter to be necessarily eternal only if we can prove it to be the sole possible means whereby the Deity can objectify Himself.   That, however, cannot be done; for Spirit may reveal itself to spirit, and *in* and *through* spirit be manifested; and a world of spirits would meet the requirements of the divine manifestation, as well as a material universe, and so the cosmos need not be eternal—the eternal may be the spirit world.

In the third view, the dependence of the world on

the Divine Mind is recognized, and a suggestive view of its origin offered. We now start with a matter that is inchoate and only gradually brought into a cosmos; and so we posit a beginning that gives scope for development and temporal evolution. The inchoate matter may be designated a "chaos"; but it is a chaos that is not absolute, but only relative. An absolute chaos would bring us back to the inconceivable and self - contradictory position of the first hypothesis. Matter as chaos can simply mean matter not yet brought into the ordered relations that we are acquainted with in the world of our experience. To us, or from our point of view, it is "without form and void";[1] yet, inasmuch as it is in relation to the Creative Intelligence, it is not the absolutely formless, but the potentially formed and implicitly rational world-mass. It is to be conceived, therefore, as implicating development and change; time being needed to make the implicit explicit, or to bring the potential into actuality. Such a conception is compatible with the revelations of modern science; and, moreover, it gives us the true philosophical signification of the Absolute, whereon the world is dependent. By the Absolute is not meant the unrelated and unrelatable, or that which is, by its very nature, out of all relation. On the contrary, it means that which is potentially relatable to everything. A being out of relation (both actual and potential) to *every*thing could never be brought into relation with *any*thing. There is nothing in itself whereby it could be done; nor is there anything outside itself whereby

[1] Gen. i. 2. This Biblical phrase the Septuagint translates "invisible and unfurnished" (ἀόρατος καὶ ἀκατασκεύαστος).

it could be done. Not in itself; for, being the absolutely unrelated, there is, *ex hypothesi*, no point of
attachment with the related. Not in anything outside ;
for, as things outside are all in relation, they could not
strip themselves of relation so as to come within range
of the non-related. The phrase "unrelated to everything" is exactly synonymous with the phrase "unrelatable to anything"; while, on the other hand, "related to anything" is synonymous with "relatable to
everything."

The fourth position is the assertion of Monism, and
is logically the declaration that one half of the dualism
of our experience is illusion. If we take the idealistic
standpoint here, then we assert that God is all, and
matter, save in appearance, is not ; if the materialistic
standpoint, then, though we may use the name God, we
empty it of its proper meaning, and assert the sole
supremacy of matter. But, either way, we merely
assert ; we do not prove. And this was what the
Stoics, especially those of the Earlier Stoa, occupying
the materialistic position, did. To them, all is matter.
Thought, reasoning, feeling, will—each is material ; as
much so as the human body or inorganic things. God
Himself is matter. But this really explains nothing.
The distinctive feature of life, or of consciousness, or of
thought, is simply ignored when it is swamped in the
same category with what is lifeless, unconscious, or
irrational. It is on the face of it plausible to declare
(as Zeno, carrying out his doctrine of strain or tension,
does) that one divine material substance pervades
everything ; appearing in the inorganic as "hold" or
ἕξις, in plants as "vital force" or φύσις, in animals as

"irrational soul" or ψυχὴ ἄλογος, and in man as "rational soul" or ψυχὴ λόγον ἔχουσα. But when we ask, What really has "hold" in common with "vital force," or "vital force" with "soul" or with "reason"? we find that we have surmounted the difficulty only in *words*. In their ultimate unity, the Stoics assumed mind, with all its characteristics, in matter; and the evolution of the world from the primal material fire became possible, only because in the primal fire are presupposed rationality and will. Yet, even thus, God is not, except in the sense of the material world; and, although to the Later Stoa (Epictetus, Seneca, etc.), and in connexion with ethics, the Deity assumed a personal spiritual aspect, He is only an impersonal force to the founders of the school, and could scarcely be other if the Stoical physics is to be strictly adhered to.

This suggests, for another point, that the physics and the ethics of the Stoics (more especially, the ethics of the Roman period) are not metaphysically of a piece: speculative materialism rules the one, intense scorn of moral materialism dominates the other. This will be impressed upon us with sufficient fulness later on. But, meanwhile, it may be well to observe that there are points in the ethical teaching that are affected for ill by the physical speculations. One such point is the conception of evil; of which cosmic pantheism, looking upon the world as perfect, could give no adequate rendering. Another has reference to the doctrine of all-controlling necessity or fate. This had sometimes a numbing influence on practice, and tended to encourage people in a too servile acquiescence in the existing state

of things.   Hence, with the exception of Epictetus
(himself originally a slave), the Stoics did not overtly
condemn slavery as an institution, but accepted it.
Nevertheless, their predominant altruism led them to
treat slaves with great humaneness and consideration,
looking upon them as friends and brothers.   This was
the result of their enthusiasm of humanity ; the purity
and fervour of which may be seen in No. 47 of Seneca's
Letters, dealing with the treatment of slaves : *unus
omnium parens mundus est.*

Still another point may be mentioned—namely, the
impossibility of progress beyond a certain limit either
to the individual or to the world, if the doctrine of
recurrent cycles be insisted on.   If each age simply
reproduces in all its details its predecessor, then the
power of Destiny is too strong to allow the number of
good men being ever increased or the number of bad
men diminished ; and as for the world itself, it must,
on this doctrine, for ever retain its included imperfections—its flaws and its defects.   "Do not hope for
Utopia"[1]—such is the counsel.   The reflection is, to
say the least of it, not stimulating and encouraging.

So much for leading conceptions.   The remainder of
the physical speculations, dealing more specifically with
the Stoic Theology, is best understood in the light of
the Ethics, and so is deferred to Chapter XI.

[1] Aurelius, *Med.* ix. 29.

CHAPTER VI

THE EPICUREAN CONTRAST

" Now, as Science demands the radical extirpation of caprice and the absolute reliance upon law in nature, there grew with the growth of scientific notions a desire and determination to sweep from the field of theory this mob of gods and demons, and to place natural phenomena on a basis more congruent with themselves."—Tyndall.

" It should never be forgotten that the natural philosophy of Epicurus is the foundation of his ethics ; its *raison d'être* is, that it renders possible a theory of conduct."—W. Wallace.

I

Like Stoicism, Epicureanism is distinctively an ethical system ; but it is ethics reposing on physics, and so implicates psychology and theory of knowledge. Like Stoicism, too, it finds the germ of both its physics and its ethics in earlier Greek systems ; the physics being derived from Democritus and the Atomic philosophers, and the ethics from Aristippus and the Cyrenaic school.[1]

Epicurus (341–270 B.C.), like the founders of Greek schools generally, was a voluminous writer—producing " three hundred scrolls," it is said,—written, as Diogenes Laërtius boasts—(x. 17), " without any cita-

---

[1] A book of Theodorus, the Cyrenaic, *On the Gods*, is said especially to have influenced Epicurus. See Diogenes Laërtius, ii. 12.

tion from other writers, but filled simply with his own sentiments (φωναί)," thereby differing, he adds, from the Stoic Chrysippus, whose writings were overloaded with quotations from other authors. But he suffered the fate of most of the others—his works are lost. We have, indeed, three letters of his and some fragments of his writings preserved by Diogenes Laërtius ; we have also the papyri discovered more than a century ago at Herculaneum ; and we have copious accounts of Epicureanism in Cicero (*e.g.*, in *De Naturâ Deorum* and *De Finibus*, etc.). But the master himself must be studied either in the writings of his followers, or in the criticism and partial accounts of subsequent philosophers (Greek and Latin), who were, to say the least of it, not always particularly sympathetic. We are fortunate, however, in possessing the philosophical masterpiece of a great Roman poet, who was, first and foremost, a follower of Epicurus — the famous didactic poem of Lucretius (95–52 B.C.), entitled *De Rerum Naturâ* ("On the Nature of Things"), in which the cosmology and general system of the Epicureans are worked out with considerable fulness and with great enthusiasm, and in which the strength of personal conviction aids the poetic imagination and adds force to the felicitous diction, so that the picture becomes at once vivid, fascinating, and impressive.

Thrown thus, to such a large extent, on Lucretius, we naturally raise the question, whether it is safe to trust him, as substantially reproducing the doctrine of Epicurus.

For one thing, we must take care not wholly to discount Lucretius himself. Lucretius was unquestionably an able thinker ; and he was, moreover, a genuine poet. And it is incredible that a disciple thus endowed should simply repeat his master. Three things, at any rate, characterize him—a clear grasp of his subject, with an extraordinary power of happy illustration (the mark of a genuine philosopher) ; an intense enthusiasm of humanity ; and a deep, poetic, speculative and scientific interest in Nature, after the manner of Wordsworth :

> " To the solid ground
> Of Nature trusts the mind that builds for aye ;
> Convinced that there, there only she can lay
> Secure foundation."—(*Miscellaneous Sonnets*, i. 34.)

He also responded unreservedly to the charm of Nature ; revelling more especially in mountain scenery and in the grander aspects of the outer world, as became a philosopher, to whom the mountain is the natural symbol of mental ascent and of wide and clear philosophical outlook, and he was attracted by every mode and form of motion, as being significant of the unceasing activity of the primordial atoms, and suggestive of life and energy.

But, on the other hand, though we must not discount Lucretius himself, we must not forget that the Epicurean school was perhaps the strictest of all schools of antiquity in insisting on the scholars adhering rigorously to the master's dogmas. Summaries of Epicurus's teaching (κύριαι δόξαι) were prescribed to be learned by heart, and little more was encouraged in the pupil than a servile repetition of the master's thought. Epicurus

himself frequently made such summaries for the use of
inquiring followers.   Three such we have, as already
hinted, in the tenth book of Diogenes Laërtius's *Lives
of the Philosophers*, in the shape of Letters giving a
sort of epitome of his philosophy—one addressed to
Herodotus, on the Epicurean cosmogony and theory
of knowledge ; another to Pythocles, regarding the
heavenly bodies, offering natural explanations of their
phenomena, so as to dispel superstition and rid the
soul of superstitious fear ; and a third to Menœceus,
on the Epicurean Ethics, or Pleasure as the Chief Good.
Moreover, every Epicurean had for the master the most
ardent personal devotion.   He even exalted him to the
place of deity in his veneration.   This comes out again
and again in Lucretius, whose language in extolling
Epicurus is that of the enthusiastic worshipper, dis-
closing whole-hearted and unbounded admiration.[1]   He
is not even second in this respect to Lucian, who
designates Epicurus " a saint indeed, who was inspired
in the highest sense ; who alone combined, and taught
others to combine, the good with the true, and was
thus the deliverer and saviour of those who would consent to learn from him " (see his *Alexander of Abono-
teichus*).

Furthermore, it was characteristic of the disciples of
Epicurus that they had likenesses of the master " not
only in pictures, but even on their goblets and rings "
(Cicero, *De Finibus*, v. 1).

Taking all these things into consideration, then, and
remembering also that the teaching of Lucretius, in

[1] See, particularly, the prologues to Books I. III. V. and VI.

so far as it can be tested by the letters and fragments of Epicurus himself, stands the test, we may safely enough accept Lucretius as a faithful expositor, even while we do not ignore Lucretius's own ability and originality.

Trusting thus to Lucretius, let us now give an outline of the physical and the intellectual parts of the system,[1] so as to point the contrast to Stoicism.

II

We begin with the Atomic theory, as explanatory of the origin and formation of the world.

Basing his physics on the principle *Ex nihilo nihil fit, in nihilum nil posse reverti*, "Out of nothing, nothing comes ; into nothing, nothing can be turned (οὐδὲν γίνεται ἐκ τοῦ μὴ ὄντος, οὐδὲν φθείρεται εἰς τὸ μὴ ὄν),"[2] Epicurus begins by positing Atoms and the Void (τὸ κενόν)—*i.e.* atoms *in motion* and empty space— as the sole existences. Not atoms as material particles alone are sufficient ; they must be presumed to be in motion : and not atoms and motion are enough ; there must also be empty space, else how could motion be possible, or how could an explanation be given of such physical facts as the different weights of bodies similar in size or bulk ? Furthermore, this space must be taken as infinite or unbounded. As to the atoms, they are conceived as absolutely dead things —exceedingly minute, invisible, solid, material bodies, qualitatively identical, but quantitatively different— different, that is, in shape, size, and weight. They

---

[1] The ethical part is, at present, outside our consideration.
[2] See Epistle in Diog. Laërt. x. 38.

are eternal or uncreated, and indestructible—"strong in their solid singleness." This last property of indestructibility, implying in it indivisibility, belongs to them because of their exceptional hardness and solidity : they have no void or empty space within them ; therefore they cannot be broken up (hence the name ἄτομος, *atom*). Their motion, too, is indestructible. They are infinite in number, and have an indefinite (unlimited, though not absolutely limitless) number of shapes, sizes, and weights. They possess no secondary qualities—such as colour, taste, smell. They move naturally in parallel straight lines downwards, like rain falling perpendicularly from the heavens to the earth. And yet, if this perpendicular downward motion were the sole one, it would be impossible for matter to form into masses—there could be no such thing as aggregation, and the formation of the world would be impossible. Accordingly, a further supposition is necessary—namely, that the atoms have in them the power of swerving or declining from the straight line, even though it be but to the smallest possible extent— the power of passing out of the orderly march of the regular atomic dance, symbolized by the motes in a sunbeam, and so of crossing each other and of coming into contact and collision, thereby rendering combination and interaction possible.

"This point of the subject also," says Lucretius (ii. 216–224), "we wish you to understand—namely, that atoms, when they are borne straight downwards through the void by their own weight, do usually, at an uncertain time and at uncertain places, push themselves a little from their course, just so far that you can call it a change of inclination. If they were not in the habit of swerving thus, they would all fall straight down through the deep void ; and no clashing would be effected nor collision produced among the primary elements : in which case, Nature would never have produced anything (*ita nil unquam natura creasset*)."

This clashing and concourse of atoms is "uncertain," both as to place and as to time ; that is, it is casual or fortuitous—it is owing to chance, is haphazard, or occurs at random. Purpose or final end in nature, there is none. On the contrary, Nature's characteristic is, that it is uniform or is subject to law: it is the grossest superstition (so Lucretius holds) to look upon it as in any way manifesting design—*that* leads to the demoralizing and baneful doctrine of the existence and overruling care—therefore, in Lucretius's view, capricious interference—of the gods,—a doctrine that had so cramped and terrorized and debased mankind, but which must be got rid of at all costs. Indeed, it was one of the chief recommendations of the Atomic Theory to the Epicureans that it enabled them to dispense with the supernatural—not, however, with the *existence* of the gods, but with their *interference* in mundane affairs. Nature is ruléd by law, and no supersensible being can in any way alter that fact or counteract it. Hence, Epicurus located the gods in the *intermundia*, or spaces between the worlds (for there are many worlds, as he taught, and not one only) ; allowing them a life of placid ease and comfort, such as Tennyson pictures in his "Lucretius"— above the turmoils and trials of earth, and indifferent to the sorrows and the hardships and the fate of men.

> "The gods, who haunt
> The lucid interspace of world and world,
> Where never creeps a cloud, nor moves a wind,
> Nor ever falls the least white star of snow,
> Nor ever lowest roll of thunder moans,
> Nor sound of human sorrow mounts to mar
> Their sacred everlasting calm!"

The apparent design manifest in the universe is explicable on purely naturalistic principles. "For, certainly, not by design (*nam certe neque consilio*) did the primary elements of things dispose themselves each in their own order, after sage deliberation (*sagaci mente*), nor, indeed, did they settle by agreement what motions each should produce; but because, on account of their great number and the variety of the changes that they undergo, they are for an indefinite length of time agitated, through the excitation of blows all the world over, they do at length, after having experienced every kind of motion and combination, settle into those positions, whereby this world of ours is produced and exists" (Lucretius, i. 121–128). . . . . "For," he says in another place (v. 187–194), "the primary elements of things were so many in number, and excited by blows in so many ways, through untold time, and were accustomed so to be borne and carried forward by their own weight and to meet in all manners and to make all kinds of trial of what their combinations might be able to effect, that it is not surprising if they fell at last into such positions and acquired such motions as those by which this universe of things, by renovation, is now carried on."

In other words, it could not but be that an infinite number of atoms, combining in all possible ways during an infinite time, should hit upon combinations so regular and orderly as to appear to us to be works of deliberate purpose and prevision. Such is the combination, or rather countless number of combinations, that goes to form what we understand by the universe.

Thus, then, out of atoms in motion and the void, according to fixed immutable laws, the whole material universe, in the view of Lucretius, was constructed; the mode of formation being to him and to the Epicureans in general, as to Democritus, very much that which has been insisted on by modern science. In Democritus and Epicurus and Lucretius, we have the undoubted precursors of Tyndall, Huxley, Büchner, Haeckel. Indeed, it has been roundly maintained that " the general outlines of the atomic doctrine has been long accepted as in the main true; in all important features it is superior to any other physical theory of the universe which existed up to the seventeenth century. In his theory of light, Lucretius was in advance of Newton. In his theory of chemical affinities (for he describes the thing though the nomenclature was unknown to him) he was in advance of Lavoisier. In his theory of the ultimate constitution of the atom he is in striking agreement with the views of the ablest living physicists. The essential function of science—to reduce apparently disparate phenomena to the expressions of a single law—is not with him the object of a moment's doubt or uncertainty." [1]

How far the Atomic theory needs to be modified

[1] J. W. Mackail, *Latin Literature*, p. 44.

8

in the light of the phenomena of radio-activity recently discovered, is not here the question. Enough that the Electron theory now definitely formulated by physicists simply modifies; resolving the atom into minuter particles, and proving that it is not the ultimate unit of matter.

III

But atoms and the void, if they are effective thus far, can also (according to the Epicureans) go farther—they can explain to us the nature and phenomena of Life and of Mind.

In this view, Life is simply the result of particular collocations of particular atoms; and human consciousness, sensation, perception, reflection—the soul, with all its properties and functions—are the product of the elementary material particles, variously combining and reacting: life and consciousness alike are but "modes of motion."

Let us see, then, the Epicurean account of Psychology, as given by Lucretius.

The Soul or Mind is, of course, material. There is nothing in existence that is immaterial, save empty space, the void; and the void can of itself effect nothing. But the soul is an efficient agent. Therefore, it is material. As material, it is constructed out of four elements—namely, heat, air, vapour, and a fourth substance to which no name is given (*east omnino nominis expers*). To this unnamed constituent is assigned the higher functions of the soul—feeling, intellection, volition.

Nevertheless, the soul differs from grosser material

things in being composed of exceedingly minute, smooth, round atoms (the very swiftness of thought proves the extreme fineness and subtlety of the mental particles); and, though far lighter in itself than the body,—so light, indeed, that when at death it departs from the body, the body is practically as heavy as it was before,—it is, yet, so intimately connected with the body, so closely conjoined with it and perfectly adapted to it (*tam conjuncta atque uniter apta est*), that it can move, support, and even lift the body. Notwithstanding, it perishes along with the body. No part of it survives death. As being wholly dependent on the body, it is mortal. Still, the distinction between the rational and the irrational part of the soul, although both parts are mortal, is a very valid and a highly important one. The rational or higher soul Lucretius calls *animus* or *mens*; the irrational or lower soul is to him *anima*. The former is seated in the breast; the latter is diffused throughout the body.

Sensation belongs neither to the soul alone nor to the body alone, but to their mutual motions and interactions. It is generated, in true Epicurean fashion, following Empedocles, by material effluxes and pores; and the phenomena of the different senses — sight, hearing, etc.—are simply owing to difference in the number, shape, motion, and mode of arrangement of the atoms, just as different arrangement of the letters of the alphabet produces different words. From all objects of sense, effluvia or tiny films are incessantly passing off in countless numbers and in all directions. These ''images'' or εἴδωλα, when they strike the eye, pass into the pre-adapted pores, and thereby produce the sensation of vision. So that it is not the object itself that we directly see in visual perception, but the images from it. Between the percipient and the external object come the material species or forms; thereby rendering sense-perception an indirect or representative process. Nevertheless, as the images are material effluxes from bodies, perception, though indirect, is trustworthy; just as our knowledge of a person from his portrait solely is, to that extent, trustworthy. In this way, Sensation may very well be taken as the Criterion of Truth—at any rate, it is the highest criterion that we have, and the testimony of the senses cannot be gainsaid. We must stand *some*where; we cannot help taking *some*thing as true. For, as Lucretius puts it, "if any one thinks that nothing can be known, he is ignorant also of whether *that* [namely, that nothing can be known] can be known, since he confesses that he knows nothing"; and he refuses to argue with such a man, inasmuch as he occupies an inverted position (iv. 468–470). In other words, absolute scepticism is suicidal. You must, therefore, assume truth somewhere; and this somewhere reflection and experience prove to be the senses.

But may not the senses be refuted? No; for what would be the means of refutation? Not reason; for reason has arisen from the senses, and if these be false, so too must it be. Not the senses themselves, set in opposition one against the other; for each sense has its own faculty and its own province and cannot be interfered with by any of the others—the ears cannot refute the eyes, or the touch the ears, or the taste the touch. Nor yet, again, the whole of the senses taken in a body ; for, as each must be trusted equally, there is no ground for distrusting them collectively. "What, therefore, at any time whatsoever has seemed to them true, is true (*proinde quod in quoquest his visum tempore, verumst*)."[1] Sensation, then, is everything ; and even the higher intellectual processes (conception, thought, etc.) are dependent on it, and their truth must ultimately be tested by it. They are all, moreover, simple functions of the atoms, differing in number, shape, size, and combination.

But this very doctrine of the atoms itself—how can it be testified by sensation, or brought to the touchstone of sense-perception, seeing that atoms are invisible and, in a sense, imaginary? All opinion or belief, whether referring to the future or to the invisible, says Epicurus, is, if true, verified by sensation either directly or indirectly. It is verified directly, when we can test it by actual experience (I believe, say, that to-morrow will be fine ; and this belief is true if, when to-morrow comes, the day proves to be fine) ; it is verified indirectly (in cases where direct verification is out of the question, as in the hypothesis of the atoms), when sense-experience has nothing to say against it (ἢ μὴ ἀντιμαρτυρῆται).[2]

But if intellect and sense can thus be explained on the Atomic theory, so can pleasure and pain.

---

[1] *De Rerum Nat.* iv. 476–496.
[2] The handling of the Criterion of Truth was designated by the Epicureans " Canonic," and corresponded in great part to the " Logic " of the Stoics.

To the Epicurean, pleasure means simply the harmonious and orderly movement of the atoms ; while pain is the feeling that ensues when there are jarring and discord among them.

The case of Will is peculiar.

The Epicureans strenuously upheld, against the Stoics, the conception of Free Will. They would not allow fate to be absolutely supreme : there was a province rescued from its grasp. This was the province of inward mental freedom,—where we find a principle that can " break the laws of fate," the iron bonds of invariable sequence (*quod fati fœdera rumpat*). Lucretius distinctly designates it *fatis avolsa potestas*—" the power wrested from the fates." The proof of such a power the Epicureans found, in the first instance, in man's consciousness of effort in deliberation and of causality in volition—in the effect of will in moving and guiding the body.[1] But not here alone, if the Atomic theory is to be thoroughgoing and effective. For, man's soul is made up of material particles. Free will, then, must ultimately be an inherent property of the soul-atoms. But if of the soul-atoms, then also, more or less, of all atoms whatsoever ; for soul-atoms differ from others (organic and inorganic) simply in degree of fineness, size, and shape, not in essential quality. Hence, the Epicureans held—inconsistently with their primary position that atoms are absolutely dead things—that atoms, taken in themselves and apart from their aggregation into masses of matter (which aggregation nullifies or counteracts their inherent spontaneity)

[1] Lucretius, ii. 257–262.

possess intrinsically a certain power of free will. This, in its first original form, is their power of declination or swerving from the straight line—of breaking the law of gravity which is nature's "necessity," and of introducing "freedom," thereby making a cosmos possible. This power, of course, unlike free will in man, is unconscious in the atoms ; but, nevertheless, it is to be subsumed under the same category.[1]

Free will in man, like thought and the higher mental functions, attaches to "the fourth principle of the soul," by means of which it acts upon the various elements of the *anima* scattered throughout the body and produces bodily movements.

IV

In his physical speculations, Epicurus was deeply indebted to Democritus (born about 460 B.C.) and his school. The Atomic theory was the great distinctive feature of Democritus's teaching, as it was of his master Leucippus ; and Epicurus accepted it, though with important differences. He was no mere literal repeater of the doctrine, but transformed it at vital points, and adhered to it with a motive of his own.

In the first place, the interest of Democritus in Nature was purely scientific : he had no ulterior end in physical research—" Science for science's sake " was his motto. To Epicurus, on the other hand, the Atomic theory commended itself, not primarily for any scientific or speculative reason, but, first and chiefly, because of its ethical and religious bearings. It seemed to him to be

[1] This point has been admirably worked out by Dr. John Masson in his *The Atomic Theory of Lucretius*, chap. vii.

most consonant with the theory of pleasure as the *summum bonum*, which was the ruling feature in Epicurus's philosophy, and it struck at the root of religious superstition by excluding the gods from arbitrary and capricious interference with the government of the world. This was a point of great importance, in face of the base and debasing religious notions, beliefs, and practices of the age.

But, next, Epicurus, while adopting the Atomic theory generally, made important alterations on it.

For one thing, he denied that atoms falling perpendicularly down would ever come into collision, and so that a cosmos could ever be formed on that sole assumption. In order to cope with the difficulty, Democritus had imagined that atoms differed from each other in their velocity. Some fell more swiftly than others; and so the swifter would overtake the slower, and thereby collisions would occur. This appeared to Epicurus to be an erroneous interpretation of falling bodies. A famous passage in the second book of Lucretius (225–239) puts the argument in a vivid form. No doubt, it is there maintained, difference in velocity is in point when you are dealing with bodies falling through air or through water, where you have to take into account the resisting medium. But this does not hold in the case of a pure vacuum. "A pure vacuum can afford no resistance to anything in any place, or at any time, but must go on allowing a thing what its own nature demands." Now, "what its own nature demands" is, according to Epicurus, free movement or liberty to the atoms to swerve from the vertical, even to the slightest imaginable extent, to begin with.

Consequently, on the basis of this physical doctrine of atomic declination, Epicurus went on to establish his doctrine of free will.

To Democritus, there was no such thing as free will : the uniformity of nature and the reign of law, extending to every being and to all departments of existence, forbade that. This teaching, in the view of Epicurus, neglected to take account of the testimony of consciousness. Free will is a fact of our experience, and the great fact on which ethics reposes ; and as ethics was the prime consideration for Epicurus, this fact must be conserved, and, if conserved, explained : and the explanation seemed to him to be found in atomic declination—in the supposition of an innate spontaneity in the atoms, whereby atomic combinations and interactions might be rendered possible.

There was also a difference between Epicurus and Democritus as to the composition of the soul. As has been seen, Epicurus demanded four elements—heat, air, vapour, and an unnamed fourth. To Democritus, the soul was "a kind of fire ($\pi\hat{v}\rho\ \tau\iota$)." It consisted, therefore, wholly of atoms the same in shape as those of fire—namely, round ; and the only differences between soul-atoms and fire-atoms that he allowed were differences of arrangement, and, probably, of size—the soul-atoms being the smaller.

V

Now, reverting to the Epicurean teaching, the contrast to Stoicism at crucial points will be apparent. There is, first, the conception of the formation of the universe by the fortuitous concourse of atoms, thereby excluding providence and all teleological reference; there is, next, the erection of sensation into the criterion of truth, or test of the validity of knowledge; and, further, there is the characteristic doctrine of free will.

With regard to the first of these, it may be allowed that the fortuitous clash of atoms, although originally undesigned, might conceivably give rise to a cosmos, in so far as the mere collocation of material bodies is concerned—their aggregation into masses, their mechanical and chemical actions and reactions. Modern science admits this: even Lord Kelvin, with all his insistence on teleology as necessary to the explanation of the world, allowed as much in certain recent utterances. But although this infinite dance and collision of atoms, continuing from all eternity, might, owing to the infinity of combinations accidentally stumbled into, end in the present arrangement that we understand as the material cosmos, nevertheless there is no explanation here of the vital and conscious phenomena of our experience. How, from the mere fortuitous dance and interminable clash and jostling of dead material particles, is Life generated? There is more than matter and motion here; there is spontaneous movement and purposive selection. Vitalism is not mechanism, as even great chemists like Professor Bunge[1] in Germany and Professor Japp[2] in Scotland are forward to allow. The physiologist also

---

[1] See his *Text-book of Physiological and Pathological Chemistry*, Lecture I.

[2] See his Presidential Address to the Chemical Section of the British Association, in 1898, on *Stereochemistry and Vitalism*.

knows that even the phenomenon of nutrition is not wholly explicable by chemical and physical laws, inasmuch as the wall of the intestine refuses to behave like a mere dead membrane ; and the botanist, just because he is here dealing with living membranous tissue, has ceased to explain the rise of the sap in a tree simply by endosmose. The intervention of life in the membrane makes all the difference. How, again, in the case of Sensation, do atoms that are themselves colourless, scentless, soundless (for, as said, they have no secondary qualities), give rise by mere collocation to colour, scent, sound? How, still more, do we get in this way the higher processes of Mind,—conception, judgment, reasoning, thought,—so different, not only in quantity, but in kind, from the properties of inorganic matter? In consciousness and self-consciousness and the processes of reflective thought, we have reached something of the nature of an organic unity, whose ruling feature is internal purposive development and spontaneous activity. These chasms—namely, between the lifeless and the living, on the one hand, and, on the other hand, between the merely animate or living and the conscious thinking life — are the standing difficulty for the Epicurean physics, as for pure material-ism in whatsoever age. If man is not "a mere automaton," if consciousness be more than a bare "epiphenomenon" or useless adjunct of brain process, then mechanism cannot fully explain him, or account for his distinctive mental characteristics. "Ex nihilo nihil fit" is the great principle that Lucretius is con-stantly · using. Nowhere is it more applicable than here, against himself.

The obvious way of surmounting the difficulty is by tacitly assuming that, in the atoms themselves, after all, there is contained the germ of life and consciousness. And this is what Epicureanism did; but it was done illogically. Frequently does Lucretius apply to atoms such terms as "seeds," "seeds of things," "procreative matter (*genitalis materies*)," "concert (*concilium*)," "generative concert," and so on; and, as we have seen, he endows them with "will." But this is virtually to acknowledge that atoms (which he began by maintaining to be absolutely dead things) and the void are not, after all, sufficient to explain the whole phenomena of our experience; that, for the world as we know it—at all events, for the organic and conscious parts of it—there is needed a force or power other than what is material (call it by whatever name you please), adequate to give the explanation of, or to account for, the "inner design" that life and mind, biological and psychical facts alike, display. In other words, the highest facts in our experience are not explicable by the principles of Epicurean physics, but are simply slurred over in it; and what plausibility the explanation possesses is got from the circumstance that it assumes those higher facts in the lower, and thereby obtains for the lower a greater potency than rightfully belongs to them.

But the Epicurean Criterion of Truth—what of it?

Certainly, knowledge begins with sensation; Stoic and Epicurean were agreed on that. But the Stoic insisted that, although sensation is indispensable, it cannot by itself explain experience to us, or show how

knowledge is possible. In all knowledge, there is a
mental element that must be taken account of, as well
as a sense element ; and the native activity of the mind
is a fundamental fact that must be duly appraised.
Hence the Stoic's insistence on the mind's assent in
knowledge, and of the power it has of grasping reality
and truth in the various ways laid down in his Epistemology, as we have detailed in Chapter IV.

Nor is the Epicurean doctrine of free will very
satisfactory.

It was vigorously attacked in ancient times (as we
see in Cicero, for example), and the Stoics opposed it.
And there is real ground for this.   Although the theory
may be said to be in line with that of unconscious will
in Schopenhauer, it is far from impregnable.   No light
is really thrown upon the problem by simply designating the power of declination in the material atoms
"will"; nor is man's volitional freedom explained
by being referred back to such declination.   If "the
bonds of fate" are to be broken, it certainly cannot be
done in this way.   To subsume two such things as the
unconscious swerving of dead material particles from
the vertical and the *intensely conscious* purposive
determination of a man in making a choice, under the
same category "will," seems very like juggling with
words.   There is no true explanation in this ; and
Aristotle's criticism of Plato's Ideas at once suggests
itself as applicable here—"mere empty talk and
picturesque metaphor (κενολογεῖν ἐστι καὶ μεταφορὰς λέγειν
ποιητικάς)."

Section C.—MORALITY AND RELIGION

CHAPTER VII

PREDECESSORS OF THE STOICS IN ETHICS

"Nec philosophia sine virtute est, nec sine philosophia virtus."—Seneca.

"Above all things, the Cynic's ruling faculty must be purer than the sun."—Epictetus.

"Diogenes, one terrible frosty morning, came into the market-place, and stood naked, shaking, to show his tolerance. Many of the people came about him, pitying him : Plato passing by, and knowing he did it to be seen, said to the people, as he went by : 'If you pity him indeed, let him alone to himself.'"—Bacon.

I

In recounting the probable sources from which the Stoics drew their ethical doctrines, in so far as they were dependent on ethicists that had preceded them, we naturally think first of Plato and his transcendent system, so grandly set forth in the *Dialogues*. To us who owe so much to Platonism, who find Platonic thought and conceptions woven into the very texture of Western culture and civilization, including law and jurisprudence, no less than metaphysics, morality, and religion, it would seem impossible that a great ethical school, created shortly after Plato's time, and on the very spot, should not have drunk in the Platonic spirit and drawn freely from the Platonic fountain. But that was not the way of the schools of ancient Athens ; and, as a matter of fact, neither the Stoics,[1] nor any of the early post-Platonic sects, owned a large debt to Plato. On the contrary, they went, for the most part, on entirely different lines, and reverted to the views of pre-Socratic thinkers, who, one would have supposed, were superseded. In Stoicism, the spritualism of Plato was supplanted by materialism, and his imposing Theory of Ideas was not merely ignored but deliberately rejected. This certainly needs explanation, and more reasons than one immediately suggest themselves. On the one hand, there is the consideration that the Platonic teaching, being so supremely speculative, was little in touch with common life and the everyday world. Plato was " the dragon "—to use a simile of Confucius, when comparing Laotsze with himself—he soars in the air, ignoring *terra firma*. Neither the mode of thinking nor the subject-matter of thought was the same to Plato as to the Stoics : it is very much the difference between viewing ethics from the high contemplative and purely theoretical side (including its æsthetic aspect), and viewing it as a practical thing, designed as a rule of life and a guide to conduct. On the other hand, the Platonic ethics subordinated the individual to the State, and hardly recognized him as an individual at all ; whereas the moment had now come (politically determined) when individualism in Greece had strongly asserted itself (just as it did, centuries afterwards, in Western Europe, at the time of the Renaissance and the Reformation), and Zeno and his immediate successors

---

[1] Things were different, of course, with the later Eclectics, such as Seneca.

were under the power of this impulse. The worth of
the individual, and his destiny, and how best he was to
achieve his perfection — these were the points that
occupied the first place in the Stoic's interest.[1] Nor,
further, must we forget that if Plato was studied by
the Stoics as interpreted by his successors in the
Academy, there were sufficient grounds for refusing to
accept him as an unerring and satisfactory guide.

But, be the explanation what it may, the fact
remains: Plato's was not an outstanding influence to
the Stoics. Nevertheless, he did to some extent affect
them—that was inevitable. They accepted his definition of virtue as knowledge or insight ; they reproduced
his doctrine of the cardinal virtues ; his anthropology
left traces on their teaching ; they were affected by
some of his sociological views as set forth in the
Republic ; and they shared with him the recognition of
the world as a living being and the conception of the
anima mundi. Yet, even while accepting these views,
the Stoics modified and handled them in a fashion of
their own. Such an argument, for instance, as the
following, to prove that the world is rational, put into
the mouth of Zeno by Cicero (*De Nat. Deor.* ii. 8),
would sound strange in Plato : "That which reasons is
superior to that which does not reason. But nothing
is superior to the world. Therefore, the world reasons."
Or this : "Nothing that is itself destitute of life and
reason can generate a being possessed of life and
reason. But the world generates beings possessed of
life and reason. Therefore, the world is itself possessed

[1] Compare this with Christianity, when the individual again
emerges.

of life and reason." The poetic glow of a great imagination (working by intuition and suggestion rather than by analysis) is here replaced by dry logical ratiocination : the cramped view of the formal dialectician takes the place of the wide synthetic sweep of the philosopher.

As with Plato, so with Aristotle. Although Aristotle's physics and his logic left their mark on Stoicism (the latter more especially through Chrysippus), and although it would not be difficult to trace the working of his psychology in the Stoic handling of the human impulses and desire, his ethics had only a very limited influence. Indeed, the distinctive Aristotelian positions—such as, that virtue is a habit,[1] and that it resides in the mean, and that it requires favouring fortune (good health, external goods, and such like) for its proper development—could not well fit into the Stoical scheme. They were necessarily uncongenial to thinkers who dealt so largely with the *ideal* of virtue (non-empirically constructed), and whose object was to raise men to a platform where worldly prudence and calculation of consequences and dependence upon fortune and environment were waived aside.

Moreover, with Aristotle intellect or contemplation was the chief thing, and he held it to be the highest aim of man to achieve the contemplative disposition. That he regarded as the characteristic of the philosopher; and he "thought that the highest aim for a State was to turn out philosophers, and that the highest aim for

---

[1] Of course, the Stoics recognized habit in the formation of character.

an individual was to be a philosopher."[1] He even conceived the Deity solely from this standpoint of contemplation, not defining Him as an *ethical* being, but as self-reflective, as "thinking upon thought."[2] The Stoics, on the other hand, viewed man first and chiefly from the side of his activities; perceiving rightly enough that these are what have for him the greatest interest and mould his destiny. Volition comes first; practical interests come first. So that, what we find is this, the battle of intellectualism *versus* voluntarism going on then, as it goes on now; and pragmatism, for the time being, had gotten the victory.[3]

II

But if Plato and Aristotle had only a modified and indirect influence on Stoical ethics, a very direct and effectual influence came from the Cynics.[4]

This may have been accidental, as the story about Zeno's first introduction to philosophy through Crates seems to suggest. It is recorded by Diogenes Laërtius (vii. 3) that Zeno, on his arrival at Athens, after shipwreck, in pursuit of business, happened to take up the *Memorabilia* of Xenophon, at a bookseller's stall, and, on reading part of it with interest and appreciation, desired to know where such men as there depicted were to be found. Crates, the Cynic, chanced to be passing at the moment, and the bookseller pointed to

[1] Sir A. Grant, *Aristotle*, p. 101. [2] *Metaphysics*, xi. 9.
[3] See Appendix.
[4] The name Cynic is likely derived from the gymnasium Cynosarges, which the Cynics frequented; although the personal habits and temper of the Cynics went far to justify opponents in applying the term as though it were derived from κύων, a dog.

him. Zeno joined him and became his disciple, and thus started his life of philosopher under the Cynic banner.

Whether this story be literally true or not, it declares the undoubted fact that the Cynics, who claimed to be the only real representatives of the Socratic teaching, greatly impressed the Stoics, beginning with the founder Zeno.

What, then, was the Cynics' view of life, and of man and his aspirations and his relations to nature and to God? for these are the main questions that engaged the attention of the Stoics.

In the *Symposium* of Xenophon, Antisthenes, the founder of the Cynic school, is introduced as upholding the thesis that his wealth is the thing of which he is most proud, and, at the same time, he expresses himself shocked at the principle of Callias that the way to make men just and upright is by giving them money. The seeming paradox is resolved by observing the double meaning of "wealth" or "money." You cannot buy uprightness with *material* coin; but you may be wealthy, though poor and lacking such coin, in *spiritual* riches. "I hold to the belief," he says, "that wealth and poverty lie not in men's estate but in men's souls," "wealth of my sort will make you liberal of nature." The soul is the great thing, and its health the first concern; and the discourse on this text that he gives is an advocacy of the wisdom, for the soul's sake, of sitting loose to the pleasures of the world, of moderating and suppressing one's desires, of finding the source of happiness and peace in the mind and inward being, not in external circumstances or the so-called good things of life, which are variable and uncertain and which perish in the using, leaving one unsatisfied. It is the characteristic of the wise man that he is self-sufficient—independent of fortune's favour and of everything outside himself: he is master of the world by being master of his own desires. Hence, he can endure hardness without repining and can even rejoice in it ; and asceticism is his natural element.

This is robust moral teaching. But there are dangers attaching to it. The self-sufficiency of the wise man, if not carefully watched and guarded, may degenerate into pride and self-satisfaction and ostentation (as too frequently it did among the Cynics), and, consequently, into contempt for others. There is a story of Antisthenes, recorded by Diogenes Laërtius (ii. 5), which illustrates this. One day Antisthenes was seen turning the torn part of his cloak towards the spectator, so as to attract his attention and, doubtless, to draw forth his regard. Whereupon Socrates, exactly gauging the situation, remarked, " I see your vanity through your cloak." Another illustration refers to Diogenes the Cynic. Once, on entering Plato's house, he ostentatiously trampled on his fine carpet, remarking, " Thus I tread on Plato's pride." "Yes, Diogenes," was Plato's answer, "with another pride of your own" (Diog. Laërt. ii. 53). Here, Cynicism has become rudeness ; which is further exemplified by a familiar incident in the life of Diogenes. When Alexander the Great visited him, as he lay basking in the sun, at Corinth, Alexander saluted him, and desired to know if there was anything that he wanted. To this Diogenes brusquely replied: "Only that you stand out of my sunshine." Certainly, good manners did not characterize the sage from Sinope.[1]

Further, the Cynic, bound up in his self-sufficiency, was narrow-minded and despised things of the intellect. He contemned learning, and spurned speculation. But, worst of all, in reducing his creed to practice, he set conventionality at defiance, gave his tongue undue licence, and gloried in offensive bodily habits,—forgetting that "cleanliness is next to godliness." Diogenes lived in a tub; the decencies of life were scarcely observed by him or by others of his persuasion; and opponents had just ground for the attacks that they made in this connexion. Moreover, the Cynics were a kind of "mendicant order in philosophy," and begged their bread. The wallet was their badge. No very high conception of independence here!

But take the Cynic doctrine of self-sufficiency at its highest and best, stripped of the debasing aberrations which attended the attempt to carry it out into practice, often rendering the nobility of it unrecognizable (just as the shell-fish and seaweed and pebbles and other marine things that gathered around Glaucus and adhered to him transformed the sea-god almost past recognition[2]), and we see that its nature is to purify and ennoble him who entertains it and tries to mould his life accordingly. With true Socratic earnestness (and the leading Cynics were earnest), it inculcates patience and endurance and a contempt for self-indulgence and for pleasure that produces strength

---

[1] See Cicero, *Tusc. Disp.* v. 32; and Arrian, *Anabasis*, vii. 1.
[2] See Plato, *Republic*, x. 11.

and beauty of soul. "I would rather be mad than pleased (μανείην μᾶλλον ἢ ἡσθείην),"[1] said Antisthenes; and thereby he showed, at least, that he aimed at raising character high.

In all this, we have the first draft of the Wise Man, which the Stoics accepted and took over but improved upon, and which explains to us how "the Cynic" became to them the technical name for the Ideal Sage.[2]

But, next, in order to a happy life for the individual, the Cynics dwelt much on the necessity of living in accordance with nature; and it was, doubtless, from this source that the Stoics derived the conception and the formula. Yet, between the teaching of the two schools there was a great contrast. The "nature" to which the Cynics wished to return was that of unrestrained unconventional living. Hence, Antisthenes took as a model for civilized man the life of the lower animals and of primitive man; thereby interpreting nature in a way that did not safeguard the higher morality, but might be looked upon as sanctioning immorality and licentiousness. "The Cynics took the savage as their teacher in all seriousness, just as Diderot and Rousseau did in a later age. They glorified the state of nature with inexhaustible eloquence and ingenuity, and they never wearied of anathematising the pernicious influence of civilisation."[3] Thus, they cast aside the sound Aristotelian dictum that the

---

[1] Diog. Laërt. vi. 4.
[2] See Epictetus, *Dissertations*, iii. 22.
[3] Gomperz, *Greek Thinkers*, vol. ii. p. 144, Eng. tr.

true test of what is natural is the end or τέλος, and that you are to interpret the lower by the higher, and not, contrariwise, the higher by the lower ; so that man is to be estimated, not by what he was or even by what at any moment he is, but by what he has it in him to be or to become.

In their doctrine on this point, the Stoics were wiser. They looked to the ideal, and refused to copy the habits either of the lower animals or of primitive man. Hence, they rose to the conception of a pure and noble individual, sharer in the divine, and of a universal brotherhood of mankind, and preached the necessity of the individual regarding himself as a citizen of the world and discharging social duties. The Cynics, on the other hand, were strictly individualistic in their teaching. Personal freedom, individual independence, was to them the great thing, and of the salvation of the community or of the world they were sceptical. Hence the Cynic was anti-social in his tendencies, and lived as much outside society as he could, avoiding social duties and renouncing family ties, devoid of patriotism and devoted to criticism of accepted ideals, living as a wanderer and a beggar. Only contemning the general run of mankind, whom he regarded as deluded, he contracted a spirit of sourness and censoriousness, which frequently expressed itself in bitter satire, thus justifying the modern acceptation of the term "cynical" as synonymous with acerbity and malignant utterance. Whatever the Stoics were, they were not cynical in this sense ; and it signalizes their philosophy that, in Marcus Aurelius, it could produce a "philosopher-king"—a man of gentle, noble nature, who could both devote himself to statesmanship and to the furtherance of the interests of the empire, and could carry the spirit of his philosophy into the discharge of his onerous duties.

But there is a further point to be noticed in connexion with Cynicism—namely, its attitude towards the popular religion. As it was the Cynic's function to criticize and oppose established customs and accepted ideals, it might naturally be supposed that he would disown religion and make a speedy end of the gods and of the heroes of mythology. This, however, was not what he did; and, when we remember his acceptance of primitive man as his model for life and conduct, we can readily see that he could not consistently have done it. For, to primitive man were due the gods and the accredited mythologies; and so these mythologies must somehow be accepted, if we are to return to a life conformable to nature. Obviously, however, they could not be accepted by philosophers in their bare literality, and so they must be allegorized. The allegorical method, consequently, was the great method in the hands of the Cynics, and those stories of the gods and of the heroes which appealed so forcibly to the untutored fancy became the subjects of rationalistic interpretation—were taken as the mere popular expression of philosophical conceptions.

To the Cynics the Stoics were here indebted; for this same allegorical method came to play a great part in their religious philosophy, keeping them philosophers while they also remained loyal citizens; and through them it was handed on to Philo the Jew, who applied

it to the Old Testament—to its early historical records
and its anthropomorphic way of viewing the Deity;
and thence to Origen and the Catechetical school of
Alexandria, who included the New Testament in their
scope; and thence to Biblical critics in later ages—so
that the principle has permanently affected Christian
exegesis.

In these respects, at any rate, there is a real affinity
and causal connexion between Cynicism and Stoicism,
though it would not be difficult to show that the Cynics
also found the germs of their system in previous philosophic thought. But with essential affinities there are
also essential differences, which will be obvious as we
proceed; and " perhaps we nearest touch the spring of
difference," as Sir Alexander Grant puts it (*The Ethics
of Aristotle*, vol. i. pp. 317, 318), " by observing that
Cynicism is essentially mere negation, mere protest
against the external world; while Stoicism is essentially
positive, essentially constructive, and tends in many
ways to leaven the external world. Cynicism despised
the sciences, disdained politics, exploded the social
institutions, and ridiculed patriotism or the distinctions
of country. Zeno, on the contrary, rearranged the
sciences according to his views: he enjoined the wise
to mix in affairs; and he conceived not a mere negation
of patriotic prejudices, but the positive idea of cosmopolitanism. Cynicism, therefore, is a withdrawal from
the world into blank isolation, while Stoicism is the
withdrawal into an inner life, which forms to its votaries
an object of the highest enthusiasm. Hence the elation,
often hyperbolical, which tinges the Stoical austerity;

hence the attractiveness of the doctrine and its spread over the world. And connected, too, with the positive and constructive impulse of Stoicism, we may reckon its plastic character, its external eclecticism, and its tendency to be influenced and modified by the course of surrounding civilisation."

III

One other name needs here to be mentioned—namely, that of Heracleitus. We have already seen how deeply indebted the Stoics were to Heracleitus's physics (see p. 87). It is most likely that they were influenced also by his ethics ; at any rate, he held views allied to theirs, and was the first in Greek philosophy to express such. These were associated with his doctrine of *logos*, or the universal reason. The world, according to him, is permeated by reason. This all-pervasive reason is not simply intellectual, but also ethical. Order as natural law exists everywhere in the universe, but that order is beneficent and rewards him who subjects himself to it. The phenomena of nature have an ethical significance, and may be interpreted as a guide to human conduct. "The wise man will despise that for which the masses strive, as a worthless and perishable thing. He will not take his own caprices, but the common law, for his standard ; will avoid nothing more than presumption, the overstepping of the bounds which are set for the individual and for human nature ; and in thus subjecting himself to the order of the whole, he will reach that satisfaction which Heracleitus is said to have declared to be the highest end of life. It depends only upon man himself whether he is happy.

The world is always as it ought to be ;[1] it must be our part to accommodate ourselves to the universal order ; the character of a man is his dæmon [is a god, ἦθος ἀνθρώπῳ δαίμων]."[2] This means, at any rate, that the world is so constructed as that character may appear and develop in it, and that the crowning glory of human beings is character—is their right relation to one another, to the whole, and to the supreme reason in which they share.

This was the pronounced teaching of the Stoics also. To them, too, the world-order is ethical, and character is man's highest concern and his greatest achievement. To Heracleitus and to Zeno alike—more still, perhaps, to Cleanthes, as judged by his *Hymn to Zeus*—the universal logos guides all things wisely and for the best ; and by all alike Matthew Arnold's definition of the Supreme would have been accepted—"the Eternal not ourselves that makes for righteousness." Ethics conditions their pantheism, and makes it glow.[3]

---

[1] This is viewed from the side of God, or *sub specie æternitatis*, as Spinoza would put it ; it is only from man's standpoint that some things appear just and others unjust.

[2] Zeller, *Pre-Socratic Philosophy*, vol. ii. pp. 97–98 (Eng. tr.).

[3] The conception of God as "Moral World-Order" was reproduced by Fichte in modern times. Wherein ethical pantheism is inadequate, I have tried to point out in *Theism as grounded in Human Nature*, pp. 394–396.

CHAPTER VIII

ETHICS : EXPOSITION

"And virtue is self-sufficient for happiness."—ZENO.

"This very place, which you call banishment, is fatherland to those who inhabit it. So, nothing is wretched, unless you think it ; and, on the other hand, every lot is blessed if it be borne with equanimity."—BOËTHIUS.

"Non qui parum habet, sed qui plus cupit, pauper est."—SENECA.

"The aids to noble life are all within."—MATTHEW ARNOLD.

I

IN their analysis of human nature, the Stoics started with the Platonic conception, that man is a compound being consisting of two parts, a body and a soul. In one place, indeed, Marcus Aurelius seems to make a threefold division of man. "Body, soul, mind," he says (*Med.* iii. 16), "these three" ; but immediately he adds, "to the body belong sensations, to the soul impulses, to the mind principles"—thereby showing that it is not a true trichotomy that he has in view, but simply a loose classification of psychical processes into sense, impulse, and intellection. "The impressions of sense," he continues, "we share with cattle of the field: the pulls of impulse with brute beasts, with catamites, with Phalaris, or Nero ; and mind is still the guide to obvious duties, even for the atheist, the traitor, and for those who lock the door for sin." To the same import is the other passage (*Med.* xii. 3), where a similar trichotomy occurs: "You consist of three parts—body, breath, mind. The first two are yours, to the extent of requiring your care: the third only is properly your own." Here, body and breath go together as constituting the mere animated corporeal instrument, and mind stands opposed as reason.[1]

But, while starting with the Platonic conception of man in his twofold nature, the Stoics further followed Plato (at least, the Plato of the *Phædo* and allied dialogues) in looking on the body as a hindrance or impediment to the soul, or, at any rate, the tool that the soul employs to effect its ends. "That which pulls the strings, remember," says Marcus Aurelius (*Med.* x. 38), "is the power concealed within; there is the mandate, the life,—there, one may say, the man. Never confound it with the mere containing shell, and the various appended organs. They may be compared to tools, with this difference, that the connexion is organic. Indeed, apart from the inner cause which dictates action or inaction, the parts are of no more use than the weaver's shuttle, the writer's pen, or the coachman's whip." To Seneca, in like manner, the body is but the clog and prison-house and punishment of the soul; or it is the fetter that deprives the soul of its liberty; or, again, it is an inn which the soul in its sojourn occupies but for a brief moment (see *Epp.* 65 and 102).

---

[1] There is only a superficial resemblance between these trichotomies and that of St. Paul in 1 Thess. v. 23—"Spirit and soul and body (τὸ πνεῦμα, καὶ ψυχή, καὶ τὸ σῶμα)."

This, apparently, was to depart from the original position of Zeno, that man was wholly formed out of the divine essence, and that there is nothing inherently derogatory in matter, and serves to show that the strict physical speculations of the school had ultimately but a feeble hold on the Ethics.

The soul, on the other hand, is that part of man which contains the master-faculty of reason, characterized by self-consciousness and moral perception (see Epictetus, *Diss.* i. 1), and therefore the authoritative and ruling principle in man (τὸ ἡγεμονικόν), that which guides him to right thought and right action. It is one, permeating the whole body; though to the later Stoics, influenced by Plato, more especially to Seneca,[1] it assumes a twofold character, inasmuch as man's nature is cleft asunder and reason is opposed to appetite and passion, and the battle in the individual, as experience testifies, is unceasing between the higher and the lower —between the spirit and the flesh. These two terms, indeed, "spirit" and "flesh," are found as a contrast in Seneca, and they signify much. The ruling faculty is "the diviner part" of man—is "the god within"; and it is man's peculiar glory to be swayed by it. Hence, in distinctive Stoic phraseology, it is man's prerogative "to live agreeably to nature" (ὁμολογουμένως τῇ φύσει ζῆν, *vivere convenienter naturæ*).

Now, what is "living agreeably to nature"? It is, in the first place, according to Cleanthes, living conformably to the course of the universe; for the universe is under the governance of reason, and man has it as

[1] See, *e.g.*, *Ep.* 71.

his privilege to know or become acquainted with the world-course, to recognize it as rational and cheerfully to conform to it. This, according to him, is true freedom of will—not acting without motive, or apart from set purpose, or capriciously, but humbly acquiescing in the universal order, and, therefore, in everything that befalls one here : " *in regno nati sumus: deo parere libertas est.*" [1]   In the next place, it resolves itself, in Epictetus's favourite phrase, into the right use of appearances, *i.e.*, into a correct insight into true values, which is conditioned by our clearly perceiving what is and what is not in our power, and by our regarding the latter as wholly indifferent (neither good nor bad), neither to be eagerly avoided nor earnestly pursued), while scrupulously laying hold of the former. In this second sense, it consists in what Chrysippus held to be its chief meaning [2]—namely, in living agreeably to *human* nature, which, again, he interpreted as meaning conformably to the nature of a being who, unlike the brutes, not only uses appearances but also understands and interprets them. [3]   In this case, true freedom consists in emancipation from the thraldom of irrational desires (wealth, lust, domination, the passions), in the eradication of our desires and the reduction of our wants to the smallest possible number, and in subjection to the will under the supremacy of reason. [4]

[1] Seneca, *De Vita Beata*, 15.

[2] " By that nature in accordance with which we are to live, Chrysippus understands both the common nature and the human in particular " (Diog. Laërt. vii. 53).

[3] See Epictetus, *Diss.* i. 6 and 13.

[4] See *ibid.* ii. 1.   This doctrine of the right use of appearances as constituting freedom was shared by the Stoics with the Cynics.

These two views of the life according to nature, though distinct, are not antagonistic. On the contrary, the one is the necessary complement of the other— "the way of both is one." [1] The first is the interpretation of the rational life from the standpoint of the universal or the whole, and the second is its interpretation on the level of human nature, a part of the whole and meaningless if divorced from it. The first is ontological, and determines the Stoic theology; the second is psychological, and gives us the Stoic theory of virtue and happiness—their theory of Conscience, for "the ruling faculty" is "conscience," and the very term conscience (συνείδησις) seems to have been coined in the Stoic mint and to have come to us from thence. [2]

It is the second of these interpretations that is at present before us, as we sketch the Stoic ethics.

II

The ethical teaching of the Stoics, as of all great moralists, centred in consideration of man's happiness and its relation to virtue. To them, as to Aristotle, happiness was something that must be self-sufficient,— which, again, resolved itself into the position that "a good man shall be satisfied from himself" (*Prov.* xiv. 14). "Dig within," says Aurelius (*Med.* vii. 59).

Diogenes claims to have been taught it by Antisthenes. See Epictetus, *Diss.* iii. 24.

[1] Aurelius, *Med.* v. 3.

[2] "The most important of moral terms, the crowning triumph of ethical nomenclature, συνείδησις, *conscientia*, the internal, absolute, supreme judge of individual action, if not struck in the mint of the Stoics, at all events became current coin through their influence" (Lightfoot, *St. Paul's Epistle to the Philippians*, p. 301).

"Within is the fountain of good; ever dig, and it will ever well forth water." Happiness consists, therefore, not in the possession of anything external, but in control of a man's own self, in strength of will illuminated by reason. It is inward, and resides in his ability to estimate the true worth of things and to act accordingly. Says Epictetus (*Diss.* iv. 4): "There is only one way to happiness, μιὰ ὁδὸς ἐπὶ εὔροιαν (let it be ready to hand in the morning, during the day, and at night)—namely, to turn away from what is beyond the power of choice, to regard nothing as one's own, to give over all things to the divinity (τῷ δαιμονίῳ), to fortune, making them the superintendents of these things, whom Zeno also has made so." This presupposes the distinction that there are some things "in our power" (τὰ ἐφ' ἡμῖν) and others "not in our power" (τὰ οὐκ ἐφ' ἡμῖν). Health, wealth, property, friends, the body, death, and such like, are outwith us and beyond our command—they "depend on chance," as Cicero puts it: therefore, we are to sit loose to them, to use them as things "indifferent." But our own will, and the formation of judgments and opinions, assent and approval—these are in our power, and in the proper management of them consists our felicity and peace.[1] In our power, in particular, is virtue and the choice of what is right and good; in the pursuit of which lie man's distinction and his bliss. "Take care, when you see a man honoured above others, or great in power, or otherwise esteemed, that you do not regard him as happy, being carried away by the appearance. For if the essence of the good be in those things that are in our own power, neither envy

[1] See Epictetus, *Diss.* i. 1 and iv. 1.

nor jealousy has any place, and you yourself will not desire to be a general, a president, or a consul, but to be free. And to this there is one road, scorn of the things that are not in our own power" (Epic. *Encheir.* 19). Control the desires, then ; yea, as the older Stoics held, eradicate them. Therein lies the secret of happiness : " Seek not that the things which happen should happen as you wish, but wish the things which happen to be as they are, and you will have an even flow of life " (*ibid.* 8).

Now, let us look more narrowly at this doctrine of the source of man's happiness, after premising that, unlike Buddha and Schopenhauer, the Stoic started with the acknowledgment that life is good and worth living, and that man naturally desires happiness and aims at it. The first impulse of every animal, as Chrysippus said, is to preserve and to protect itself— " the first thing proper to it is its own existence and the consciousness thereof" (Diog. Laërt. vii. 52). This means that its primary aim is to live, to obtain food and drink, to reproduce its kind, and, in a word, to find and continue the adaptation of internal to external relations. In success lies its happiness ; in failure its unhappiness.[1] Otherwise put, the good is naturally attractive, and we are drawn to it when we perceive it. " For, as the money-changer is not allowed to reject Cæsar's coin, nor the greengrocer, but if you show the coin, whether he will or not, he must give up what is sold in exchange for the coin, so it is also in

---

[1] Cf. Spinoza's doctrine of *conatus* in his *Ethica* (see, *e.g.*, Pars i. prop. 18).

the matter of the soul. When the good appears, it immediately attracts to itself; the evil repels from itself. But never will the soul reject the manifest (ἐναργῆ) appearance of the good, any more than people will reject Cæsar's coin. Thence is derived every movement both of man and of God " (Epictetus, *Diss.* iii. 3).

It is not in inclination towards the good that there is any difficulty, according to the Stoics. Where difficulty arises is in the application to particular cases. Some men place the good in outward prosperity; others in internal character. Philosophy begins only when the contradiction between these two is felt and the reason of it inquired into; and it is the aim of philosophy to establish that the good is internal and resides in the will, and not external or dependent on things beyond us.

Well, then, to face directly the point before us—the source of man's happiness.

Pleasure, Apathy, Desire

First of all, as we have seen, nothing external can really affect us : it is only what we ourselves allow our mind, and, therefore, our desire, to rest upon and entertain that can either injure or benefit us. " The view taken is everything ; and that rests with yourself. Disown the view, at will ; and behold, the headland rounded, there is calm, still waters and a waveless bay " (Aurelius, *Med.* xii. 22).

Hence the correct notion of pleasure and pain. While the one is in itself no good, the other is not in itself an evil ; each becomes such only through our

judgment or opinion of it. "Pain," says Aurelius
(*Med.* viii. 28, 29), "is either an evil for the body—
and if so, let the body state its case ; or for the soul—
but the soul can maintain its own unclouded calm,
and refuse to view it as an evil. For every judgment
or impulse or inclination or avoidance is within, and
nothing evil can force entrance there. Efface impressions, reiterating to yourself—It rests now with
me, that within this soul of mine there be no vice,
nor desire, nor any perturbation at all ; perceiving
the true nature of all things, I use each at its proper
worth. Remember this prerogative is yours by
nature." Cleanthes went farther, and maintained that
pleasure is not only not a good, but is "contrary to
nature" and "worthless." It was his opinion that
all the emotions (love, fear, grief) are weaknesses:
they lack that strain or tension (τόνος) which he so
persistently emphasized, and on which the strength
of the soul, no less than that of the body, depends,
and which constitutes in man self-control, and robust
moral fibre (ἐγκράτεια), and also conditions every
virtue ;[1] they are on the side of loosening and col-
lapse, not on that of coherence, persistence, and
stability. "The freehold of the mind none other may
contravene ; fire cannot touch it, nor steel, nor tyrant,
nor slander, nor any other thing ; so long as it
abides 'poised as a sphere self-orbed'" (Aurelius,
Med. viii. 41).

The doctrine under consideration is put most strik-

[1] The Stoics took over the cardinal virtues from Plato, and gave
a handling of each—wisdom, self-control, courage, righteousness
or justice.

ingly in connexion with the passionlessness or apathy (ἀπάθεια) of the ideal wise man. On him mental perturbation is without effect; for perturbation, as Zeno defined it (Cicero, *Tusc. Disp.* iv. 6), is "a commotion of the mind repugnant to reason and against nature." Desires, therefore, in so far as they are bare feelings, are no motive to him: it is only the desires of reason, such as arise from his conception of the unity and rationality of life and of the universe, that can move him. Feelings, of course, as psychical states, the sage, like every other human being, experiences—feelings of pleasure and pain; but they do not in any way disturb or unhinge him—under them he remains self-poised. It is recorded of Pompey that, when he visited Posidonius with a view to hearing him discourse on the Stoic philosophy, he found him seriously ill and much pained. He graciously saluted him, and expressed his disappointment at not being able to hear him lecture. "But you are able," was the reply, "nor can I allow that bodily pain should cause so great a man to come to me in vain." Whereupon, Posidonius proceeded to discourse to him seriously and copiously, from his couch, on the Stoic theme that nothing is good unless it be honourable; and, when interrupted by frequent paroxysms of pain, he exclaimed: "You are making no impression, pain! although you are hard to bear, I will never admit that you are an evil" (Cicero, *Tusc. Disp.* ii. 61). In this way, the wise man, being self-sufficient, alone is free and alone is a king; he is rich in the midst of poverty, and happy though in physical torment. He never yields to anger, or resentment, or envy, or fear, or grief, or even to joy or to lust;[1] nor does he experience pity or compassion, or show forgiveness,[2] for he cannot compassionate or pardon another, who, he conceives, is simply suffering from what he himself, if such suffering were his, would regard as no evil.[3] Hence, further, the ideal sage has no desire for fame, and scorns the pursuit of it, and is relieved from all anxiety above both the future and the past.[4] He is thus the equal of Zeus himself; and to him, if the doctrine is to be consistently carried out, Zeus becomes "a subject for compliments, rather than a power to be reckoned with." As Horace puts it (*Ep.* i. 1, 106–7):

> " Ad summam, sapiens uno minor est Jove, dives,
> Liber, honoratus, pulcher, rex denique regum."

"The ultimate end," said Ariston, "is to live in entire indifference towards the things that are intermediate between virtue and vice, not making any distinction between them, but treating all as equal; for the wise man is like a good actor, who, whether he personates Thersites or Agamemnon, plays the part of each fitly" (Diog. Laërt. vii. 2).[5]

It is on the ground of this same indifference towards things external that the Stoic both permitted and,

---

[1] The Stoics, according to Cicero, classified the emotions in a fourfold way; two of them having respect to goods (namely, joy and lust) and two to evils (namely, fear and grief). Under each of the four, they had many groups or subdivisions; and their delight in minute distinctions may very well be seen from examples in the *Tusculan Disputations*, bk. iv.

[2] See Seneca, *De Clementia*, ii. He calls pity "the vice of a petty spirit (*est enim vitium pusilli animi*)."

[3] See Diog. Laërt. vii. 64.   [4] See Aurel. *Med.* ii. 14.

[5] For a characterization of the wise man, see Diog. Laërt. vii. 64.

under certain conditions, counselled suicide (ἐξαγωγή).
As death is a thing destined to all, and its advent,
therefore, beyond our power to prevent,—in other
words, as it is one of the things "indifferent" (ἀδιάφορα,
res mediæ, indifferentes),—it is not to be dreaded by the
wise man. Rather, the wise man, just because he is
wise, may, if life's circumstances be such as to impede
his development or impair his usefulness, properly
enough accelerate its advent. The soul is at best but
the "hospes comesque corporis." "Hence, they say
also that with good reason may the wise man deprive
himself of life, for the sake either of his fatherland
or of his friends, or if he be suffering from very acute
pain, or from mutilations, or from incurable diseases"
(Diog. Laërt. vii. 66). This is the doctrine of what
Epictetus calls "the open door." "When he (God)
does not supply the necessaries, he gives the signal for
retreat, opens the door, and says to you, Go" (Epic.
Diss. iii. 13). "Only," he adds in another place (Diss.
i. 29), "you must not do it thoughtlessly, you must not
do it as a coward, nor on any slight pretext." So, too,
Marcus Aurelius (Med. v. 29) : "You can live here on
earth, as you think to live after your departure hence.
If others disallow, then indeed it is time to quit ; yet
even so, not as one aggrieved. The cabin smokes—so
I take leave of it. Why make ado ? But so long as
there is no such notice to quit, I remain free, and none
will hinder me from doing what I will ; that is, to
conform to the nature of a reasonable social being."[1]

[1] For an interesting casuistical discussion, turning on the fact
of individual peculiarities, of when and to whom suicide is permissible, see Cicero, De Officiis, i. 31.

Virtue and Happiness

In the next place, happiness, to the Stoic, means virtue—not something added on to it from without as its reward, but virtue itself as a realized state in the individual. Virtue, therefore, is the sole ultimate source of happiness, issuing naturally and inevitably in it : as Zeno puts it, "Virtue is self-sufficient for happiness."[1] In that case, virtue is not merely the chief but the only good ; and vice, issuing in misery, is the only evil.

Now, what is virtue? It is wisdom (φρόνησις)—*i.e.*, it is moral insight, or the clear and consistent perception of what is good and what is evil, and the eager intentional accepting of the one and rejecting of the other. As Seneca defines it (*Ep.* 20): "It is always to will and not to will the same thing. You need scarcely add the qualification that what you will must be what is right. The same thing cannot always please any one unless it be right." Virtue, therefore, lies in the will, in the disposition and the intention, and not alone in the overt action. "Character," as Stobæus expresses it (*Eclogæ*, ii. 36), "is the fountain of life from which actions severally flow."[2] "Cleanthes useth this example: 'I sent,' saith he, 'two boys into the Academy to seek out Plato, and to bring him unto

---

[1] "However, Panætius and Posidonius do not admit that virtue is self-sufficient, but that there is need also of good health and competence and strength" (Diog. Laërt. vii. 65). This reminds one of Adam Smith, who enumerates the constituents of happiness as health, a good conscience, and freedom from debt.

[2] ἦθος ἐστι πηγὴ βίου, ἀφ᾽ ἧς αἱ κατὰ μέρος πράξεις ῥέουσι.

me. The one of them sought him out in all galleries
and porches where he was wont to walk, and ran
through all other places wherein he had any hope to
find him out, and at length, being weary with his way,
and frustrate of his hope, returned home. The other
stood gazing at the next juggler, or mountebank, or
whilst he wandereth up and down and playeth with his
fellows and companions, seeth Plato passing by, and
found him whom he sought not. I,' saith Cleanthes,
'will commend that boy who performed that he was
commanded, to his uttermost, and will chastise that
other who was more fortunate in laziness. It is the
will that is the lawful mistress of these actions, the
condition whereof must be considered, if thou wilt
have me to be thy debtor. It is a small matter to
wish a man well, except thou pleasure him; it
is a small matter to have pleasured, except thou
hadst a will to do it'" (Seneca, *De Beneficiis*, vi. 11,
Thomas Lodge's tr.).   Hence, "the measure of
the man's worth is the worth of his aims";[1] and
it is only according to his purpose and intention
that a man is either to be praised or to be blamed
for his acts;[2] and "the guilty deed lies in the very
hesitation, even though it should never be actually
accomplished."[3]

This doctrine of the *inwardness* of morality was
fundamental to the Stoics,[4] and must be taken in

[1] Marcus Aurelius, *Med.* vii. 3.
[2] Epictetus, *Diss.* iv. 8.
[3] Cicero, *De Officiis*, iii. 8.
[4] As it was also to Christ, in His Sermon on the Mount.

connexion with their famous distinction of the two kinds of Duty—"the suitable" or "fitting" and "the right," καθῆκον and κατόρθωμα,—a distinction (together with the elaborate working out of it) that entitled them to be regarded as the originators of what Bentham calls Deontology or the science of duty. Indeed, the term "duty" (καθῆκον) is said to have been first employed in the technical ethical sense by Zeno, who wrote a treatise *On Duty* (Diog. Laërt. vii. 21).[1] But duty, as καθῆκον, is simply the suitable or fitting, and not that absolute rule of right that the term designates to-day. It is applicable only to things "indifferent" (*officium medium*), and signifies any action in everyday life that meets a want or serves a purpose, any line of conduct for which a reason may be given. It is not, therefore, strictly speaking, "virtue," which moves in a different and a higher sphere. Strict virtue is κατόρθωμα (*honestum*, or *rectum*, or *officium perfectum*)—duty in its purest form, which is not simply conformity to right reason, but conformity which flows from the will, the full knowledge, and the simple intention of the wise man. Hence, in this specific sense, and from the point of view of abstract theory, virtue is indivisible : there cannot be *degrees* of it. There can be degrees only in things that have relative value ; but virtue has absolute worth—it is to be sought for its own sake, and is the same under all circumstances. It is not, therefore, a "habit (ἕξις)," as Aristotle had taught—it can neither diminish nor increase: it is, in distinctive Stoic terminology, a

---

[1] The Stoic's mode of handling Duty, in all its practical detail, including the seasonable and decorous (*decorum*, τὸ πρέπον) in conduct, may be seen in Cicero's *De Officiis*.

διάθεσις, or " disposition " : [1]—*decrescere summum bonum non potest nec virtuti ire retro licet. . . . Incrementum maximo non est; nihil invenis rectius recto* (Seneca, *Ep.* 66).

But if there are not degrees in virtue, neither are there degrees in vice: all sins are equal ; omission of the most trivial duty and commission of the most glaring crime stand precisely on the same plane.[2] " They also maintain," says Diogenes Laërtius (vii. 64, 65), "that all sins are equal, as says Chrysippus in the fourth book of his Ethical Questions and Persæus and Zeno. For if what is true is not more than true, nor what is false more than false, so also a deceit is not more than deceit, nor a sin than sin. For he who is a hundred stadia distant from Canopus and he who is only one are both equally not in Canopus ; and so also he who commits a greater and he who commits a less sin are both equally not in the right path. As a stick must be either straight or crooked, so a man must be either

---

[1] Diog. Laërt. vii. 89.

[2] See Sextus Empiricus, *Opera*, vii. 453 (422–23). Compare St. James (ii. 10) : " For whosoever shall keep the whole law, and yet stumble in one point, he is become guilty of all." On the other hand, it is interesting to observe that Calvinism, which has so much in common with the stern side of Stoicism, viewing sins from the standpoint of Theology, makes distinction between them. In answer to the Question, " Are all transgressions of the law of God equally heinous in themselves, and in the sight of God ?" the Westminster Divines have no difficulty in replying, in *The Larger Catechism*, " All transgressions of the law of God are not equally heinous ; but some sins in themselves, and by reason of several aggravàtions, are more heinous in the sight of God than others " ; and, immediately after, they proceed to enumerate the kinds and sources of aggravation—namely, " the persons offending," "the parties offended," " the nature and quality of the offence," and " circumstances of time and place."

just or unjust, and cannot be more just than just or more unjust than unjust."[1] This carries with it the paradox that there are two, and only two, classes of men—the good and the bad, or, as the Stoics called them, "the wise" and "the foolish."[2] The good are wholly good, the bad are wholly bad ; for, at this high ethical level, the alternative is, either perfection or nothing at all. As Cicero puts it (*De Finibus*, iv. 19) : " All who are not wise are equally miserable ; all wise men are perfectly happy: all actions done rightly are equal to one another ; all offences are equal." Hence Zeno's paradox, that "those who are not wise are unfriendly and hostile, and slaves, and aliens to each other, parents to children, and brothers to brothers, and relatives to relatives ; while the wise alone are citizens and friends and relatives and free ; so that to the Stoics parents and children are enemies, for they are not wise " (Diog. Laërt. vii. 28).[3]

This stern doctrine was further intensified by the teaching that the vast majority of men belong to the class of the foolish—that, indeed, human nature in general is utterly depraved, and that there seems little hope of reformation. On this topic Seneca loves to dwell ; and, not unnaturally, considering the times in which he lived and the state of Rome in the days of

---

[1] " Heracleides of Tarsus, however," he adds, " the acquaintance of Antipater of Tarsus, and Athenodorus say that sins are not equal."

[2] See Stobæus, *Eclogæ*, ii. 7. 11. Compare Christ's teaching in the Parables.

[3] That the good or wise alone can be friends, was a prominent Stoic doctrine, previously maintained by Aristotle. See, *e.g.*, Epictetus's famous chapter on Friendship (*Diss.* ii. 22).

Nero, he appeals to experience in confirmation of his view. "Hereof our ancestors and predecessors complained, hereat we ourselves are aggrieved; and for this will our successors sigh, because good customs are abolished, impieties have pre-eminence, and human affairs grow worse and worse, and men leave no wickedness or sin unsought after. . . . In a word, we may always boldly say thus of ourselves, that we are evil, and (unwillingly I speak it) we always shall be" (*De Ben.* i. 10). He also maintains (*ibid.* iv. 27): "We do not say this, that all vices are in all men as particular vices are in some; but that a wicked and foolish man lacks not any vice. . . . All vices are in all men, but not all are prominent in each." Upon this Zeller remarks: "It hardly requires to be noticed how nearly this view coincides with that of Augustine on the virtues of the heathen, how close a resemblance the Stoic doctrine of folly bears to the Christian doctrine of the unregenerate, and how the contrast between wisdom and folly corresponds to that between the faithful and unbelievers."[1]

But now, if virtue be the sole source of human happiness, certain things follow.

In the first place, time or the length of a man's days on earth has nothing to do with it. For happiness, or "even flow of life" ($\epsilon \check{\upsilon} \rho o \iota a \ \beta \acute{\iota} o \upsilon$), it is all one whether we have lived a single day or a hundred years, if within the single day our life has been full, its quality perfect: it is quality, not quantity, that determines. Hence it is only in *duration* that Zeus in his goodness

[1] *The Stoics, Epicureans, and Sceptics* (Eng. tr.), p. 275, n. 1.

excels the good man. "Life is long," says Seneca
(*Ep.* 93), "if it be full ; but it is full when the mind has
achieved its development and realized it capacities. . . .
As a man of small stature may be a perfect man ; so,
in a small measure of time, life may be perfect. Age is
among things external to us. How long I may live is
an accident ; but how long I may be a man depends
upon myself." Again, he says (*Ep.* 74) : " The highest
good is neither diminished nor increased. . . . Whether
you make a circle larger or smaller is but a matter of
size, not of shape ; and though the one remain a long
time, and you immediately obliterate the other and
reduce it to the dust on which it was inscribed, yet
each was the same figure. That which is right is not
a matter of magnitude or of number or of time ; it can
neither be extended nor contracted. Take an upright
life of a hundred years' duration, or whatsoever number
you choose, and reduce it to a single day ; the one is
as upright as the other." [1]

This is precisely the doctrine of "the eternity"
of the soul espoused by Spinoza, ages after, in his
Ethica. By "eternity" Spinoza did not mean, any
more than the Stoics meant by happiness or εὔροια
βίου, *duration* : he meant, as they meant, *quality* of life
—not *length* of days, but *kind*.[2]

---

[1] See also Aurelius, *Med.* ii. 14.

[2] "By eternity," he says (*Ethica*, i., Def. 8), " I understand
existence itself, so far forth as it is conceived to follow necessarily
from the definition alone of the eternal thing.—Explanation.—For
such existence, like the essence of the thing, is conceived as eternal
truth, and, consequently, it cannot be explained by duration or
time, even although the duration be conceived as without beginning
or end."

In the next place, it is only another aspect of the Stoic doctrine when we say that virtue is its own reward ; or, to put it otherwise, that man is made to be virtuous—virtue is the function of his soul.   But an organ is not paid for discharging its function : the reward lies simply in its service.   Says Marcus Aurelius (*Med.* ix. 42) : "When you complain of some breach of faith or gratitude, take heed first and foremost to yourself.   Obviously the fault lies with yourself, if you had faith that a man of that disposition would keep faith, or if in doing a kindness you did not do it upon principle, nor upon the assumption that the kind act was to be its own reward.   What more do you want in return for a service done ?   Is it not enough to have acted up to nature, without asking wages for it ? Does the eye demand a recompense for seeing, or the feet for walking ?   Just as this is the end for which they exist, and just as they find their reward in realising the law of their being, so too man is made for kindness, and whenever he does an act of kindness or otherwise helps forward the common good, he thereby fulfils the law of his being and comes by his own." [1]

But if virtue is its own reward, vice is its own severest punishment.   "As Zeus has ordained, so act. But if you do not act so, you will suffer loss, you will be punished.   What will be the punishment ?   Nothing else than not having done your duty : you will lose fidelity, modesty, decency.   Do not look for greater penalties than these" (Epictetus, *Diss.* iii. 7).

Moreover, the worth of virtue is independent of man's appreciation of it.   A thing is what it is, and is neither

[1] See also vii. 73, 74 ; also, Epictetus, *Diss.* iii. 24.

better nor worse for being praised. "True beauty
needs no addition, any more than law, or truth, or
kindness, or self-respect. For which of these can
praise beautify, or censure mar? Is the emerald less
perfect for lacking praise? or is gold, or ivory, or
purple? a lyre or a poniard, a floweret or a shrub?"
(Aurelius, *Med.* iv. 20).[1]

Epicurean Hedonism

The Stoic doctrinc of virtue as the ethical end will
still further be elucidated, if we refer to the contrasting
doctrine of pleasure. To the Epicurean teaching of
pleasure as the *summum bonum*, the Stoics were in
entire and absolute opposition. They attacked it with
unwearied persistence, and with many arguments—the
most striking of which were drawn from the psychology
of pleasure and pain.

(1) In the first place, they objected to the term "pleasure" as being ambiguous. It refers properly, they
maintained, only to bodily pleasures, or, in addition, to
such secondary pleasures as can be traced ultimately to
the body as their source ; but the Epicureans often gave
it a wider connotation, and thereby gained an illegitimate
plausibility for their doctrine.[2] (2) In the next place,
pleasure, even as applied to agreeable sensation, has
two meanings—(*a*) the positive signification of a settled
state, and (*b*) the negative signification of mere absence
of pain ; and these two are by no means the same thing.
(3) Again, if pleasure be the highest good, then pain

---

[1] See also Cicero, *De Officiis*, i. 4.

[2] Clearly this was an *ignoratio elenchi*. If you are to vanquish
an opponent in dialectics, you must meet him on his own ground.

must be the greatest evil—the two are incompatible ;
and so a man in pain must be the most miserable and
pitiable of beings.   But, as a matter of fact, pain is
regarded by the virtuous as quite secondary, and, while
they bear it with magnanimity, they can be entirely
happy under it, seeing that their mind or conscience is
at rest.   (4) Once more, virtue is universally admired
and praised, not because of the pleasure it procures, but
because it *is* virtue ; and if people ever suspect that a
moral hero has acted as he did simply for the sake of
pleasure, they at once cease to regard him as a hero.
(5) But, even as applied to bodily sensation, pleasure is
not the sign of health and continued efficiency, but is an
index of degeneracy and decline—it is the indication
that a faculty or organ has reached its highest point and
is on the way to decay.[1]   (6) Then, again, the doctrine
was attacked on the ground that it takes account only
of a part of human nature, and omits its altruistic and
sympathetic side.   This was a line of attack that was
possible only to developed Stoicism, when the value
of the humaner virtues came to be realized ; but it is
very frequent in (say) Epictetus.   It was aimed at the
Epicurean conception of " unperturbedness " ($\dot{a}\tau a\rho a\xi\acute{\iota}a$)
as the supreme good—the state of agreeable feeling,
unalloyed by pain ; thereby making the feelings ($\pi\acute{a}\theta\eta$)
the criterion of moral worth, and placing man's peace
of mind in something that was esentially fleeting and
unstable.   This appeared to Epictetus to be a wholly
mistaken and a very derogatory view to take.   Of it he
said contemptuously, that Epicurus had placed man's
good in " the husk " (meaning the body), and so had to

[1] This is not psychologically correct.

maintain that, though a social being, a man must not
yield to his social affections, or his social impulses,
otherwise he will disturb his tranquillity (taking upon
him the burdens and sorrows of others), and so fail to
reach the state of ἀταραξία. For this reason, he must
cease caring for his offspring, as well as refuse to take
part in public affairs—all such duties would interfere
with his personal tranquillity and ease. On this
Epictetus makes a vigorous onslaught (*Diss.* i. 23)
from the side of altruism and the sympathetic emotions,
insisting that nature is too strong for Epicurus here.
For, he says, "Epicurus knows that if once a child is
born, it is no longer in our power not to love it, or to
care about it"; and he concludes with a striking home
thrust—"For my part, I think that, even if your father
and your mother had been told by an oracle that you
would say these things, they would not have cast you
off." Thus, truth, according to Epictetus, may be
found in other parts of human nature than reason—the
social instincts at any rate can guide us. "Thus also
Epicurus mutilated all the offices of a man and those of
the head of a house, and of a citizen, and of a friend,
but human desires he did not mutilate, for he could not"
(*Diss.* ii. 20). (7) Then, lastly, another argument may
be mentioned. If pleasure be the chief good, it was
urged, as by Cleanthes (see Stobæus, *Floril.* vi. 37),
that wisdom had been given to men for evil.

Enthusiasm of Humanity

This brings us to a further point in the Stoic characterization of virtue, a point that took firm hold of the
later Stoics in particular—namely, that virtue is a social

thing, and that the individual's good is bound up in that of the community : what is good for the community is good for him ; what is good for him is good for the community. " What is not good for the swarm is not good for the bee " ; " all that befalls the individual is for the good of the whole " (Aurelius, *Med.* vi. 54 and 45).

" Zeus," says Epictetus (*Diss.* i. 19), " has made the nature of the rational animal such that it cannot obtain any good proper to itself, unless it contribute something to the common interest. In this way, it is no longer unsocial for a man to do everything for the sake of himself. For what do you expect ? that a man should stand aloof from himself and his own interest? And how in that case could there be one and the same principle to all—namely, the principle of affection (οἰκείωσις) for themselves ? " And, again (*ibid.* ii. 5) : " What are you ? A man. If you look at yourself as separate from other men, it is according to nature to live to old age, to be rich, to be healthy. But if you look at yourself as a man, and as a part of a certain whole, for the sake of that whole it may now become you to be sick, at another time to sail the seas and to run into danger, at another time to be in want, and, perchance, to die before your time."

Yea more, it is only by Altruism that the individual's own highest good can be realized. " Nor can any one live happily who looks only to himself, who turns all things to his own advantage : you must live for others, if you wish to live for yourself " (Seneca, *Ep.* 48).

Hence the relation between self-interest and altruism, according to Stoic teaching. Self-interest is a necessity

—a man must attend, and should attend, to his own interest and preservation ; but, in doing so, he is also furthering the interest of others.   The two are mutually implicated, and there is no true severance between them.   " If, after all, they (the gods) take no thought for anything to do with us, then it is in my own power to take thought for myself ; and what I have to consider is my own interest ; and the true interest of everything is to conform to its own constitution and nature ; and my nature owns reason and social obligation ; socially, as Antoninus, my city and my country is Rome, as a man, the world.   These are the societies, whose advantage can alone be good to me " (Aurelius, *Med.* vi. 44).

This raises the question, then, in general, What is the community in whose interest is bound up that of the individual ?   In the first instance, no doubt, it is a man's family ; then his tribe ; then his city or his nation—the particular people to which he himself belongs.   But there is no logical stopping-point even here.   You must go on from people to people, and from race to race, until you have embraced mankind.   It is not blood-relationship, but community of reason, that makes men brothers.   And so the Stoic said, Every man is a citizen of the world : he finds in every other man a brother and a friend—as Musonius puts it, " The world is the common fatherland of all men." [1]   He even went farther, and maintained that every man is a citizen of a still larger world.   Says Epictetus (*Diss.* ii. 5) : " Do you not know that, as a foot alone is no longer a foot, so you alone are no longer a man ?   For what is

[1] Κοινὴ πατρὶς ἀνθρώπων ἀπάντων ὁ κόσμος ἐστίν.

a man ?   A part of a State—first of that which is made
up of gods and men ; then of that which is said to be
next to the other, which is a small copy of the universal
State."   Also, " The greatest and most powerful and
most comprehensive of all is the community ($\sigma\acute{\upsilon}\sigma\tau\eta\mu\alpha$)
that is composed of men and God " (*Diss.* i. 9).

Humanity, then, is, to the Stoic, more than a collection of human beings—it is an organism ; and each unit
is more than a part—it is a member ; and humane offices
of man to man are more than acts of duty—they are
the promptings of love : *membra sumus corporis magni*
(Seneca, *Ep.* 95).[1]   " If you substitute *meros* for *melos*
—part for member—you do not yet love men from your
heart ; you have yet no certitude of joy in doing kindness ; they are still bare duty, not yet a good deed to
yourself" (Aurelius, *Med.* vii. 13).

This doctrine contained in it the condemnation of
Slavery—not of slavery in the sense of gradation of
ranks and classes in society, but of slavery in the sense
that one's subordinate and servant is in his nature an
inferior being, a mere implement, to be disposed of and
used precisely as his master or his owner chooses,—
just as to the modern employer of labour his workmen
are merely "hands."[2]   "How, then," asks Epictetus
(*Diss.* i. 13), "shall a man endure such persons as this
slave ?"   "Slave!" he replies, "will you not bear with
your own brother, who has Zeus for his progenitor,
and has been begotten as a son from the same seeds
and of the same descent from above?   But if you have

[1] The similarity of this teaching (metaphor and substance alike)
to that of St. Paul is obvious.
[2] That was Aristotle's view, and is disowned by Stoicism.

been put in any such higher place, will you immediately make yourself a tyrant? Will you not remember what you are, and whom you rule? that they are kinsmen, that they are brethren by nature, that they are the offspring of Zeus?—But I have purchased them, and they have not purchased me? Do you see where you are looking? that it is towards the earth, that it is towards the pit, that it is towards those wretched laws of dead men? But towards the laws of the gods you are not looking." It was in answer to the question whether a master may not sometimes accept a favour from his slave that Seneca made the beautiful reply— " There is one parent of us all, the world (*unus omnium parens mundus est*)." [1]   Purchase, property, of one man by another is now seen to mean nothing as to real proprietorship: the superior is acknowledged to be as dependent on the inferior as the inferior on the superior; the power of helping is not confined to one class, but the lower may bless the higher, as the higher the lower. That was a great step gained in the advance of the larger thought. A common parentage means mutual helpfulness and mutual love.

This cosmopolitanism and enthusiasm of humanity had for the Stoic far-reaching consequences. It shaped anew his doctrine of forgiveness of `injuries; making him no longer stand aloof and refuse forgiveness to an offending brother, but urging him to extend compassion, on the plea that the injurer and the injured are both akin—sharers in the same nature, members of the same family. It taught him, besides, the true function and

[1] *De Ben.* iii. 28.

the correct conception of punishment. "Society," says Seneca (*De Ira*, ii. 31), "cannot continue, if the parts of it do not assist and maintain one another. We will not, therefore, strike a man because he has offended, but that he may offend no more ; nor should punishment ever refer to the past, but to the future, for it does not minister to anger but is preventive (*non enim irascitur sed cavet*)." This might have been a sentence from Austin the jurist, or a quotation from J. S. Mill's *Utilitarianism* ; or it might have been taken from More's *Utopia*, where we read that the end of punishment "intendeth nothing else but the destruction of vices and saving of men : with so using and ordering them, that they cannot choose but be good, and what harm soever they did before, in the residue of their life to make amends for the same."

The Stoic's altruism also seems to have justified to him the position, that no one willingly inflicts an injury on another—a position that the later Stoics, such as Epictetus and Marcus Aurelius,[1] make a great deal of. As it is man's nature to be social, and as his reason shows him that sociality is a law of the universe, and what he rationally sees he naturally submits to, the person inflicting an injury does so from ignorance, not knowing what he does.

This same deep-seated altruism produced in the Stoic that wide charity and generosity of spirit that so frequently, especially among the Roman Stoics, characterized him, and prevented his becoming either a bigot or an ascetic. His tolerance was a conspicuous

[1] See Epictetus, *Diss.* i. 18 and 28, and ii. 26 ; also, Aurelius, *Med.* ii. 1, iv. 3, etc.

feature, not disproved even by Aurelius's persecution of the Christians; for that did not proceed from religious intolerance, but was dictated by political motives, supported by the belief (mistaken, no doubt, yet real) that the Christians did not act from inward conviction, but from "mere perversity."[1] In the true cosmopolitan spirit, Epictetus counsels us, when any one speaks evil of us, to harbour no ill-will against him, but to bear a gentle mind towards him, consoling ourselves with the reflection, "So it appeared to him" (*Encheiridion*, 42). This, of course, might be simply the gracious condescension of the superior person contemptuous of those who differ from him or who criticize him. But, as a matter of fact, it was not. The Stoic was no cynic (in the modern sense of that term), and his charity was genuine. On the other hand, the Stoic was no hermit. Although the wise man, being self-sufficient, is independent of all forms of government and of distinctive nationality, nevertheless his philosophy taught him that for the generality of people a man should remain in the State and perform faithfully his duties as citizen, whatever they might be—"staunchly every hour, as a Roman and a man, resolving to do the work in hand, with scrupulous and unaffected dignity, affectionately, freely, justly" (Aurel. *Med.* ii. 5); should marry also, if there were no sufficient reason to the contrary, and enter into the various home and family relationships, discharging conscientiously his part as husband, father, friend;[2] and when, after years of toil, he might rightfully seek a haven of rest,

---

[1] Aurelius, *Med.* xi. 3.
[2] See Cicero, *De Finibus*, iii. 20, 68; Seneca, *De Otio*, iii. 2.

he is counselled to do it, not out of dislike of mankind, but simply for satisfaction and repose.   His philosophy taught him, further, that if by a selfish act he sinned against the community and thereby forfeited his place and cut himself off as a member from the whole, he might yet be reinstated in his organic position : that is his special privilege.   " Have you ever seen a dismembered hand," asks Aurelius (*Med.* viii. 34), " or foot, or decapitated head, lying severed from the body to which it belonged ?   Such does a man, so far as he can, make himself, when he refuses to accept what befalls, and isolates himself, or when he pursues self-seeking action.   You are cast out from the unity of nature, of which you are an organic part ; you dismember your own self.   But there is this beautiful provision, that it is in your power to re-enter the unity. No other part of the whole doth God privilege, when severed and dismembered, to reunite.   But consider the goodness of God, with which he has honoured man : he has put it in his power never to be sundered at all from the whole ; and if sundered, then to rejoin it once more, and coalesce, and resume his contributory place." [1]

---

[1] It is a disputed point how far the Stoic Cosmopolitanism was due to the non-Hellenic nationality of the leading Stoics ; but, anyhow, the fact of non-Hellenic nationality is very noteworthy. " Zeno was from Citium, a Phœnician colony in Cyprus, and himself belonged to the Semitic race. . . . Of his disciples, Persæus came also from Citium ; 'Herillus was from Carthage ; Athenodorus from Tarsus ; Cleanthes from Assus in the Troad.   The chief disciples of Cleanthes were Sphærus of the Bosporus, and Chrysippus from Soli in Cilicia.   Chrysippus was succeeded by Zeno of Sidon, and Diogenes of Babylon ; the latter taught Antipater of Tarsus, who taught Panætius of Rhodes, who taught

Moral Progress

The Stoics took over from Socrates the doctrine that virtue may be taught. The proof they gave of this position was the fact that "bad men may become good" (δῆλον ἐκ τοῦ γίνεσθαι ἀγαθοὺς ἐκ φαύλων) ; and the great proof of the reality of virtue adduced by Posidonius was the fact that "Socrates and Diogenes and Antisthenes made progress in it" (Diog. Laërt. vii. 54).

This conception of progress (προκοπή) in the moral life toned down the original sternness of the Stoic teaching of the absolute nature of virtue, and became the great source of moral impulse to the unsophisticated —to struggling and imperfect humanity. Many of the most telling passages in Seneca have reference to this very subject.

But though the Stoics thus acknowledged the possibility of teaching virtue and upheld the fact of progress, and, therefore, the potency of habit, in the upbuilding of character, they were divided in opinion as to whether virtue could be lost ; Chrysippus holding

Posidonius of Apamea in Syria.   There was another Athenodorus, from Cana in Cilicia ; and the early Stoic Archedemus is mentioned by Cicero as belonging to Tarsus.   The names of Nestor, Athenodorus, Cordylion, and Heraclides may be added to the list of Stoical teachers furnished by Tarsus.   Seleucia sent forth Diogenes ; Epiphania, Euphrates ; Scythopolis, Basilides ; Ascalon, Antibius ; Tyre, Antipater ; Sidon, Boëthus ; Ptolemais, Diogenes. We see then what an Oriental aspect this catalogue presents. Not a single Stoic of note was a native of Greece proper" (Sir A. Grant, *The Ethics of Aristotle*, vol. i. p. 307).   The genuine Greek despised the Barbarian (even Plato and Aristotle did), and made a very marked distinction between the freeborn citizen and the slave.

that it could, and Cleanthes that it could not—"the one saying that it can be lost by drunkenness and melancholy, the other that it cannot, on account of the firm perceptions" (Diog. Laërt. vii. 65).

The difficulty that confronted them here was real, and was precisely that which later Christian times had to face with regard to salvation and divine grace; and the solution in both cases was substantially the same. If the Stoic school was divided over virtue, Christian theologians have been equally divided over salvation; some upholding the dogma of "the perseverance of the saints," and others maintaining the possibility of finally "falling away."

Preference and Avoidance

But practical morality was further encouraged when the doctrine of "indifferent" things was revised and developed, as it soon came to be. The dogma in its original form—such, possibly, as it came from the hands of Ariston of Chios, to whom Diogenes Laërtius [1] ascribes the origination of it—made a sharp and uncompromising division between things in our power and things not in our power, including in the latter class the vast majority of things that people in general most desire (health, bodily vigour, favourable circumstances, etc.), and maintained that things of this class were wholly "indifferent," having no real value whatever, and allowing of no degrees or grades among them. This was soon found to be too drastic and too much opposed to ordinary experience and regardless of the plain man's capacity; and so the important concession

[1] See vii. 31.

was made that, *in special connexions and for definite purposes*, some indifferent things (such as mental ability, health, bodily vigour, favourable circumstances) were better than others, and therefore were to be pursued, while their opposites (mental impotence, ill-health, feebleness of body, etc.) were to be eschewed. This was the famous distinction between "things to be preferred" (προηγμένα, *præposita*) and "things to be avoided" (ἀποπροηγμένα, *rejecta*), which allowed a man living in the world and wishful to discharge his duties to society and to himself to cultivate aptitudes, to make selection among circumstances, to husband resources, and to follow definite objects with zest and appreciation. A certain number of indifferent things were now conceived as having "value" (ἀξία), and so were regarded as being "according to nature," whereas only those things that "have no value" (ἀπαξία) were relegated to the category of "contrary to nature."[1]

But though these things having value might be preferred, nothing must be done or chosen or accepted that would lead to the deterioration of character—that was an indispensable restriction. "What, then, if a dried fig should fall into your lap? Take it and eat it; for thus far may you value even a dried fig. But if I shall stoop down and overturn another, or be overturned by another, and shall flatter those who have entered in, neither is a dried fig worth that nor any of the things that are not good, which the philosophers

---

[1] There was also a third class of indifferent things recognized—namely, those that were "absolutely indifferent" (τὰ καθάπαξ ἀδιάφορα), such as, whether the hairs on one's head are in number odd or even.

have persuaded me not to regard as good " (Epictetus, *Diss.* iv. 7).

This sphere of "indifferent things," as thus interpreted, is the sphere of "duty," as καθῆκον, to which we have already referred ; the conception of which brought the Stoical ethics into close contact with morality in everyday life. It was the acknowledgment that counsels of perfection are valuable and may be appropriate for the select few ; but that, for the many, there are needed counsels that are in sympathy with the efforts and aspirations of frail and feeble mortals —counsels that pay some consideration to the circumstance that, while the spirit is willing, the flesh may be weak.

CHAPTER IX

ETHICS: SPECIAL POINTS

" It is from considering the relations which the several appetites and passions in the inward frame have to each other, and, above all, the supremacy of reflection or conscience, that we get the idea of the system or constitution of human nature. And from the idea itself it will as fully appear, that this our nature, *i.e.*, constitution, is adapted to virtue, as from the idea of a watch it appears, that its nature, *i.e.*, constitution or system, is adapted to measure time."—BUTLER.

" In regno nati sumus : deo parere libertas est."—SENECA.

" The seat of law is the bosom of Almighty God."—HOOKER.

BEFORE proceeding, it may be well to emphasize and further explain one or two of the leading positions in the Stoical Ethics.

I

And, first of all, the formula, " *Live agreeably to nature.*"

Many people have stumbled at this phrase, regarding it as indefinite, and unsuitable to express the central thought of the system. Now, it is quite true that the term " nature " is ambiguous : it may be used in a wider and in a narrower sense, as designating the whole or as indicating merely a part. But, in either case, the meaning is perfectly plain, and the two significations are complementary of each other. If "nature" be taken in its wider sense, as designating the whole, then the life that is counselled in the injunction "live agreeably to nature" is that of law and order, conscious and willing conformity to the processes of the universe, to the general course of things; and as the order of nature (in this sense) is conceived by the Stoic as rational, it means submission to reason in all the modes of its manifestation. If, on the other hand, "nature" be interpreted as *human* nature, then the phrase is equally intelligible, if we avoid the Cynic error of making savage and uncultured nature the type, and place the type in developed civilized nature, and especially in man's ideals and aspirations. The meaning now is, that man has a distinct place in the world, as a social being endowed with reason—is a member of a corporate whole whose good is the supreme end and in which the individual's good is inseparably bound up. He is thus conceived as a complex of many powers and principles, duly graded, with the supremacy accorded to conscience or the practical reason. That is the conception of a system or constitution that Butler afterwards so lucidly defined.[1] Viewing the matter thus, the Stoic raised no question as to the legitimacy of the hierarchy of principles that human nature disclosed. He was undisturbed, on the one hand, by any troublesome problems about origin, such as have perplexed later moralists (origin of moral ideas and guiding axioms), and, on the other hand, by any doctrine of evolution—biological or other. He took his stand firmly on the empirical position; accepting human nature as something given, which it was his duty to analyze and try

[1] See Preface to his *Sermons.*

to understand, and in the analysis and understanding of which he rested content.

And there is no doubt that his analysis was remarkably striking, and his teaching, on its practical side, salutary to a degree. He clearly saw the supreme value of the ethical side of man's constitution, and set himself to advocate its significance accordingly. Hence, Stoicism is and ever must be an important element in philosophy ; and it has exerted immense influence in moulding philosophical teaching in the past. All the great ethical philosophies of Western Europe have been indebted to it. Need we refer to Kant and to Butler ? or is it more than necessary to allude to Thomas Reid and the Scottish philosophers generally ? No one can read the last part of the *Ethica* of Spinoza without being struck with its purely Stoic aspect ; and Stoicism is very apparent in the Ritschlian teaching of " value-judgments " at the present day. If we turn to poetry, it will be sufficient to instance Pope's *Essay on Man*, which is simply Stoicism in verse, although Pope has in part misconceived the doctrine of *apatheia* ; and Matthew Arnold is a Stoic poet in chief, and his prose, too, bears impress of the Porch.

II

Nor is the Stoic doctrine of the Will without significance. Untrammelled by any abstract theory of volitional freedom, as also by the false antithesis between internal and external motives that has so frequently played havoc in ethical systems, no less than by the question as to whether motives are really causes, the Stoics went direct to the psychological and experiential fact that man, as a rational being, has the power of recognizing the rationality of the cosmic order and of cheerfully submitting to it, and, in the sphere of ethics, that he has a conception of the ideal good, and the power of identifying himself therewith. This doctrine British philosophers of to-day are in the habit of associating specially with T. H. Green[1] and his followers. But it is Stoical in its essence, and was then, as it is now, the main cause of the stimulating energy that high ethical teaching possesses, and of its wholesome elevating influence on life and practice.

This doctrine of the will must be taken in connexion with the Stoic psychology of Desire. Although not essaying an elaborate analysis, such as we find in Aristotle, partly in the *Nicomachean Ethics*, partly in the *De Animâ*, the Stoics made desire and the right handling of it practically the centre of their system. According to this, they determined merit and demerit, gauged impulse and allied processes, and appraised the ethical character of an act. " In comparing sins—so far as they admit of general comparison—Theophrastus sagely observes that sins of desire are more heinous than sins of passion. For passion is an estrangement

---

[1] " The motive which is thus necessarily involved in the act of will, is not a motive in the same sense in which each of the parties to the controversy constantly uses the term. It is not one of the mere desires or aversions, between which the advocate of ' free-will ' supposes a man to exercise an arbitrary choice, and of which the strongest, according to the opposite view, necessarily prevails. It is constituted by the reaction of the man's self upon these, and its identification of itself with one of them, as that of which the satisfaction forms for the time its object " (*Pro-legomena to Ethics*, bk. ii. chap. 1).

from reason, accompanied by sense of pain and inward
constriction ; but sins of desire, in which pleasure gets
the better of us, imply more of feminine incontinence.
And surely it is right and philosophical to say that
sinning with pleasure is more culpable than sinning
with pain.   The latter is like acting under provocation,
and being driven into passion by pain : the former is a
spontaneous impulse towards wrong, driving one to
satisfaction of desire " (Aurelius, *Med.* ii. 10).

III

Again, a very strong point in Stoicism was its
attempt to withdraw mankind from the futile pursuit of
happiness in varying and uncertain circumstances, and
its locating true felicity in the mind, and especially in
the virtuous disposition.   This, of course, did not
originate with the Stoics.   Nothing, for example,
could surpass the beautiful prayer of Socrates at the
end of the *Phædrus*: " Beloved Pan, and all ye other
gods who haunt this place, give me beauty in the
inward soul ; and may the outward and inward man
be at one.   May I reckon the wise to be the wealthy,
and may I have such a quantity of gold as a temperate
man and he only can bear and carry."   But what
characterized the Stoics was the emphasis that they
laid on this doctrine, the variety of applications that
they made of it, and the noble way in which they
unweariedly insisted that the source of the highest
human bliss is the mind conscious to itself of right.
" Remember that your Inner Self is inexpugnable,
when once it rallies to itself and consistently declines
to act against its will, even though the defiance may

be irrational. How much more, then, when its judgment is rational and made with circumspection?
Therefore the mind free from passions is a citadel;
man has no stronger fortress to which he can fly for
refuge and remain impregnable. Ignorant is he, who
has not seen this; unhappy he, who, having seen, yet
flies not to the refuge" (Aurelius, *Med.* viii. 48). This
was their protest, true and emphatic, valid for all time,
against moral materialism — against the degrading
tendency to place genuine worth in the accessories of
ethical life, instead of in the life itself. Right well did
the Stoic see that, when a man fixes his heart on anything outside his character, farewell to all high moral
action and to noble thought. "Alexander suffered
great misfortune when the Greeks came upon the
Trojans and destroyed Troy, and when his brothers
perished? By no means; for no one is harmed by the
action of another, and what happened then was only
the destruction of the storks' nests. But his misfortune
was when he lost modesty, fidelity, hospitality, and
decorum. When did Achilles suffer misfortune?
When Patroclus died? Not so; but when he began
to be angry, when he wept for a maiden, when he
forgot that he was at Troy, not to get possession of
mistresses, but to fight. These things are the mis-
fortunes of men, this is beleaguering, this is destruction,
when right opinions are pulled down, when they are
corrupted" (Epictetus, *Diss.* i. 28).[1]

---

[1] " Resolve to be thyself; and know that he
Who finds himself, loses his misery."
                (Matt. Arnold, "Self-dependence.")

IV

A fourth striking peculiarity is the Stoic's insistence on altruism—his cosmopolitanism and doctrine of the universal brotherhood of man: " We are made for co-operation, like the feet, the hands, the eyelids, the upper and the lower rows of teeth " (Aurelius, *Med.* ii. 1). This struck at the very root of selfishness; and by teaching the individual habitually to view his actions in the light of deeds done by one who was yet not isolated and independent, but part of a body, in living communion and intercommunion with the whole, enunciated a truth of the greatest practical significance. Morality now became the chief concern of life, for morality was essentially social; and the notion of virtue was widened, so as to have a really ennobling effect on character. No cramped, stunted ethics was offered to mankind, but an expansive ethics—social, universal; the true import of which would be apparent to the world only as thought matured and men tried to adjust their practice to their profession. The contrast was explicitly to Epicureanism—not so much, however, in the area that ethical action covered (for the Epicurean, too, recognized the social character of morality), as in the motive and disposition: it was the exaltation of unselfishness against egoistic hedonism and selfishness. In this respect, Stoicism showed a distinct parallel to Christianity, and, as a matter of fact, is very likely to have affected the early Christian teaching—more especially that of St. Paul, who himself belonged to a city that was a chief seat of Stoicism (namely, Tarsus), and who could, on occasion, as in the Areopagus at

Athens, turn his Stoical knowledge effectively to account. Only, there is this great difference, that the Christian enthusiasm for humanity originates in love for the personal Christ, in devotion to a divine Person, and is stimulated by His example. Natural fellow-feeling and brotherly affection thus becomes intensified ; and it is rendered effective in a way that nothing else can do when it is based in personal religion. At all events, it was this very sentiment of universal brotherhood, prompted by true altruistic motive, that broke down the distinctions of caste among the Stoics, putting Epictetus, the lame slave, on a level with Marcus Aurelius, the Roman Emperor, on the principle that

> " The rank is but the guinea stamp,
> The man's the gowd for a' that " ; [1]

and that enabled Aurelius himself to work steadily towards the realization of his own ideal—" The conception of an equal commonwealth based on equality of right and equality of speech, and of imperial rule respecting first and foremost the liberty of the subject " (*Med.* i. 14). And it is the same sentiment, working slowly yet surely, that in Christian lands has procured the abolition of slavery, has made consistently for freedom (social, political, and religious), obliterating class animosities, and stirring the spirit of philanthropy so deeply as it does in Christendom at the present day.[1]

[1] Burns.

[2] For a laudation of the social duties and the proof of their pre-eminence, see Cicero, *De Officiis*, i. 43-45.

V

Once more, Stoicism, like Christianity, was distinguished by its appreciation of man's dignity and worth.
The Stoics conceived men to be akin to God, rays
from the divine light, parts of the primal substance,
even children of the one great Father—"for we also,"
said Cleanthes, "are Thy offspring."

As a consequence of this, they strenuously insisted
upon the cultivation of self-respect and of an independent spirit, in a way and with an urgency that would
have satisfied Kant himself or the poet Burns. To
them, as to Kant, self-respect was not so much a virtue
as the foundation of all virtue. In the 25th section of
the *Encheiridion*, Epictetus puts it in a very homely
way: "How much are lettuces sold for? An obolus,
perhaps. If any one, then, give up the obolus and
receive the lettuces, and you do not give up and receive,
think not that you are worse off than he who receives.
For, as he has the lettuces, so you have the obolus,
which you did not give. Likewise, also, in the other
matter. Have you not been invited to the feast of so
and so? It was because you did not give to him who
issues the invitation the price at which the supper is
sold; and he sells it for flattery, he sells it for obse-
quiousness. Give then the price, if it will profit
you, for which it is sold. But if you will not give the
price and yet will have the things, you are greedy
and fatuous. Have you nothing, then, in lieu of the
supper? Yes, indeed, you have this, that you have
not flattered him whom you would not; you have
this, that you have not endured his door-attendants."

"This do, my Lucilius, vindicate thy dignity (*vindica te tibi*)."[1]

They counselled, also, in the spirit of a rational ethic, rather than in the merely sentimental fashion of the present day, kindness to the lower animals. Naturally enough, in conformity with their system, the brute creation was conceived as being subservient to the uses of man. As the Stoic physics was geocentric, so the ethic was homocentric: "Is it not palpable that the lower forms exist for the higher, and the higher for one another? And things with breath of life are higher than things without; and things with reason than with breath alone" (Aurelius, *Med.* v. 16). But they said, "You have reason; unreasoning creatures and the world of material things have none: therefore in your dealings with them rise superior and free " (*ibid.* vi. 23).

As another consequence of their appreciation of man's worth, they maintained the indissoluble connexion between ethics and religion. The law of the universe, they held, is the law of God; and the bindingness of morality on us is the bindingness of rationality, echoing or reproducing the divine reason. And even human laws, they taught, are to be obeyed by men because they are not arbitrary enactments of the individual with a view to his own selfish ends, but embodiments of the universal reason subservient to the interests of the whole. Law, therefore, is one with God ; at all events, where law is, God is. Jurisprudence, as much as cosmic order, or the rational conduct of the individual, implies the Deity: "the seat of law," as Hooker afterwards put it, "is the bosom of Almighty God." Heracleitus, too, had said that

[1] Seneca, *Ep.* i.

"all human laws are nurtured by the one divine law; for this prevails as much as it will, and suffices for all, and has something over." Nor was this a mere sentiment with the Stoic, but a living, operative, principle, turned to great use. It was embodied by the Emperor Aurelius in his State legislation. Need we wonder that the great jurists of the second and third centuries of the Christian era worked under the impulse of Stoic principle? Who but the Stoically-minded were thus competent? None were so able to enshrine the moral law that legislated within in the form of the actual law operating without; and none were so successful in bringing State and conscience into unison and harmony.

VI

Particularly noticeable is the Stoic's appreciation of the regenerative power of a virtuous life in the world. He maintained that virtue could be taught; but, though not despising theory and theoretical teaching, he held that the most potent schoolmaster is the life of individual men clearly displayed. We learn by copying, more than from prelection. Hence, (a) in the first place, he had certain moral heroes, certain supreme examples of strenuous moral living, whom he held up for imitation—such as Socrates, Hercules, Antisthenes, Diogenes. These he set forth as models. For this purpose he had to idealize them. He was not unaware of defects in the actual men: Seneca, for instance, admits that Socrates had flaws and shortcomings, and these are not to be followed.[1] But though the models

---

[1] That there never was a perfect concrete example of the Stoic Wise Man, is strongly urged by Lucian in his *Hermotimus*.

may not have been absolutely flawless, they were supremely worthy of imitation, and were set forth accordingly. Even a halo was thrown round them, just as was done by the great Church painters with mediæval Christian saints. Thus the account of Diogenes, the Cynic, that Epictetus gives us is considerably different from that which common history owns. The asperities, bohemianism, and rudeness of that rugged character are passed by, and in their place we find the following: "But come now, Did Diogenes love nobody, who was so gentle and humane that, for the sake of men in general, he gladly undertook so great labours and hardships of the body? But how did he love? As became a minister of Zeus, at the same time concerned for men and also as subject to God. Therefore, the whole earth was fatherland to him alone, and no selected place; and being taken prisoner, he did not long for Athens or his acquaintances and friends there, but he made acquaintance with the pirates themselves, and tried to reform them; and when he was sold later on, he lived in Corinth as before at Athens, and he would have done exactly the same had he gone to the Perrhæbi. Thus is freedom acquired" (*Diss.* iii. 24).

But, (*b*) next, the Stoic pointed to right living as a model in whatsoever Stoic it was found, however humble he might be. We have already seen (Chapter III. p. 52) how strict he was in demanding purity of life in the philosopher and professional teacher, but he aimed at high achievement in all. Hence, he counselled the progressive and aspiring to keep constantly before him some real example as known to him in life; as says Marcus Aurelius (*Med.* vi. 48), "Nothing is more

cheering than exemplifications of virtue in the char-
acters of those about us, suggesting themselves as
copiously as possible. We should keep them always
ready to hand ": and that he acted on his own counsel
is evident from the beautiful picture that he draws of
Antoninus Pius in Book I. of the *Meditations*, and from
the glowing tribute that he pays to his mother and to
all the instructors that helped to mould his character,
out of a full and grateful heart.

And there is no question that the most effective way
of teaching morals is by example. Precept is not to be
contemned; but precept divorced from practice is a
weak force compared with high doctrine embodied in a
life. Such life embodiment is what people can see and
understand; and, coming into immediate contact with
it, they can feel its power and inspiration. It thus
comes to them with warmth, clothed in flesh and blood,
and thereby influences.

VII

Yet again, the Stoic made it his special endeavour to
be helpful to the earnest; and so put his principles to
practical use all round. He condescended to teach the
duties of everyday life. We do not, indeed, find in
any of the masters an elaborate classification and
handling of duties such as is given us by Kant[1] or by
Richard Price,[2] or such as may be found in Bishop
Martensen,[3] or in Professor Newman Smyth,[4] or in Dr.

---

[1] *The Metaphysic of Ethics* (Semple's translation).
[2] *A Review of the Principal Questions in Morals.*
[3] *Christian Ethics* (Eng. tr.).
[4] *Christian Ethics.*

W. S. Bruce;[1] but we do find, even in the earliest writers (such as Zeno and Cleanthes), analyses and definitions of the four cardinal virtues (which was then the recognized and authoritative enumeration of duties), and we find division of virtues into primary and secondary, or subordinate, with explications;[2] and there are abundant instances of counsels, though not in systematic fashion, but thrown out at all points, regarding numerous social and religious duties.[3] The Stoic preached the necessity of a man's attending to his own highest interest and of developing his better self to the fullest extent—only thus can virtue be realized; he sketched his functions as a worthy member of the community, with social obligations of the various relationships in life (citizen, husband, father, friend) laid upon him; and, suffused as he was with piety and devotion, he enforced the duty and the privilege of serving God. This gives the nucleus of the threefold classification of man's duties current in modern treatises on practical ethics—duties to oneself, duties to one's neighbour, duties to God. And, indeed, the Stoic teacher would have been untrue to his great purpose of reclaiming the fallen and of purifying society, if he had not legislated for man as man and turned his attention to the remedy of clamant evils in everyday life.

[1] *Social Aspects of Christian Morality.*

[2] The primary are the four cardinal virtues (wisdom, self-control, courage, righteousness); to each of which is attached a list of species or varieties, duly discriminated, which constitute the secondary or subordinate virtues. See Diogenes Laërtius, vii. 92; Stobæus, *Ecl.* ii. 60, 9 W.

[3] Stoicism is, in this respect, like the Bible; and it finds its parallel in Proverbs in O.T. and in St. Paul's practical counsels in N.T.

CHAPTER X

ETHICS : DEFECTS

"Et in seipso totus, teres atque rotundus."—HORACE.

"In lazy apathy let Stoics boast
Their virtue fix'd ; 'tis fix'd as in a frost."—POPE.

"Certainly, Vertue is like pretious Odours, most fragrant, when they are incensed, or crushed : For *Prosperity* doth best discover Vice ; But *Adversity* doth best discover Vertue."—BACON.

BUT with all these merits (and they are great), the Stoic Ethics had its weak points ; and to these it now becomes necessary to advert.

I

For one thing, it over-emphasized the stern, austere, unsympathetic side of morality in its paradoxical doctrine of the Wise Man, and thereby disturbed the true balance of human nature, and, to a certain extent, rendered its own teaching impracticable. If it was the fault of Epicureanism that it made too much of pleasure, it is certainly the fault of Stoicism that it made too little of pain. This was, doubtless, an inheritance from Cynicism. Its dogma of Passionlessness or ἀπάθεια— its contempt for pain and pleasure and its indifference towards objects of affection—is in an extreme : it is too unbendingly Puritanical. Of it one might say, what Stoicism itself said of Epicurus's counsel that parents should not bring up their children, "Nature is too strong for it." Their apathy, although not "lazy" (as Pope designated it), is certainly "virtue fix'd" and "fix'd as in a frost." [1] It was originally circumscribed and frigid, and, even to the end, it failed to appreciate the multifarious interests of human nature. When Epictetus counsels (*Encheir.* iii.), "If you love an earthen jar, say, 'It is an earthen jar that I love,' for, when it is broken, you will not be disturbed ; if you kiss your little child or your wife, say that it is a human being whom you are kissing, for, when either of them dies, you will not be disturbed," [2] he simply lays bare, in concrete form, the fundamental weakness of the Stoical indifference. For, surely, child and wife are more to father and husband than "a human being" ; and even the earthen jar, through the power of association, becomes more to us than a mere thing of earth and clay, valuable simply for its utility. Again, it may very well be true that, if a man is unhappy, it is his own fault, for God has made all men to be happy ; but it does not follow, as Epictetus makes it, that his unhappiness is no concern of yours (*Diss.* iii. 24) ; and if a man grieves at being parted from you, his friend, it is but harsh consolation to tell him that "he simply suffers the consequences of his own folly," for he should never have supposed that you two could remain together for ever.

The defect of the Stoical Ideal is that it does not sufficiently recognize *the emotions*. A large section of human nature (and that a most important one) was

[1] *Essay on Man*, ii. 101.   [2] See also *Diss.* iii. 24.

practically cut off from the wise man's cognizance: he
lived according to a mere part of his nature and ignored
the rest.   The great power of an ideal lies in the fact
that it addresses itself to the heart—lays hold of the
affections and stimulates our aspirations.   But bare
emotionlessness cannot do this.   Apathy, at best,
attaches itself to the heroic side of our being; but it is
impotent to *attract* us, like the amiable and gentle
virtues: it is stern and unlovable, and lacks the milk
of human kindness.   Hence it is suitable (and has been
found to be so) to men in times of great turmoil, hard-
ship, and persecution, when the world seemed so much
out of joint that it would not tolerate high principle, or
give quarter to any one who would not accept might for
right, and fall in meekly with the prevailing vices and
oppressions.   It was precisely the philosophy for Epictetus, the lame slave, over whom Epaphroditus acted
the part of tyrant; for Seneca the tutor and hapless
guide of Nero—uncertain of royal favour, with the
prospect of untimely death before his eyes, and the
thought of it never long absent from his mind; for
Boëthius, the martyr of Ticinum, barbarously used by
the untutored Ostrogothic king.   Men of the heroic
stamp, when heroism was supremely needed, found in
it a consolation and a power which gentler natures,
under more favourable circumstances, scarcely discovered.   In the midst of Neronic cruelties and injus-
tices, or in the battlefield or camp (as was the case with
Marcus Aurelius), among the Quadi, or at Carnuntum,
the Stoic found his solace in withdrawing into himself
and making himself realize that happiness resides in the
soul and not in external fortune, and that inward recti-

tude is beyond the reach of tyrant, of untoward circumstance, or of war. But, in happier days, this solace is
less required ; and then men come to feel that there is
such a thing as the *beauty* of virtue (in distinction from
its *sublimity* and *grandeur*), and the soothing influence
of goodness most effectually exerts itself when no sharp
line is drawn between inward felicity and outward
circumstances—when the two are felt to be in harmony,
and the latter ministers to, and does not oppose, the
former, man and his environment being reconciled.

In this connexion, it is interesting to compare the
early Stoic contempt for the sympathetic and amiable
virtues with the position of Christianity, which has
elevated humility, meekness, and the passive graces
(patience, long-suffering, and the like) to the highest
place. The Christian, like the Stoic, aims at being
self-sufficient ; but what a difference there is between
the two kinds of self-sufficiency ! The difference has
been admirably expressed by Professor Findlay in the
contrast that he draws between the Pauline and the
Stoic conceptions of self-sufficiency or αὐτάρκεια, thus :
"The Christian self-sufficiency is relative ; it is an
independence of the world through dependence upon
God. The Stoic self-sufficiency pretends to be absolute.
The one is the contentment of faith, the other of pride.
Cato and Paul both stand erect and fearless before a
persecuting world : one with a look of rigid and defiant
scorn ; the other with a face now lighted up with un-
utterable joy in God, now cast down with sorrow and
wet with tears for God's enemies. The Christian
martyr and the Stoic suicide are the final examples

of these two memorable and contemporaneous protests against the evils of the world" (*Christian Doctrine and Morals*, p. 34).[1]   So, further, there is an absolute contrast between Stoicism and Christianity in the matter of the kindlier feelings.   There is nothing in the Stoic teaching like the sentence, "He shall not break the bruised reed, nor quench the smoking flax"; nor like this, "If thine enemy smite thee on the one cheek, offer him the other also"; nor like this, "Be ye kind one to another, tender-hearted, forgiving each other, even as God also in Christ forgave you" (*Eph.* iv. 32).

Yet the need for recognizing the sympathetic and tender side of human nature came more and more to be felt by the Stoics; and, as time went on, they tried to adjust their teaching to this requirement.   It is noteworthy that the Roman period of Stoicism is far more expansive and humane than the earlier Greek period. The meaning of this is that, pressed, on the one side by the demand to show some living example of the ideal wise man, and, on the other side, by the constant cry of the emotions for a more adequate recognition, they made important alterations in their system, which had indeed the effect of rendering it more popular, but at the expense of consistency.   It may reasonably be doubted whether any system should be finally condemned on the simple ground that it has failed to produce any man who lived exactly up to its highest precepts.   For the use of an ideal is precisely to show what should be done, or what ought to be aimed at,

[1] See also Lightfoot, *St. Paul's Epistle to the Philippians*, p. 303.

and to stimulate to a nearer and nearer approach to that, acting all the while as a beacon and a lure ; and it is enough if this ideal embody desirable elements that are realizable, though never actually realized by the individual here,—and if it elevate and encourage and improve him who strives to attain to it. We need not, then, lay great stress on the fact that, when the Stoics pointed to Hercules, or to Socrates, or to any other of the very few saints of their calendar, you were able to establish shortcomings and failings in the example, and to prove that each was far from perfect. But it is different if we are able to prove that some of the elements in the ideal are either not realizable, or are such as, if realized, are not desirable—would not expand our nature, but cramp and contract it. And this, or something like it, might be done in the case of the ideal sage. In some respects, his is a non-human and an unattainable condition, and a condition which, if attained, would not be wholly desirable : at best, it is agreeable only to a side of man's nature.

Hence, the Stoics, even in Zeno's time, amended their doctrine of indifferent things, or things not in our own power ; admitting that a relative value exists among them : there are *grades* of indifference ; some things being preferable to others, and, therefore, in certain circumstances and for certain ends, to be more or less eagerly pursued. Indeed, the later Stoics went so far in their endeavour to adapt their conceptions to the notions and customs of the vulgar, that they virtually split up Stoicism into an esoteric and an exoteric portion.[1] The result was that even great teachers

[1] See Cicero, *De Officiis*, ii.

lent the weight of their authority to doubtful practices
—as when Penætius, if Cicero is to be relied on,
justified the advocate or *patronus* in his practice
of defending the plausible, even when it was not
true.

Again, the Stoics (as we have already seen) had by
and by to admit that there are degrees in virtue and
in vice, as well as in pleasure and in pain. And
when they perfected their teaching of Altruism, and
emphasized the fact that every man is a citizen of the
world, with privileges and obligations corresponding,
they paid homage to the affections in a way that
struck at the root of their fundamental dogma. Their
system now became far more effective, but it became
inconsistent.

So, in like manner, their doctrine of moral progress
(προκοπή, *profectus*), and their counsel of daily self-
examination (after the manner of the Pythagoreans),
carried faithfully out by the conscientious Stoic, so as
to gauge his shortcomings and stir him up to amendment, were concessions to practical human needs, and
gave working power to what might otherwise have
been an inoperative abstract teaching.[1] If men can
advance in character, if habits may be formed and
count for much,[2] if the "foolish" may become "wise,"
there are degrees in virtue and in vice ; and, as virtue
is by degrees contracted, vice is by degrees abandoned.
That is not a doctrine of theoretical perfection, but a
fact of moral experience ; and the recognition of it gave
a great fulcrum to Stoic Ethics.

[1] See Epictetus, *Diss.* i. 4 ; iii. 2.
[2] See Epictetus's wise handling of habit in *Diss.* ii. 18.

II

Another point in which Stoicism erred was its doctrine that injury is done only *unwittingly*. It taught that a man who harmed another did so from ignorance, and, therefore, unintentionally.[1] " If others are doing right, you have no call to feel sore ; if wrong, it is not wilful, but comes of ignorance. Just as *No soul wilfully misses truth*, none wilfully disallows another's due " (Aurelius, *Med.* xi. 18). This was a remnant of the old Socratic teaching (as laid down in the *Protagoras*, for instance), that no man sins willingly, or that vice is ignorance and virtue knowledge ; but it assumes a new aspect in its Stoical setting.

The position may be met by the rejoinder that, as a patent fact of our experience, native bad principle exists, and that a man, from the very circumstance that his nature is depraved,—that he is possessed of malevolent, as well as of benevolent, affections,—may take real conscious delight in injuring another and in gratuitously inflicting pain.[2] The beast in him, or the fiend in him, is a factor that you cannot ignore, and which you certainly do not eliminate by simply slurring over.

The ground of the Stoic dictum is, that a man is a member of society, and, therefore, his good is bound up with the good of every other member of society. And so, when one man injures another, he is thereby

---

[1] See Epictetus, *Diss.* i. 28.

[2] See this point very ably argued by Professor Bain in his *Dissertations on Leading Philosophical Topics*, pp. 84–104.

injuring himself, for his own good and the good of the other are one ; and if he clearly saw this, he would refrain from injuring, inasmuch as no man wishes evil to himself. "It is man's special gift to love even those who fall into blunders : it operates as soon as it suggests, that men are your brothers, that sin is of ignorance and unintentional, that in a little you will both be dead, that, above all, no injury is done you ; your Inner Self is not made worse than it was before" (Marcus Aurelius, *Med.* vii. 22).

And, no doubt, if man were purely a rational being, this appeal to reason would be enough and effective. But man is not purely or solely rational—he is emotive and emotional also, and is moved by inclination and desire ; and the malignant emotions are a part of his nature, as has just been said, and must be taken account of. That being so, it is no comfort to me, when injured by some one, to suppose that the injurer acts ignorantly ; for such may not have really been the case : his inclination may have mastered his judgment. And as for the offender himself, the way to gain him is, not to prove to him that his conduct is irrational, as being really against his own self-interest, but to win him to oneself, or to the right, by love and kindness. The road to reformation lies through the affections, more than through the reason, as Epictetus clearly saw when he said : "Every thing has two handles— one by which it may be carried, and the other by which it may not be carried. If your brother wrongs you, take it not by this handle, that he wrongs you, for that is the handle by which it may not be carried ; but take it rather by this handle, that he is your brother, nourished along with you, and you will take it by the handle whereby it may be carried " (*Encheir*. 43).[1]

Furthermore, this doctrine of injury as involuntary regards sin as a mere defect, just like blindness in a man bereft of sight, and it led to counsel that, if consistently acted on, would have undermined morality itself. Both Epictetus and Marcus Aurelius frequently give us the advice to take no heed of the man who harms us, inasmuch as he has no power to hurt our soul. But, surely, he *has* power to hurt our soul if his injuring us simply leads to our passively ignoring him, instead of our actively attempting his reformation, by resistance or merited punishment, in whatsoever form. Our generosity must not be allowed to degenerate into spiritual pride, or into selfish disregard of our brother's highest good, or even into passive acquiescence in wrong out of mistaken deference to the doer. There is something noble in Epictetus's deliverance, but it is inadequate (*Encheir*. 30): "Duties are in general measured by relations. A man is a father. The injunction is to care for him, to submit to him in all things, to suffer him when he rebukes, when he strikes.

---

[1] The later Stoics in general came to acknowledge this. See, *e.g.*, Aurelius, *Med.* xi. 18: "Kindness is invincible if only it is honest, not fawning or insincere. What can the most aggressive do, if you keep persistently kind, and as occasion offers gently remonstrate, and seize the moment, when he is bent on mischief, for trying quietly to convert him to a better frame of mind? 'Not so, my son, we are made for other ends ; you cannot hurt me, you hurt yourself, my son.' Then point him gently to the general law of things, that neither do the bees act so, nor any of the gregarious animals ; but avoid any touch of irony or fault-finding, and be affectionate and conciliatory in tone; not in schoolmaster style, or to show off before others, but quietly in his own ear, even if others are standing by."

'But he is a bad father.' Were you then by nature settled with a good father? Nay, but with a father. 'My brother wrongs me.' Preserve then your own position towards him, nor scrutinize what it is that he is doing, but what it is necessary for yourself to do that your will may be according to nature. For another will not damage you, unless you yourself will it; but *then* will you be damaged when you imagine that you *are* damaged."

III

Valuable as the doctrine of *adiaphora* or indifferent things was as a protest against moral materialism and self-indulgence, still, in its strictest form, it was too unbending; and, even to the end, the Stoic Ethics never shook itself entirely free of inadequate notions of some of the things that it regarded as indifferent. It is obvious to remark that the doctrine, unless properly safeguarded, might easily lend itself to abuse and lead to antinomianism; and, as a matter of fact, it did so lead among the Stoics themselves in particular cases. But the conclusion is by no means necessary or logical. The most that can be said is, that the doctrine affords a ready excuse, though no real justification, to him who wishes to live loosely, and that it does not sufficiently conserve the ordinary civilities and proprieties of life.

Two views of the Stoics in special, in this connexion, call for remark—their view of the Body and their view of Death.

As being one of the *adiaphora*, the Body was conceived as alien to man, enslaved to disease and evil chance,

a clog and hindrance, and gladly to be thrown off
like a worn garment.   "What am I? '*A poor soul
laden with a corpse*'—said Epictetus " (Aurelius, *Med.*
iv. 41).

But surely, the body is not this alien and despicable
something, to be classed among things not in our
power, along with possessions, riches, and the like,
and so to be summarily dismissed from our regard.
It is not something foreign to us and embarrassing,
but, on the contrary, a constituent part of ourselves—
helpful, controllable, desirable, to be tended and
cherished, and, as one of the most wonderful structures
of nature, to be gloried in.[1] It is not in the same
sense a thing external to us as are riches or property ;
and its health is inseparably bound up with our highest
mental and moral good and welfare. The right view
of it is that expressed by Browning in his *Rabbi Ben
Ezra* :—

> "To man, propose this test—
>   Thy body at its best,
> How far can that project thy soul on its lone way?
> .   .   .   .
>   Let us not always say,
>   'Spite of this flesh to-day,
> I strove, made head, gained ground upon the whole !'
>   As the bird wings and sings,
>   Let us cry, 'All good things
> Are ours, nor soul helps flesh more, now, than flesh
>   helps soul.'"

For one thing, however, the Stoics are to be
commended : they absolutely condemned slovenly
neglect of the body (thereby differing from the Cynics)

---

[1] So Athenagoras and the early Christian Apologists generally
(Justin Martyr, etc.) saw.

and strictly demanded personal cleanliness or purity.
This they did on two grounds : "first, in order that you
may do the acts pertaining to a man ; then, in order
that you may not be offensive to those with whom you
come in contact." Although it does not quite reach
the doctrine that "cleanliness is next to godliness,"
the teaching in the chapter in Epictetus on the subject
(*Diss.* iv. 11) is in striking contrast to the doctrine of
"the sanctity of dirt" preached and practised by
mediæval ascetics. "If nature entrusted you with a
horse, would you overlook him and neglect him ? And
now think you that you have been entrusted with your
own body as with a horse. Wash it, wipe it, take care
that no one turn away from you, that no one get out of
your way. But who does not get out of the way of
a dirty man ?" Further still, the Stoics maintained
that the man who neglects his body is lacking
in the perception of beauty, and so rules himself
out of court so far as philosophy is concerned. "For
not even by the appearance of the body ought we
to drive away the many from philosophy ; but, as in
other things the philosopher should show himself
cheerful and undisturbed, so also in things relating to
the body. 'See, ye men, that I have nothing, that I
want nothing ; see how I am houseless and cityless
and a fugitive, if so it be, and without a hearth I live
more free from trouble and more prosperous than all of
noble lineage and than the rich. But look at my little
body also that it is not spoiled by my austere mode of
life.' But if a man says this to me who has the
appearance and countenance of a condemned man,
which of the gods will persuade me to approach

philosophy that makes men such persons? Not so; I would not do it, even though I were going to become a wise man."[1]

In like manner, Death is not the thing "indifferent," to which we may sit so loose that we may lawfully court it when we think fit. The countenancing of suicide (ἐξαγωγὴ) is a chief blot in the Stoic Ethics.[2] Doubtless, it fell in with the Stoic teaching about *adiaphora*: we are not to fear death, but, seeing that it must come to us some time, must be ready to meet it at any time. But it is really subversive of the Stoics' great principle that a man is sufficient for himself—that inward calm may be maintained, and complete satisfaction found in the soul. To despise death, or not to dread it, when it comes in the course of nature, is one thing; to court death, and of our own accord to effect it, is quite another. We have a duty towards life, as well as towards death; and we must take care that courage as it faces the latter do not mean cowardice turning away from the former.[3] Moreover, as Plato urged, a man's life is not his own, but God's, and can be given up only when He recalls it. This the Stoics, being thoroughly

[1] For the remainder of the passage about the unkempt young man, see Chapter III. p. 55.

[2] Spinoza, who had so much in common with the Stoics in Ethics, says of suicide: "Persons who kill themselves are impotent in mind, and have been thoroughly conquered by external causes repugnant to their nature" (*Ethica*, iv. 18).

[3] Speaking of courage, Aristotle very fitly says (*Nic. Eth.* iii. 7): "To seek death as a refuge from poverty, or love, or any painful thing, is not the act of a brave man, but of a coward. For it is effeminacy thus to fly from vexation; and in such a case death is accepted, not because it is noble, but simply as an escape from evil."

conversant with the thoughts of Plato, quite well knew : Cato of Utica spent a portion of the night on which he committed suicide by reading the *Phædo*. But they met the objection with the rejoinder that suicide is permissible only when the suicide recognizes that it is God's will that he should go. Yet, when we remember that Zeno, the founder of the Stoic school, suffocated himself in old age, because, through a fall, he had broken one of his fingers ; and that Cleanthes, for even less reason, continued his abstinence till he died of starvation, we have difficulty in seeing how so trivial a cause could be regarded by earnest and thinking men as a sign from the Deity, or as sufficient justification for an act so solemn as self-murder. The story about Cleanthes, as recorded by Diogenes Laërtius (vii. 7), is that, suffering from swollen gums, he was enjoined by his physician to fast for two days. At the end of that time, he had so far recovered that permission was given him to return to his former habits. But he refused, saying that he had now thus far traversed the way, and, consequently, continued his fast till he died. "Indifference" of that sort, doubtless, seemed to exhibit moral freedom and strength of will ; but it may be taken rather as proving how inadequate the Stoic's estimate of human life still was, and how far short he fell of grasping the full meaning of his own doctrine of man's dignity and of apprehending the true nature of God. And even the deed itself was frequently spoiled by being done theatrically. This, at any rate, applies to Stoics of the Roman period. The suicide of Cato of Utica was dramatic ; so, too, was that of Seneca ; so of others. On reading the narrative of these and similar cases, one cannot help feeling that there was an element of acting that is out of place.[1]

On the same lines, we find a further proof of the Stoic's inability to estimate human life at its true value, in the fact that he made no definite stand against infanticide. Even the humane Seneca defends the practice. "Children," he says, "if they are born weakly and deformed, we drown. It is not anger but reason to separate the useless from the sound" (*De Ira*, i. 15).

IV

Last of all, the Stoics, despising pleasure and uncompromisingly upholding virtue, could hardly fail to be unjust to the Epicurean ethical end. Many of their criticisms, indeed, of pleasure as the *summum bonum* might find a place in so subtle a modern book as Sidgwick's *Methods of Ethics*, and are effective; but it was still open to an Epicurean to argue that *his* conception of pleasure did not tally with that of the Stoics, and, consequently, that many of the criticisms had no relevance to him—they were simply beside the point.

In the first place, the Stoic, entertaining a low opinion of the body, could not place a very high price on pleasure. Pleasure must needs seem to him to be little more than a synonym for selfishness, and so required to be fought with outright from the beginning. But in pleasure, it might be rejoined, there is nothing in itself

---

[1] Epicurus had a summary way of getting rid of the fear of death, without invoking suicide. He reasoned, "While we exist, death is not present; and when death is present, we do not exist; therefore, death is nothing to us."

either selfish or unselfish, but merely a fact of the human constitution, necessary and natural, and so to be accepted like every other natural fact, and to be made the most of. There is no demerit in being pleased: pleasure is simply an indication that our organism is working harmoniously and well. But there is no merit in being pained : pain in itself is simply an indication that our system is out of sorts—that something has gone wrong. To hug pain as a virtue is the sign of an unhealthy and abnormal subject. This was the position that the Epicurean took up, and in which he occupied strong psychological ground.

In the next place, the Stoic laid the stress on the lower pleasures, and, noting the tendency in man to exceed in them, set forth pleasure as in itself debasing and derogatory to man. That there are debasing pleasures, the Epicurean readily admitted ; but he did his very utmost to counteract them—he denied that man's real happiness resided in these. The greatest calumny on Epicurus is to identity him with the sensualist or the epicure. This will best be seen, if we turn to Epicurus himself. In his letter to Menœceus, as given in Diogenes Laërtius (x. 27), he thus defines pleasure in its ethical aspect :—

" When, then, we say that pleasure is the chief good, we are not speaking of the pleasures of the profligate or those that lie in sensual enjoyment (ἀπολαύσει), as some who are ignorant and not of our way of thinking, or interpreting us in the worst sense, suppose, but freedom of the body from pain and of the soul from per- turbation (ἀλλὰ τὸ μήτε ἀλγεῖν κατὰ σῶμα μήτε ταράττεσθαι κατὰ ψυχήν). For it is not continuous drinkings and

carousals, nor the enjoyments of boys and women, nor
of fish and other such things as a lavish table affords,
that produce a pleasant life, but sober reasoning (νήφων
λογισμὸς) which both searches for the reasons of every
choice and avoidance and banishes opinions, from which
the greatest confusion lays hold on souls."

He then goes on, in the same section, to set forth
prudence as the leading virtue, from which the other
virtues spring; for it is not possible, he maintains, to
live pleasantly unless one also live prudently and
honourably and justly, and it is not possible to live
prudently and honourably and justly without also living
pleasantly: for "the virtues are connate (συμπεφύκασι)
with living pleasantly, and living pleasantly is inseparable from them."

This gives a different complexion to the matter, and
shows, at any rate, that not all the Stoic criticisms of
Epicurean hedonism were just. There is need here, as
in so many other cases, of the logical *distinguo*.

The same is seen if we turn to Desire. From the
Stoic criticism, one would infer that Epicurus had
only a very low and unworthy doctrine of desire. But
the contrary is the fact: his views on this important
topic are extremely high. He divided desires into three
classes: (1) those that are natural and necessary,
(2) those that are natural but not necessary, (3) those
that are neither natural nor necessary. "He regarded
as natural and necessary those that remove pains, as
drink when one is thirsty; as natural but not necessary,
such as merely vary the pleasure without taking away
pain, as very expensive foods; and as neither natural
nor necessary, such things as crowns and erection of

public statues" (Diog. Laërt. x. 31). These differ in their psychological significance. The first class are easily satisfied and at small expense ; nor is there very great difficulty in satisfying the second. It is the third class that create the supreme difficulty ; for they are "vain" desires, and have neither limit nor moderation.[1] Resist transgression of the limit, then. On the duty of moderating the desires, if true happiness is to be secured, Epicurus insisted with as great pertinacity as the Stoics, and he gave utterance to many sage maxims which even the Stoics did not disdain to make use of. Thus, one saying of Epicurus, Seneca loves to quote —namely, "If you wish to make Pythocles happy, add not to his riches, but take away from his desires." Nothing could go more direct to the heart of the matter than that. Seneca could only paraphrase it when he said, "It is not he who has little, but he who desires more, that is poor." And there is shrewd pagan wisdom in this of Epicurus :—"We are born once, twice we cannot be born : for eternity we must be non-existent. Yet thou who art not master of to-morrow puttest off the right time. The life of all of us is ruined by procrastination, and it is on this account that each of us dies before he is ready."

The truth is that hedonism is not incompatible with high moral efforts and aspirations, and Zeno and Epicurus were not so far apart as themselves supposed ; and, when the day of eclecticism arrived, this became apparent. "Says Epicurus—'When I was sick, I did not converse about my bodily ailments, nor discuss such

[1] See Cicero, *De Finibus*, i. 13.

matters with my visitors; but continued to dwell upon the principles of natural philosophy, and more particularly how the understanding, while participating in such disturbances of the flesh, yet remains in unperturbed possession of its proper good. And I would not,' he adds, 'give the doctors a chance of blustering and making ado, but let life go on cheerily and well.' Imitate Epicurus—in sickness, if you are sick, or in any other visitation. To be loyal to philosophy under whatsoever circumstances, and not join the babel of the silly and the ignorant, is a motto for all schools alike. Stick only to the work in hand, and to the tool you have for doing it." So wrote Marcus Aurelius (*Med.* ix. 41).

CHAPTER XI

THEOLOGY AND RELIGION

" Estne Dei sedes nisi terra et pontus et aer
  Et cælum et virtus? Superos quid quærimus ultra?
  Juppiter est quodcunque vides quodcunque moveris."
                                                    LUCAN.

" Cujus rei ordo est etiam prædictio est."—SENECA.

" From Nature's chain whatever link you strike,
  Tenth, or ten thousandth, breaks the chain alike."
                                                    POPE.

" We are Thine offspring, alone of mortal things that live and
walk the earth, moulded in image of the All."—CLEANTHES.

WE return now to the subject of ontology, or speculation on being, which we so far considered already under
the heading of Physics, in Chapter V. ; and we do so
with the advantage of approaching the problems through
a previous knowledge of the Stoic Ethics. For, as we
have seen, the ruling formula, " Live agreeably to
nature," is susceptible of a twofold interpretation, and,
according as we accept the one or the other, we are
brought face to face with the psychology of ethics or
with ethical ontology. If by " nature " we mean solely
or chiefly human nature, then the formula introduces us
to ethics as psychology ; if we give it the wider signification, and understand by it the world-order, then we have
presented to us ethics as metaphysics. Supposing,

however, the question to be asked, in due modern fashion, Can there be ethics without metaphysics? then the Stoic answer would unquestionably be, "No; morality is rational, and so is founded on cosmology and the intellectual interpretation of the universe. In its higher reaches and in its deeper foundations, ethics is justified only by a reference to the Whole, and the world-order is necessary for the explanation of the ethical order."[1]

It is the metaphysical aspect, then, that now engages us. What is "Living agreeably to nature" in its ultimate ontological signification?

I

On this head, the teaching of the Stoics was as follows :—

The World one and perfect

The world is a cosmos or universe—a whole consisting of interrelated parts and, consequently, informed by reason: there is a world-course, a system of universal causation. As Marcus Aurelius puts it (*Med.* vii. 9), "All things intertwine one with another, in a holy bond: scarce one thing is disconnected from another. In due co-ordination they combine for one and the same order. For the world-order is one made out of all things, and God is one pervading all, and being is one, and law is one, even the common reason of all beings possessed of mind, and truth is one : seeing that truth is the one perfecting of beings one in kind and endowed with the same reason." "All that now happens follows in the train of consequence ; else you must deny reason

[1] This answer goes back to Heracleitus. See Chap. VII. p. 138.

14

to the sovereign ends which guide the impulse of the World-soul" (*ibid.* 75).

Hence, taken in its entirety, the world is perfect (this is the view *sub specie æternitatis*). This means that there is really no such thing as evil in it; for what is real is true—it *is* as it *must* be. Pain and suffering, indeed, there are; but these are not evils, because necessary and conducive to ultimate good: they are only the "masks" that children use with which to frighten us. They are even necessitated by the law of relativity, or the principle that a relative implies a corelative—pleasure would have no meaning, if there were not pain; up involves down; valley needs hill: "take away one and you take away all" (Aulus Gellius, *Noctes Atticae*, vii. 1). Neither are sin itself and sinful actions a real evil, being necessary. "When some piece of shamelessness offends you, ask yourself, Can the world go on without shameless people? Certainly not!—Then do not ask for the impossible. Here you see is one of the shameless, whom the world cannot get on without. Similarly in any case of foul play or breach of faith or any other wrong, fall back on the same thought. When once you remember that the genus cannot be abolished, you will be more charitable to the individual" (Aurelius, *Med.* ix. 42). Again, "The gourd is bitter: drop it then! There are brambles in the path: then turn aside! It is enough. Do not go on to argue, Why pray have these things a place in the world? The natural philosopher will laugh at you, just as a carpenter or cobbler would laugh, if you began finding fault because you saw chips or parings lying about their shop. And yet they have a place for the rubbish; but Nature has nothing outside herself. Herein is the marvel of her handiwork, that thus self-circumscribed she yet transmutes into herself every content that seems corrupt and old and useless, and from the same materials recreates afresh: so as to avoid the need of fresh substance from without, or of some place for her refuse. Her own space, her own material, and her own handiwork suffice " (*ibid.* viii. 50).

Providence: Optimism

The World-course, proceeding uniformly, and not capriciously or at mere random, is synonymous with the presidency and overruling providence of God. The course of the world is teleologically determined. " Thee doth all this system that rolls round the earth obey in what path soever Thou guidest it, and willingly is it governed by Thee" (Cleanthes, *Hymn to Zeus*). Nature's uniformity bespeaks both wisdom and goodness; and this means the Divine Reason in its prevision and pre-arranging. Hence, the individual and the community alike are under the rule and forethought of the Supreme: *i.e.*, in regard to great things, for small things seemed to the Stoic (though not at all times) too insignificant to attract the divine care — *magna di curant, parva negligunt.*[1] In this way, Providence being both universal and special, no man should be over-anxious about what is to happen to him here: all is graciously and wisely ordered. A man's lot and the circumstances of life are both in the hands of the Deity. He is part of the whole; and God cares for the whole, and, therefore, for the parts. " For each is best, what

[1] See Cicero, *De Nat. Deor.* ii. 66.

Nature brings: and best too at the time, when Nature brings it. 'Earth is in love with rain, and holy æther loves.' Yes, the world-order is in love with fashioning whatever is to be. To the world-order I profess, 'Thy love is mine.' Is there not a truth implicit in the familiar 'as it listeth'? Either—You live on where you are; to that you are well used: or—You move off, and so doing have your wish: or—You die, and your service is finished. There is no other alternative. So be of good cheer" (Aurelius, *Med.* x. 20–22).

This optimism was characteristic of the Stoics in their speculative moods; although, when they were confronted by the actual experience of life's pains and hardships and by the deep-rooted depravity of human nature, they could not help sometimes giving expression to pessimistic thoughts. This is very noticeable in Seneca, who, even when administering comfort in bereavement, cannot help being despondent. "There is nothing so deceitful," thus he consoles Marcia on the loss of her son (*Ad Marciam de Consolatione*, 22), "as human life, nothing so insidious: nor would any one, in sooth, accept it, were it not given us without our knowledge. Therefore, if it is happiest of all not to be born, it is next best, I think, to be quickly restored, after a brief life, to the Whole again." "Think of bathing," says Aurelius (*Med.* viii. 24), "and its accessories—oil, sweat, filth, foul water, and all things nauseating. So is it with every part of life, and each material thing." However, this pessimism is not a fixed creed, but a mere transient state—not the basis for a philosophy, but a fleeting mood (such as we find in a poet like Byron); and optimism was the prevailing temperament of the Stoic, producing in him a cheerful and willing acquiescence in the ways of Providence: *non pareo deo, sed adsentior* (Seneca, *Ep.* 96). "So long as things that are to come are unknown to me," said Chrysippus, "I hold always by the things that are more favourable for obtaining the things that are according to nature; for God Himself made me such as to choose these." "But if, indeed," adds Epictetus, "I knew that it were now fated for me to be sick, I would even myself move to it; for the foot also, if it had intelligence, would move to be mired" (*Diss.* ii. 6). "I am in harmony with all, that is a part of thy harmony, great Universe," said Aurelius (*Med.* iv. 23). "For me nothing is early and nothing late, that is in season for thee. All is fruit for me, which thy seasons bear, O Nature! from thee, in thee, and unto thee are all things. '*Dear City of Cecrops!*' saith the poet: and wilt not thou say, 'Dear City of God'?"

This Stoical optimism is a most significant fact, and has a lesson for the present time. Among other things, it gives us in a very striking fashion a practical refutation of the theory frequently advocated to-day, that "temperament and circumstance, not logic, make the difference between a pessimist and an optimist."[1] That temperament and circumstance count for much, is quite true; but, were they all-potent, Stoicism ought to have been the most pessimistic of creeds, for there have seldom been darker, sadder times than those in which it was propagated at Rome. If ever it were justifiable for a man to take the worst possible view of the government of the universe and to maintain on

[1] Leslie Stephen, *An Agnostic's Apology*, p. 177.

system that life is utterly detestable and bad, it was while Nero and the other human monsters occupied the Imperial throne, and when pagan society was rotten to the very core. Yet, those were the times when Stoical optimism was strenuously preached, and when faith saw, behind the corruption and brutalities and inhumanities of life, the universal righteousness and wisdom.

Is God personal or impersonal?

Nevertheless, whether the supreme providence is a living personal God or merely an impersonal principle, the course of nature, or the universe itself, is very doubtful. Had the Stoic physics ruled the ethics, there would have been no doubt. *There* the law of causation and the uniformity of nature are supreme, and the Ethereal Fire is impersonal. There, too, the term *Cosmos* was used indifferently, as by Chrysippus, of the ordered universe, which consists of heaven and earth and all that they contain, or of God, the source from which the ordered universe proceeds and whereby it is perfected. But the physics did not drastically rule the ethics. The conception of the Deity as primitive ethereal fire came to be practically regarded as an intellectual speculation merely, with little or no influence on the ethical doctrine; and the conception of the Divine personality, as distinct from the universe, became more and more articulate. Accordingly, Epictetus speaks, almost uniformly, in language of the most fervent theism. To his intensely religious nature, God is personal ever-present " Father," " Creator," " Ruler," " Guardian," seeing our every deed, knowing our every thought, and holding us responsible to Him for our character and conduct. He is omnipresent, and, like the Deity of Butler, rules through conscience. "So that," he counsels us (*Diss.* i. 14), "when you have shut the doors and made darkness within, remember never to say that you are alone; for you are not, but God is within, and your Dæmon[1] is within, and what need have they of light to see what you are doing? To this God you ought also to swear an oath, just us the soldiers do to Cæsar. . . . And what shall you swear? Never to disobey, and never to make accusations, and never to find fault with any of the things that have been given by him, and never unwillingly to do or to obey any of the things that are necessary."

Marcus Aurelius, on the other hand, is, for the most part, a pantheist. Yet, the pantheism that appeals to him is based less on the hylozoism of the earlier Stoics than on the rationality of the All, intellectually conceived: it is spiritualistic or idealistic rather than physical or materialistic. "You exist but as a part inherent in a greater whole. You will vanish into that which gave you being; or rather, you will be retransmuted into the seminal and universal reason" (*Med.* iv. 14).

One main difficulty in precisely determining the Stoic conception of the nature of God arises from the fact that, apart from the philosophical doctrine of the Deity, the Stoics accepted the popular notion of the existence of "the gods." They accepted even the popular mythology, but were very careful to interpret it in a way of their own—they used it simply as symbolical of higher truth, thereby copying the Cynics. But this

[1] This is the equivalent of "guardian angel."

fact that the Stoic acknowledged " the gods " makes it difficult to say when he is speaking philosophically of the Deity or popularly of the gods of polytheism.

Still, a Supreme Being, as Active Reason, is conceived as underlying all and guiding all ; and, even when the idea of personality is not grasped, it is the notion of a supreme all-permeating, all-comprehending essence that stimulates the Stoic and gives impulse to his aspirations. More especially is this so, when the Deity is conceived on His moral side, as purity and righteousness, and the thought of Him is given to man as a motive to the formation of right character. " You are a leading object," cries Epictetus, addressing his fellow-man (*Diss.* ii. 8), " you are a piece of God, you have in yourself something that is a part of Him. Why then are you ignorant of your high descent ? . . . Wretched one, you are carrying about a god with you, and are ignorant of it. Do you think that I mean an external god of silver or of gold? In yourself you bear Him, and you perceive not that you are defiling Him with your impure thoughts and filthy deeds." " Without Thee, O Divinity," says Cleanthes, addressing Zeus, " no deed is done on earth, nor in the ethereal vault divine, nor in the deep, save only what wicked men do in the folly of their hearts." If religion means response of the human soul to the impact of the world Spirit, there is genuine religion here.

Proofs of God's existence

The existence of God, although maintained to be so obvious as not to require a proof,[1] was, nevertheless,

[1] See Balbus, in Cicero, *De Nat. Deor.* ii.

proved by the Stoics in various ways. The physical argument, drawn from the leading doctrine of the primitive ether or all - pervading creative and pre-servative fire, was what Cleanthes laid the stress on. But countless other proofs were adduced by the school, partly inductive, partly deductive. Inductively, they reasoned from human nature, from history, from the world; deductively, from the *a priori* conception of God, and the logic of necessity.

(1) Take, first, their inductive proofs. (*a*) They had the argument from man's constitution in the form of their doctrine of προλήψεις or common notions. God *is*, they reasoned, for we have a primary notion of Him: in other words, the notion of a God inevitably arises in us during life's experiences. This, when interpreted in modern language, is just the psycho-logical position that "God is a necessity of human nature." In this connexion, the Stoics, like Kant afterwards, laid the burden of the testimony on man's moral nature: to them, as to him, God is a moral necessity, a postulate that alone is competent to solve the riddle and clear the mystery of human life. His existence is thus established on the evidence of Con-science, as Cicero explicitly puts it in *De Officiis*, iii. 10; or, as it is even more strikingly put by Seneca (*Ep.* 41), "Near to you is God; He is within you. . . . A holy Spirit dwells within us, watcher and guardian (*sacer intra nos spiritus sedet observator et custos*)." And how God operates through conscience is thus:—He notes conduct and keeps back from sin, He guards us against temptation, and He inspires us with thoughts "upright, just, and pure." The distance between this

and the famous utterance of Cardinal Newman, in his memorable *Letter Addressed to his Grace the Duke of Norfolk*, is not so very great: "Conscience is not a long-sighted selfishness, nor a desire to be consistent with oneself; but it is a messenger from Him, who, both in nature and in grace, speaks to us behind a veil, and teaches and rules us by His representatives. Conscience is the aboriginal Vicar of Christ, a prophet in its informations, a monarch in its peremptoriness, a priest in its blessings and anathemas."

(*b*) The complement of this is the argument from history, or the general consent of mankind (*consensus gentium*)—seen in the past as in the present, in this people as in that. *Quod ubique, quod semper, quod ab omnibus creditum est.*

(*c*) Teleology, or the adaptation of means to ends in the external world, gives us the third inductive proof. "How is it possible," they reasoned, "that a city or a house cannot continue, not even for the shortest time, without an administrator and curator, but this so great and beautiful structure should be administered thus orderly without purpose and by chance? There is, then, one who administers" (Epic. *Diss*. ii. 14). This reminds one of Bacon's famous utterance (in the beginning of the Essay *Of Atheisme*): "I had rather beleeve all the Fables in the *Legend*, and the *Talmud*, and the *Alcoran*, than that this universall Frame is without a Minde. . . . It is true, that a little Philosophy inclineth Mans Minde to *Atheisme*; But depth in Philosophy bringeth Mens Mindes about to *Religion*: For while the Minde of Man looketh upon Second Causes Scattered, it may sometimes rest in them, and goe no further : But when it beholdeth the Chaine of them, Confederate and Linked together, it must needs flie to *Providence*, and *Deitie*."

As part of this same teleological view of the universe, must be taken men's actual experience of the moral government of the world. Says Aurelius (*Med.* iv. 10) : " 'All that happens, happens aright.' Watch narrowly, and you will find it so. Not merely in the order of events, but in just order of right, as though some power apportions all according to worth."[1] The cosmic order, then, is moral, as well as natural ; and experience is the proof of it. We have heard the echo of this in very recent times.

(2) Take, next, the leading deductive proofs.

Deductively, God's existence is proved (*a*) by the necessity of truth, as applied to propositions regarding the future. This is Chrysippus's argument, mainly against the Epicureans, as given in Cicero, in the *De Fato*. It runs as follows :—

All propositions are either true or false. This holds of propositions that refer to the future, as much as to other kinds of propositions. But all such propositions are true only when they are necessary — *i.e.*, when what they affirm *must* come to pass ; they are false, when they affirm an impossibility. Whatever, therefore, happens must of necessity follow from the causes that produce it. This means that God, as Fate, or as Course of Nature, is.

(*b*) Again, it is proved from the very notion of the

---

[1] This is very remarkable, as basing the argument on experience, and not merely (as with Heracleitus) on metaphysics.

world as a universe. The world as a whole, it is argued, is perfect (so reasons Balbus, reproducing Chrysippus, in Cicero's *De Naturâ Deorum*, ii.). It must, therefore, contain in itself all the qualities and excellences that are to be found in its parts, only in a superior degree (in this we seem to hear Descartes speaking).[1] But reason, wisdom, and virtue are excellences that are in parts of the world: we find them in man, though imperfectly. This means that there must be a being in whom they exist perfectly. "The world, therefore, has virtue: it is also wise, and, consequently, a god."

(*c*) Thirdly, God exists, because what will necessarily come to pass is foreknown by Him: His own nature, as supreme reason, implies that.

(*d*) To which, fourthly, may be added the complementary argument, frequently insisted on by the Stoics, from Divination. Divination is; but nothing could be predicted or divined, unless things were foreordained. Therefore, God is.

These arguments have more than an historical interest; they show the human mind vigorously at work on the theistic problem, and they touch points that go to the very root of theism.

Against Agnosticism

The Supreme Being, thus proved to exist, may, of course, be known by man. The Stoics would have had little sympathy with that extreme form of agnosticism put forward by Herbert Spencer in his *First Principles*, and defended in other of his works, founded on an

[1] The view was also Scholastic.

erroneous conception of the Absolute and on a mistaken apprehension of the relativity of knowledge, and which makes the Deity absolutely transcendent, and, therefore, unknowable.[1]   He is, to the Stoic, the universal reason, immanent in the world, pervading it, and so in necessary contact with that which shares pre-eminently in itself—namely, the reason of man.   " The philosophers say that we ought first to learn this, that there is a God and that He provides for all things, and that it is not possible to hide from Him, not only our acts, but even our intentions and our thoughts.   Next, we should learn what is the nature of the Gods ; for such as they are found to be, he who would please and obey them must needs try with all his might to become like them. If the Divine is faithful, he too must be faithful ; if free, he too must be free ; if beneficent, he too must be beneficent ; if magnanimous, he too must be magnanimous ; as being, then, a follower ($\zeta\eta\lambda\omega\tau\grave{\eta}\nu$) of God, he must both do and say everything consistently with this " (Epictetus, *Diss.* ii. 14).

Yet, there is a wholesome, modified agnosticism in the Stoic theology, especially in its later Roman form, the positive conception of God being qualified by consideration of the fact that man is limited or finite in his knowledge.   Right well, for instance, does Seneca realize that it is not possible for us to comprehend fully the power that made all things, although we may discover him in part on every hand.   On two points, only, is he perfectly assured—namely, that there is a God, and that we are to ascribe to Him all majesty and goodness.

[1] Cf. my *Theism as grounded in Human Nature*, pp. 160–172.

The Deity limited by Fate

Nevertheless, the Supreme Being, in the Stoic theology, is subject to a peculiar limitation. Strangely to modern Western thought, but not strangely to any ancient Greek, He is conceived as under the sway of Fate. Behind the throne of Zeus stands Moira ; and Fate rules in the affairs of men: *irrevocabilis humana pariter ac divina cursus vehit* (Seneca, *De Prov.* v. 6). Hence, Cleanthes in his *Hymn to Zeus* speaks indifferently of "Zeus," "the Universal Reason," "Destiny."

Obviously, this conception, if strongly obtruded, or if tenaciously held and applied with logical rigour, would produce a very cramping effect upon ethics, and might be disastrous in the sphere of conduct.[1] But, with a noble inconsistency or a sublime forgetfulness, the Stoics did not allow the conception unduly to obtrude itself ; and, although they used it as a solace in the case of adverse fortune and untoward occurrences, they cast it aside, or quietly ignored it, in the province of ethical effort, in training the will and shaping the mind, in dealing with those highest of all things— "things within our own power." It is recorded of Zeno that once, when he was chastizing a slave for theft, the slave said, "It was fated that I should steal (εἵμαρτό μοι κλέψαι)." "Yes," replied Zeno, "and that you should be beaten" (Diog. Laërt. vii. 19). That, from the Stoic standpoint, is the proper answer.

---

[1] Compare with this the Calvinistic theology, which is the strictly logical outcome of its primary conception of God as Absolute Sovereign.

Mythology and Divination

Finally, the Stoics, while accepting mythology, acquiesced also in the propriety of consulting the oracles and paying regard to signs. They were—though not without great exceptions, such as Panætius—firm believers in Divination; and they supported their belief by a vast collection of instances, which might well be commended at the present day to the consideration of the Society for Psychical Research.

II

Now, on this ontological teaching several observations immediately occur.

The problem of Evil

In the first place, with regard to the problem of Evil—physical and moral.

(1) The doctrine that the universe is perfect discloses an unreconciled discrepancy between the Stoic conception of evil, especially moral evil or sin, and the dictates of conscience. Roseate optimism does not meet the necessities of the case. As the world is perfect, evil, according to the Stoics, is simply apparent and not real: it has no essential being; it is merely, from the point of view of the intellect, absence of light—shade or necessary contrast. "As a mark is not set up to be missed," says Epictetus (*Encheir.* 27), "even so the nature of evil exists not in the universe."

But this, clearly, solves nothing. To deny that sin *is*, is simply the boldness of dogmatic assertion, and contradicts our common experience. It does, indeed, get rid of one moral difficulty—the difficulty that so pained

Job, and that has weighed upon earnest souls in all ages
—namely, how, if God is, can the wicked prosper and
the virtuous be in adversity? According to the Stoics,
the so-called prosperity of the wicked is no prosperity,
for it concerns only external goods—mere *adiaphora* ;
whereas the adversity of the righteous is no real adversity, inasmuch as it does not harm the soul. But if so,
how comes it that there can be such a thing as remorse
or self-reproach? If "the thing that is shameful ought
to be blamed, and that which is blameable is worthy of
blame" (Epictetus, *Diss*. iii. 26), then sin is a reality
and mars the perfection of the universe, not being
a necessity. If the universe be perfect, "whatever
is, is right": it could not have been otherwise than as
it is ; and if mere causal sequence is to determine all,
a thing that is, being the necessary result of antecedents,
is as it ought to be. A philosophy that *submerges*
ethics, rather than assimilates it, cannot be final.

(2) There is more to be said in favour of the Stoical
position that evil is good under disguise, and is
ultimately conducive to the best. This position
Chrysippus affirmed when he compared evil to the
coarse jest in the comedy (see Aurelius, *Med*. vi. 42) ;
for, just as the jest, though offensive in itself, improves
the piece as a whole, "so too you may criticize evil
regarded by itself, yet allow that, taken with all else,
it has its use" (Plutarch, *Adv. Stoic*. 14). So, in the
Hymn to Zeus, Cleanthes, while quite admitting that
"what wicked men do in the folly of their hearts" is
not to be imputed to the Supreme Being, but to the
doers themselves, nevertheless regards the Supreme
Being as having "fitted all, evil with good, in one

great whole, so that in all things reigns one reason everlastingly." This is, doubtless, true; but it does not solve the problem—it only makes us somewhat more ready to acquiesce in the existence of evil, by making us more hopeful.

(3) It is also but the inculcation of a faith—a noble faith, no doubt, yet not an intellectual solution of the difficulty—when Seneca rises to what one might call the Scriptural height of regarding suffering as disciplinary, and as God's token of love and Fatherly affection for His children. With lucidity and light, the subject is worked out in his treatise, *De Providentia*.[1] If, on the one hand, he there maintains that "calamity is the occasion of virtue" and that "he is vanquished without glory who is vanquished without danger," he strongly insists, on the other hand, on the immense value of hardships and difficulties in forming character and in producing manly generous spirits. We are soldiers, he says, we are sailors, and need to be inured to dangers in order that we may despise them, and to be exercised in order that our faculties and organs may develop and attain perfection. We have to grow, like trees; and trees become strong and noble and root themselves securely in the earth only when exposed to frequent winds and tempests : "fragile are the plants that grow in the sunny valley." Yea, further, it is the most promising pupils to whom the master gives the hardest tasks; and sometimes, moreover, the individual has to suffer for the sake of the general, and good men are afflicted in order to teach others how to endure.

[1] Or, to give it its full title, *Quare Aliqua incommoda bonis viris accidant cum Providentia sit.*

15

All this is noble and true, and is not even marked by that incompleteness that usually characterizes pagan conceptions of suffering — namely, an inadequate realization of the fact that the sufferings of the individual may be beneficial, not only to himself, but to his fellow-men—that by a man's patient heroism mankind in general are blessed.

And Seneca's view was that of other great Stoics. Says Epictetus (*Diss.* iii. 24): "For this purpose he (God) at one time leads me hither, at another time sends me thither, shows me to men as poor, without authority, and sick; sends me to Gyara, leads me into prison; not because he hates me, far from that, for who hates the best of his own servants? Nor yet because he cares not for me, for he does not neglect any even of the smallest things; but with the view of exercising me and of using me as a witness to others."

Yet, with all this, there is no due appreciation in Stoicism of the fact that, as each individual is essentially a social being, the sufferings that he is called upon to endure are in great measure *vicarious*; and, in cases where he suffers through others' faults or sins, his sufferings are of the nature of *atonement*, thereby reacting for good upon those whose wrong-doing entailed them. This is the philosophy of suffering that is implicated in the great truth of the solidarity of mankind, and that illumines much.

(4) A word remains to be said on the Stoic position that evil, and, therefore, sin, is necessary on the law of relativity: without evil we should have no consciousness or realization of good.

The law of relativity is undoubtedly a commanding

principle in human experience—things are known by us only in relation to their opposites, and our desires repose on relativity: as Heracleitus long ago said, "sickness makes health pleasant and good; hunger, satiety; weariness, rest." But the law need not be so interpreted as to require that these opposites must be absolute contrasts. In order to consciousness, we must have change: a uniform temperature, continued indefinitely without variation, would be to us the same thing as no temperature at all. But *change* does not necessarily mean transition to the entirely opposite state. Degrees of warmth would give us consciousness of heat, as much as a temperature in which warmth alternates with extreme cold. And so we should be conscious of good without experience of positive sin or evil, if there were within good itself change from one degree to another, or if there were varieties of good. All that is required by the law of relativity is perception of difference; and that does not demand two absolutely contrasting states—it would be enough if there were two degrees of one state: I might quite well know what good is, without knowing sin or evil, if I had experience of diverse kinds of good, or if my perception of righteousness admitted of various applications or were compatible with various modes of apprehension. The world might very well be full of interest to me, though sin were eliminated, if holiness were susceptible of increase or of progressive realization.

The doctrine of Fate

Next, the Stoics' teaching about Fate creates a difficulty. We seem here to be in the iron grasp of inexorable law, from which God, in any true sense of the term, is excluded ; or, if He be included, we are in the grasp of an ultra-Calvinistic theology that seems to paralyze human freedom. "Whatever befalls," says Marcus Aurelius (x. 5), "was fore-prepared for you from all time ; the woof of causation was from all eternity weaving the realisation of your being, and that which should befall you." "Does aught befall you? It is well—a part of the destiny of the universe ordained for you from the beginning ; all that befalls was part of the great web" (*ibid*. iv. 26). And there is no doubt that, even in the greatest of the Stoic Doctors, Fate at times appears as a coercive force, or compulsive power, overriding all : *ducunt volentem Fata, nolentem trahunt*.[1] "The universal cause is like a winter torrent ; it sweeps all before it" (Aurelius, *Med*. ix. 29).

It may, however, be maintained that the Stoics at their best got beyond this position, and meant little more by Fate than that things happen in the world according to law and order, that events are part of a general plan or system, and that human actions must work out their consequences ; and, as applied to God, that not even the Deity acts arbitrarily and capriciously, but with Him, too, law and order hold, and reason guides the world. If so, they were on the track of a great truth—a truth that is seen in its fulness only when we throw into the conception of God's governance of the universe the ideas of love and mercy, as well as those of intelligence and justice. It is not

---

[1] This is the opposite of Epicurus's dictum that "we are our own masters, τὸ παρ' ἡμᾶς ἀδέσποτον" (Diog. Laërt. x. 133).

really to ascribe blind fate to the Deity, or to deprive Him of genuine freedom, to say that every evil deed on man's part, and every silly action, *must* receive its due recompense of reward. For, how else than under the conception of "must" can you suppose the Divine Government, if righteous, to be carried on? If there is order, there is necessity. This seems to be what Seneca meant when he said that, if we maintain that all the good things of life come to us from "Nature," that is simply "changing the name of God, for what else is Nature but God?" "You shall not also lie," he adds, "if you call Him fate; for, whereas fate is nothing else than a series of causes woven together, He it is that is the first cause of all and on whom all the rest depend" (*De Beneficiis*, iv. 7, 8). Moreover, though Zeno identified Fate with Providence (εἱμαρμένη with πρόνοια), Cleanthes rejected this identification, in face of the existence of evil in the world; for evil, he thought, though fated, cannot be said to owe its being to forethought or providence — though predetermined, it is not foreordained. Furthermore, Cleanthes, notwithstanding that he was strenuously materialistic in his physical speculations regarding the universe, and even in his theoretic explanation of mind, can yet infuse into his submission to the Cosmic Order such an amount of willing acquiescence as to give us the impression of the deepest religious feeling. "Lead me, O Zeus," he cries (*Encheir.* 53), "and thou Destiny, whithersoever I am ordained by you to go. I will follow without hesitation. And even if, in evil mood, I will not, none the less must I follow."

Let it be noted, however, that the Stoic acquiescence

differs from that of the Christian theist, inasmuch as it is lacking in hope and definite faith as to the future of the individual man who willingly acquiesces in his Destiny. The light of Revelation has made a vast difference in this particular, and the gain is on the side of him who has clear conviction that his lot is determined by a living, loving Person.[1]

Divination

In like manner, how can the conception of God as absolute law or order be reconciled with the belief in divination?

The two are irreconcilable, if divination be regarded in its purely superstitious aspect. But, probably, the Stoics in their philosophy did not so conceive it. They did, indeed, accept the mythology of the popular faith, but interpreted it allegorically, in Cynic fashion. And if they made much of omens, prodigies, consultations of the oracle, and such like, may it not have been in the belief that, to the sincere inquirer, God spoke in these things to the conscience; just as the dæmon of Socrates, to which they frequently referred as an example, had a moral significance? This, at all events, seems to be the suggestion in the passage on Divination in Epictetus's *Encheiridion* (chap. 32): "Come then boldly to the gods as your advisers; and, for the rest, when any advice has been given to you, remember whom you have taken as advisers, and whom you will be slighting if you obey them not."

Plausibly, it may be held that the Stoic's belief in

[1] Compare the Stoic's view of Providence with (*e.g.*) that of Ps. ciii.–cvii.

divination was nothing more nor less than his acknowledgment (half unconscious, of course) of the existence
of the supersensuous and supernatural—his mode of
expressing the fact that Revelation there is, and that
the Supreme is the source of it.[1] He reasoned that,
if God is, He must reveal Himself to man ; while, on
the other hand, if there is found to be truth in divination, God is. It is a deep thought that Balbus expressed
when he said (Cicero, *De Nat. Deor.* ii. 66) : "There
never was a great man without some divine inspiration
(*sine aliquo adflatu divino*)." At the same time, the
Stoic drew a clear distinction between the different
kinds of divination,—as we see from the first book of
Cicero's *De Divinatione.* Some kinds, he said, are
technical or artificial ; others are natural. To the
technical group belong astrology, prodigies, all the
art of the augur and the haruspex—*i.e.*, of the professional soothsayers ; and the ground of foreknow-
ledge and prediction here lies in practised sagacity and
in the lengthened and accumulated observation of many
generations of men—in other words, in general, if not
absolutely uncontradicted, experience. The diviner's
forecasts, indeed, may sometimes be wrong ; but that
is owing to one of two causes—either to ignorance of
some particular sign, or to the circumstance that there
is an unobserved or purposely concealed fact among the
facts observed or disclosed.

All this is strictly in accordance with the true
scientific method of induction—namely, trained observation and accumulation of instances ; and its value,
if any, must depend upon the number and amount

[1] See Seneca, *Naturales Quæstiones*, ii.

of proved coincidences, and upon the possibility of eliminating the fallacy of *post hoc ergo propter hoc*.

But it is different with the second group of cases, with instances of natural divination. Under this class come dreams, frenzy, vaticinations. The personal character of the instrument or agent of revelation now plays the important part. He must be a man of clear and unclouded intellect—unclouded because free from the grosser habits and passions of the body (such as are produced by gluttony and drunkenness), and a man of purity of life: " for true divination belongs rather to a sound mind than to a sick body" (Cicero, *De Div.* i. 38). This is simply saying, in a far off way and in a dim light, what is said in the full blaze of spiritual insight and supreme wisdom in the New Testament, "Blessed are the pure in heart: for they shall see God." When, therefore, it was urged against prophetic dreams, as by Aristotle, in his little treatise *On Prophecy in Sleep*, that such dreams cannot come from God because they are not given to the wisest and the best men, we can easily imagine the Stoic answer—*viz.*, The dreamer must be good, before we can trust his vision ; and the better he is, the more rational our trust in his prevision.

We are not, then, to dismiss the Stoical doctrine as pure superstition ; we are rather to see in it—in the principle of it, though not in all the details — the adumbration of a great truth. Bearing testimony as it does to the supernatural, it has only to be purified and expanded on the lines of this " natural " divination to eventuate in the conception of true prophecy ; where the religious man, delivering a heaven-sent message, becomes an authority, not because of any mere official position, such as that of priest or augur, nor yet because of nature's laws or the cosmic order having been broken in imparting to him illumination, but because the prophet himself specially reflects the divine in his own character, and, therefore, stands nearer to God and has a deeper insight into His ways and will than the majority of his fellow-men possesses.

Hence, the Stoics' proof of the existence of God from Divination, although it moved in a circle, may very well be justified. The Stoics reasoned that "as God is, Divination must be true"; and, again, "as Divination is true, God is." That is certainly a circle; but it is a circle that includes the whole universe of the realities amidst which we move. Consequently, it must return upon itself. Clearly, if there be a God, He must manifest Himself to mankind; and, again, from the manifestations of Himself to mankind, we are justified in asserting His existence. Given divination, then, as such a manifestation, the being of God is assured; or, starting with the idea of God, then divination is a manifestation of Him, if it be in the line of true inspiration. Either way, the argument holds, although the form of it be circular.

Prayer

The same acknowledgment of the supernatural that we have in the doctrine of divination (whether altogether consistently with the general philosophical system, is another matter) is made by the Stoics in the recognition of Prayer. "And the wise man, they say, will pray, asking good things from the gods, as says Posidonius in the first book of his *Duties* (περὶ καθηκόντων), and Hecaton in the thirteenth book of his *Paradoxes*" (Diog. Laërt. vii. 54).

Indeed, there are few things finer in the Greek language than Cleanthes's *Hymn to Zeus*, or than many of the impassioned prayers of Epictetus. Yet the purpose of prayer with the Stoics is a very noble one. It is not so much to obtain some object of desire as to be freed from desiring objects. "The gods either have power, or they have not. If they have not, why pray at all? If they have, why not pray for deliverance from the fear, or the desire, or the pain, which the thing causes, rather than for the withholding or the giving of the particular thing? Assuredly, if they can help men at all, this is the way of help. But perhaps you will say, The gods have put all that in my own power. Then is it not better to exercise your power and remain free, rather than to be set on what is not in your own power, and become a slave and cringer? And who told you that the gods do not assist us even to what is in our own power? Begin there with your prayers, and you will see. Instead of 'Oh! to enjoy her caresses!'—pray you against lusting after the enjoyment. Instead of 'Rid me of my enemy!'— pray you against desire for the riddance. Instead of 'Spare my little one!'—pray you that your fears may be at rest. Be this the direction of your prayers, and watch what comes" (Aurel. *Med.* ix. 40). And even where temporal things may lawfully be prayed for, it must be in the simplest, most confiding, manner. "An

Athenian prayer—*Rain, rain, dear Zeus, upon Athenian tilth and plains.* We should either not pray at all, or else in this simple, noble sort." So wrote Marcus Aurelius (*Med.* v. 7).

Reference has just been made to Cleanthes's *Hymn to Zeus.* That noble production has the merit of being the perfection of Stoic prayers ; and it also gives us a concise summary of the whole Stoic theology, as formulated in the earlier days. It is intellectual and pantheistic ; but it is touched, also, with that emotional fervour that intellectual pantheism is capable of producing. It may very well, then, be reproduced here in full, as a fitting conclusion to the chapter :—

"Above all gods most glorious, invoked by many a name, almighty evermore, who didst found the world and guidest all by law—O Zeus, hail ! for it is right that all mortals address thee. We are thine offspring, alone of mortal things that live and walk the earth moulded in image of the All ; therefore, thee will I hymn and sing thy might continually. Thee doth all this system that rolls round the earth obey in what path soever thou guidest it, and willingly is it governed by thee : so dread is the bolt thou wieldest in thy hands invincible, to do thy pleasure, that flameth double-edged and faileth never—lo, beneath its stroke all nature shivers ; therewith too thou dost regulate that Reason universal that comes and goes through all things, mingling with lights that are great and lights that are lesser . . . for that thou art so great, sovran supreme for evermore ; without thee, O Divinity, no deed is done on earth, nor in the ethereal vault divine, nor in the deep, save only what wicked men do in the folly of their hearts. Nay more, what is uneven, thy skill doth make even ; what knew not order, it setteth in order ; and things that strive find all in thee a friend. For thus hast thou fitted all, evil with good, in one great whole, so that in all things reigns one reason ever-lastingly. Now, this the wicked among mortals, for their undoing, shun till it slips from them ; who yearning ever in the quest of goods neither behold God's all-pervading law nor listen to it, though by obedience thereto noble their life might be in accord with reason. No, but of themselves are they driven, crazed, to divers vices, some exerted in unlovely striving for renown, some turned to lawless pursuit of gain, some to soft luxury and the train of sensual joys,—longing vehe-mently the while for the opposite of that they get. But do thou, Zeus, giver of every good thing, wrapt in cloud and bright lightnings, save mankind from woful ignorance ; do thou, Father, dispel it from the soul ; grant that we may attain to true judgment, which is thy stay in thy just rule of all things ; that so being held in honour we may requite thee in honour, chanting thy deeds right on, as is most fit for our mortality, since nor mortal men, no, nor gods, have any greater privilege than duly at all times to hymn the universal Law." [1]

[1] Among the many translations of the Hymn, this one—made by a former distinguished student of my own, Mr. George Watt, B.A. (Cantab.)—deserves a high place.

CHAPTER XII

PRESENT-DAY VALUE OF STOICISM

"Nunquam nimis dicitur quod nunquam satis discitur."—SENECA.

"Among the statutes of the Ephesians was an injunction, to meditate continually on some ancient model of virtue."—MARCUS AURELIUS.

"Where Gods are not, spectres rule."—NOVALIS.

I

FROM what has now been said, it will be felt that the Stoical philosophy is not a dead thing, a mere past system effete and useless, to be put aside as a relic of antiquity, arousing only an antiquarian curiosity, but is something instinct with life, and is capable of creating a genuine sympathetic interest. It breathes a fine spirit, and, in its later forms, touches the heart, while at the same time it appeals to the intellect.

What value it has as science and speculation (formulated by the founders), we saw with sufficient fulness in Chapters III. to V. In that respect, it is very much a philosophy of common sense and is the precursor of much modern theory, especially of the teaching of Thomas Reid and the Scottish School. It has both its strength and its weakness, though the former is much greater than is usually acknowledged at the present moment. It has distinct significance as Theory of Knowledge. To that we need not return.

But, looking back on its ethical and religious teaching, outlined in Chapters VIII. to XI., we may well ask, What, in this teaching, is of permanent value, and has special interest for the present day?

The answer to this question has been given from various points of view; two of them, in particular, characteristic of recent times. First, high authorities have commended Stoicism as an antidote to, or a substitute for, systematic organized religion—especially, for the Christian religion, whose pronounced supernaturalism and doctrinal theology had become offensive. Secondly, it has seemed to some that, without in any way affecting people's attitude towards the Christian religion, Stoicism may very properly be studied for its practical counsels and wise moral precepts. It was, doubtless, for some such reason as the second of these that Lord Avebury (then Sir John Lubbock), not very many years ago, when recommending to the College of Working Men in London "the Hundred best Books," included in his list Marcus Aurelius's *Meditations* and the *Encheiridion* of Epictetus. With this practical ethical view, we may readily enough sympathize; and it does not seem necessary to dwell upon it. Whatever can help one, whether Christian or not, in the effort to live a higher life, to make character stronger and conduct purer, may very safely be recommended for study and assimilation. Stoicism, especially in its later phases, can undoubtedly do this in a very marked degree.

But it is different with the first of the answers. When Stoicism is opposed to systematic theology, and particularly to the Christian faith (whether on scientific or on other grounds), critical examination becomes necessary. Marcus Aurelius is the Stoic in special now selected for our imitation,[1] and his teaching is offered us as a worthy substitute for the so-called emasculated conceptions of the dogmatic believer. No personal God, no future life, no supernatural, but morality in its virgin purity, independent of and unassisted by considerations of heaven or of hell, with a metaphysics definite enough to rescue it from being absolutely vague, yet not so precisely defined as to become dogmatic—this is the gospel that can alone avail (so we are told), and that alone is worthy of an age of emancipated thought and scientific enlightenment. Renan here leads the way. In his brilliant treatise on the great Stoic Emperor, he designates the *Meditations* (or, as he calls them, the *Thoughts*) "the gospel for those who do not believe in the supernatural," "a veritable eternal gospel, which will never grow old, for it affirms no dogma. . . . Science may destroy God and the soul, while the book of the *Thoughts* remains young yet in life and truth. The religion of Marcus Aurelius, as was occasionally that of Jesus, is the absolute religion—that which results from the simple fact of a high moral conscience placed face to face with the universe. It is neither of one race nor of one country. No revolution, no advance, no discovery, can change

---

[1] The popularity of Marcus Aurelius in Great Britain is seen, *inter alia*, by the large number of English translations of the *Meditations* made within the past ten years.

it." A similar attitude has been taken up by others, as the following sentence from Leslie Stephen's *An Agnostic's Apology* (pp. 345–346) may show: "The rationalist may well feel that on many points he would sympathise more closely with Marcus Aurelius than St. Paul. The Stoical view of the world and life may appear to him worthier, freer from antiquated mythology, and more congenial to modern thought, than that of the great Apostle." [1]

Now, there can be no doubt that, if one wish to oppose Stoicism to the doctrinal Christian religion, it can best be done by taking Aurelius as the typical Stoic. For he has thrown off much of the harshness of the older system, and yet he is far less intense in his emotional nature than (say) Epictetus or Seneca, and is more scientifically-minded, and supernaturalism does recede with him into the background. There is nothing in his *Meditations* corresponding to that vivid present-ment of the immortality of the soul and of its future state that we found, under the "Physics," in Seneca. His conception of God, too, is mainly abstract and pantheistic, and is, in part, a contrast to that of Epictetus. On the other hand, there is a calm re-iterated insistence on three great ideas, which may, indeed, be taken as the sum of his creed. First, the fleetingness of life and of the world, and, therefore, the vanity of clinging to life or of putting our trust in external things and in fickle fortune. The transitori-ness of fame, in particular, exercises his mind; and, naturally to Imperial Cæsar under the circumstances,

---

[1] The significance of Aurelius's teaching was brought out by Sir Frederick Pollock in *Mind*, 1st series, vol. iv. pp. 47–68.

he broods much over the fact of how soon even great names are forgotten. "The accustomed phrases of old days are the archaisms of to-day. So, too, the names that were once on all men's lips, are now as it were archaisms—Camillus, Cæso, Volesus, Dentatus ; and a little later, Scipio and Cato ; yes, even Augustus, and so with Hadrian and Antoninus. All things fade, as a tale that is told, and soon are buried in complete oblivion. This is true even of the shining lights of fame. As for the rest, no sooner is the breath out of them, than they are ' to fortune and to fame unknown.' And what, after all, is eternity of fame? Just emptiness" (*Med.* iv. 33). Secondly, the necessity of doing our duty now and here, not relying on the past (which is gone) nor waiting for the future (which is not ours) ; and public interest, or the good of the community, is the test of Duty. Thirdly, unqualified belief in the wisdom, righteousness, and goodness of Providence, *i.e.*, of the World-order (personality being out of count) and implicit trust therein. Whatever befalls us here, and whenever it befalls us, is and must be for the best ; for it is conducive to the good of the whole, and what is serviceable to the whole cannot be prejudicial to any one of its parts. This optimism necessarily carries, as a corollary, contentment with our lot in life and meek submission to our fate. Still, it does not paralyze us and render progress impossible. We are not to fold our hands and sleep, because all things are ordered well: on the contrary, we are to work and do our duty, and show ourselves worthy of our lot. There is no more strenuous preacher of the gospel of work than Aurelius, except Carlyle.

16

So that, thus far, we may very readily acquiesce in the verdict of Matthew Arnold, himself a Stoic in very large measure. "In general," he says, "the action Marcus Aurelius prescribes is action which every sound nature must recognise as right, and the motives he assigns are motives which every clear reason must recognise as valid. And so he remains the especial friend and comforter of all clear-headed and scrupulous, yet pure-hearted and upright, striving men, in those ages most especially that walk by sight, not by faith, but yet have no open vision. He cannot give such souls, perhaps, all they yearn for, but he gives them much ; and what he gives them, they can receive " (*Essays in Criticism*, vol. i. p. 378).

But, over and above this, there is clearly discernible in Aurelius a supernatural strain ; and neither he nor any of the greater Roman Stoics were anti-supernaturalists, in the sense of the modern rationalist or freethinker. They delighted to view the world, as Spinoza did, *sub specie æternitatis*. They were, for the most part, believers in divination and in the propriety and utility of prayer ; and even Renan has to admit that, in the *Meditations*, there is just "a little insignificant spot" of the supernatural, "which does not mar the marvellous beauty of the whole." Yea, in Epictetus and in Seneca, the world and its governance are set forth in a view that comes remarkably near St. Paul's conception of the God in whom we live and move and have our being; and their ethical theory, with its pronounced altruism and doctrine of the solidarity of the race, might, but for the inversion of historical sequence, be designated emphatically

Pauline. No wonder that the *Encheiridion* should have been "adopted as a religious work in the early Christian Church," and should have been twice paraphrased about the sixth century of our era,—once specially "for the use of monastic bodies!"[1] Human nature was not to the later Stoic, any more than it is to the Christian, summed up in the one word "reason"; and the religious, no less than the moral, sentiments, were duly recognized and definitely provided for by him.

II

Hence, the answer to our question must not lay the stress on the absence of dogmatism in Stoicism; nor must it put the Stoical philosophy in flat opposition to modern dogmatism. The "spot" to which Renan refers, even in Marcus Aurelius's *Meditations*, is more than "little" and "insignificant"; and if it be the criterion of "a veritable eternal gospel, which will never grow old," that "it affirms no dogma," then Aurelian Stoicism cannot stand the test—no philosophy can, which bases its positions on metaphysics: would it be a real *gospel* (good news) if it did? Moreover, if religion results "from the simple fact of a high moral conscience placed face to face with the universe," that conscience must discern under the universe a *Person*, for moral relations can exist only between *persons*, and, however much you may *admire*, you cannot *worship* abstract law or order. But what the answer must emphasize are points such as the following, each of which has its own significance for to-day.

[1] Simplicius's famous commentary on the *Encheiridion*, from the Neo-platonic point of view, belongs to the same sixth century A.D.

First, its vivid realization of the universe as a whole, a system consisting of interrelated and mutually necessary parts. "Subsequents follow antecedents by bond of inner consequence ; it is no mere numerical sequence of arbitrary and isolated units, but a rational interconnexion. And just as things existent exhibit harmonious co-ordination, so too things coming into being display not bare succession, but a marvellous internal relationship" (Aurelius, iv. 45). That is both scientific and philosophical, nor could either the modern scientist or Spinoza himself have put it more felicitously.

Next, its deep sympathy with Nature, and its clear insight into Nature's workings and processes. There is a note of modernity here, too, that is very striking. On the one hand, we have anticipation of the man of science of to-day, demanding facts and concrete experience ; and, on the other hand, we have Wordsworth and the poets of Nature foreshadowed. "Watch well," counsels Aurelius (*Med.* iii. 2), "the grace and charm, that belong even to the consequents of nature's work. The cracks, for instance, and crevices in bread-crust, though in a sense flaws in the baking, yet have a fitness of their own, and a special stimulus to tickle the appetite. Figs, again, just at perfection, gape. In ripe olives, the very nearness of decay adds its own beauty to the fruit. The bending ears of corn, the lion's scowl, the foam that drips from the wild boar's mouth, and many other things, though in themselves far from beautiful, yet looked at as consequents on nature's handiwork, add new beauty and appeal to the soul, so that if one attains deeper feeling and insight for the workings of the universe, almost everything, even in its consequents and accidents, seems to yield some pleasing combination of its own. Thus the actual jaws of living beasts will be not less picturesque than the imitations produced by artists and sculptors. The old woman and the old man will have an ideal loveliness, as youth its ravishing charm, made visible to the eyes that have the skill. Such things will not appeal to all, but will strike him only who is in harmony with Nature, and her sincere familiar."

This shows great observation of Nature and intimate communing with her, but there is wanting that keen appreciation of the *beauty* of Nature as manifesting the divine and the ideal that is characteristic of modern philosophy. The beauty recognized is that of suitability to circumstances or adaptation of means to ends, rather than the beauty of shade and colour, seen in the clouds and the sunset, etc.,—it is scientific more than æsthetic. This is in line with the Stoic's central conception of morality, which emphasizes the *grandeur*, rather than the *beauty*, of holiness. Order and harmony, in nature and in morals alike, are to him supreme: the artistic side of either is only secondary—hardly even that.

Again, its intensely experiential character. Both its psychology and its ethics, no less than its religion, are based on, and tested by, experience. Human nature as we find it, and the external world as known to ourselves through inductive study of it, are the stable foundations of the Stoic philosophy; and speculation and theory are only subsequent and grounded on our knowledge of these.

This also is very modern. The "reign of law" in
Nature which science postulates, is the very keystone
of Stoicism ; and the Stoical conception of the cosmic
process as ethical or righteous, reached through in-
tently watching the outcome of occurrences and events
and the trend of human history, is a clear anticipation
of Fichte and Matthew Arnold, a clear recognition of
"the eternal not-ourselves that makes for righteousness," a finger-post to Hegel and the philosophy of
history.

A further point is its unwearied insistence upon
Character as the supreme concern for man. This gives
a distinctive note to Stoicism, and marks it off from
the opportunism of other creeds and other times. "No
compromise" was here the motto,—"no tampering
with principle." Hence the stimulating power that
Stoicism has had in every age when men have shown
themselves to be really in earnest, and the standing
rebuke it has been to worldly-mindedness and in-
differentism. "Live as on a mountain. It matters not
whether here or there ; everywhere you are a citizen of
the city of the world. Let men see and witness a true
man, a life conformed to nature. If they cannot bear
him, let them make away with him. Better that, than
life on their terms" (Aurelius, *Med.* x. 15).

Further, its reverent and devout spirit, and, in
particular, its acknowledgment and keen appreciation
of the psychological basis of religion, and, therefore, its
recognition of the need of religion for man. To the
Stoics, God is a necessity of human nature ; which is

technically expressed by saying that He is a πρόληψις or primary conception of the mind, and, popularly, in the argument known as *consensus gentium*, or the general consent of mankind. No great help, however, was given by Stoicism in determining the idea of God, inasmuch as the Stoics oscillated between pantheism and monotheism, and seemed not to feel the need of an absolutely definite conception. Nevertheless, the idea had for them ethical or moral, as well as intellectual, content, so that the nature of man that craved for or demanded a Deity was his *whole* nature, not merely a part of it—not the intellect alone (as with Aristotle), nor the conscience alone (as with Kant), nor feeling chiefly (as with Schleiermacher). Not a little of their theistic reasoning would commend itself to the modern theist, who essays above all things to find a thorough-going basis in human nature (feeling, intellect, and will alike) for his Natural Theology.[1]

Next, its firm belief in the World as a manifestation of Divine Order, and man's life and human society as a plan of God. " Order is Heaven's first law "; and social order is binding, not simply through its utility, but because it comes with the divine sanction—law in every form means God. The consequence of this conviction was an optimism which was both invigorating and robust, and a trust and submission so unflinching that even to come into contact with it elevates and stirs. " Man, be desperate now, as the saying is, on behalf of happiness, on behalf of liberty, on behalf of high-mindedness. Lift up your head at this time as one

[1] Cf. my *Theism as grounded in Human Nature.*

released from slavery.　Dare to look up to God and say, ' Use me for the future for whatsoever purpose Thou willest, I am of one mind with Thee, I am Thine ; nothing do I refuse of the things that seem good to Thee ; whithersoever Thou willest, lead me ; in whatsoever dress Thou willest, clothe me.　Dost Thou will me to hold a position of authority, to live as a private individual, to remain here, to go into exile, to be poor, to be rich ?　I will be Thy advocate for all these positions to men ; I will show the nature of each of them what it is ' " (Epictetus, *Diss.* ii. 16).

" Man, you have been a citizen of the great world city—" so does Aurelius close his *Meditations.*　" Five years or fifty, what matters it ?　To every man his due, as law allots.　Why then protest ?　No tyrant gives you your dismissal, no unjust judge, but nature who gave you the admission.　It is like the prætor discharging some player whom he has engaged.— ' But the five acts are not complete ; I have played but three.'—Good : life's drama, look you, is complete in three.　The completeness is in his hands, who first authorised your composition, and now your dissolution ; neither was your work.　Serenely take your leave ; serene as he who gives you the discharge."

There is here a very noble trait of Stoic teaching. What alone is wanting in this matter of willing acquiescence in the Deity and one's destiny is the hope or faith as to the individual's future that characterizes the modern theist, or the thinker who has a firm apprehension of the personality of God.　The ultimate destination of the present world, according to Stoical notions, is to be burned up at the Great Conflagration, and yet, in the cycle-revolution, to be reproduced again with all its imperfections. The sinful, troubled, sorrowing individuals that now are, will be reborn to the same sins, troubles, sorrows, time after time ; no progress being made in the future, nor advance of any kind. This, certainly, should have toned down the Stoic's optimism ; it might have been expected, at any rate, to strip it somewhat of its exuberance. It was, perhaps, some such feeling as this that led a section of the later Stoics—notably Panætius—to dissent from the doctrine of World-cycles, which had so fascinated the founders of the School, and had been so carefully and fully elaborated by Cleanthes. But their implicit trust in the World-order remained, notwithstanding ; and the Stoic's attitude has its lessons for the moderns.

Once again, the high estimate that the Stoics entertained of human nature itself, as partaking of the divine. Human reason is a part of the κοινὸς λόγος, or universal reason : " Each man's mind is god, an efflux of deity " (Aurelius, *Med.* xii. 26). Hence man's dignity and worth,—especially on the side of virtue and will-power or self-control. "Virtue and truth are the same in man as in God." There is no great step from this to the Scriptural teaching of man as made in the image of God—" in our image, after our likeness."[1] It is a noble view to take of a man—(a) that he need not, if he care, break the law of righteousness at all ; but, (b) that, if he do break it, he has it in his power to retrace his steps and to regain his position. Only to a being of transcendent worth could the motto be given as

[1] Gen. i. 26.

his rule of conduct, "Bear and forbear (ἀνέχου καὶ ἀπέχου)."

Lastly, the vivid apprehension (in the case of the later Stoics) of the dependence of true happiness, on the one hand, on cheerful submission to the course of the world, as being a manifestation of Divine law and rule, both wise and good ; and, on the other hand, on realization of the fact of the brotherhood of man, "not by blood or physical descent, but by community of mind" and "partnership with the Divine," and willing performance of the duties thence arising, on the ground that society or the community is an organism, part of the Divine order, and subservient to the highest good.   Peace within is the great thing ; and peace within can be got only from a high conception of Duty and an effort faithfully to do our work.   We have here a voice from the past meeting a voice in the present.   "There is in man a Higher than love of Happiness : he can do without happiness, and instead thereof find Blessedness !   Was it not to preach forth this Higher that sages and martyrs, the Poet and the Priest, in all times, have spoken and suffered ; bearing testimony, through life and through death, of the Godlike that is in Man, and how in the Godlike only has he Strength and Freedom ?   Which God-inspired Doctrine art thou also honoured to be taught ; O heavens ! and broken with manifold merciful Afflictions, even until thou become contrite and learn it !   O, thank thy Destiny for these ; thankfully bear what yet remain : thou hadst need of them ; the Self in thee needed to be annihilated.   By benignant fever-paroxysms is Life rooting out the deep-seated chronic disease, and triumphs over Death. On the roaring billows of Time thou art not engulfed but borne aloft into the azure of Eternity. Love not Pleasure ; love God. This is the Everlasting Yea, wherein all contradiction is solved : wherein whoso walks and works, it is well with him " (Carlyle, *Sartor Resartus*, ii. 9).

Again, could anything, on high religious lines, be nobler than the following utterance of Epictetus about Duty, and about the privilege of man as a rational being to live in conscious union with the Supreme and to joyfully serve Him ? "For," he says, "had we understanding, ought we to do anything else, jointly and severally, than hymn the divine, and praise Him, and rehearse His benefits ? Ought we not, when digging or ploughing or eating, to sing this hymn to God ? 'Great is God, inasmuch as He has given us those instruments whereby we till the earth. Great is God, inasmuch as He has given us hands, and swallowing, and a belly, and the power of growing secretly and breathing while we sleep.' These things it were meet that every one should praise, and should chant the greatest and most divine hymn, inasmuch as He has given us the faculty of understanding these things and of using the proper way. What then ? Since the majority of you are blinded, ought there not to be someone to fill this place, and, on behalf of all, to sing the hymn to God ? For what else can I do, an old lame man, than sing hymns to God ? If, indeed, I were a nightingale, I would do as a nightingale ; if a swan, as a swan. But now I am a rational being ; it behoves me to sing of God.

This is my work ; this I do, nor will I relinquish this post, so long as I am permitted, and you I exhort to join in the same song " (*Diss.* i. 16).

III

In all these respects, then, Stoicism may be confidently affirmed to have perennial value ; and, in particular, its ethico-religious interpretation of the universe, not only stands as a notable landmark in the history of philosophy, but possesses the illuminating and inspiriting power of a great truth, to which modern philosophy is again reverting, and which, one would fain believe, will continue to exert an influence so long as sane thought and right reason retain their hold on mankind. And, coming down to practice, when we look at such treatises as the *Dissertations* and the *Encheiridion* of Epictetus and the *Meditations* of Marcus Aurelius, as aids to practical ethics, we see that these can never die : the wisdom that is enshrined in them is for all ages. If, in the words of Farrar, " the *Manual* [of Epictetus] was to antiquity what the *Imitatio* of Thomas à Kempis was to later times, and what Woodhead's *Whole Duty of Man*, or Wilberforce's *Practical View of Christianity*, have been to large sections of modern Englishmen " ; so also it is the case that " no systematic treatise of morals so simply beautiful was ever composed [as the *Encheiridion*], and to this day the best Christian may study it, not with interest only, but with real advantage. It is like the voice of the Sibyl, which, uttering things simple, and unperfumed, and unadorned, by God's grace reacheth through innumerable years " (*Seekers after God*,

p. 222). And if so with Epictetus, so too with Aurelius:
not even the best Christian need despise the high
ethical teaching of the *Meditations*, which fair-minded
thinkers like John Stuart Mill (see his posthumous
essay on the *Utility of Religion*) have deemed worthy
of being brought into comparison with the Sermon on
the Mount, all the more so that the author's life was
conscientiously moulded on his own precepts. As well
despise the Book of Proverbs, or the Epistle of St. James,
or the exhortations of St. Paul, as the *Meditations.*

Nor can the philosophical writings of Seneca be
other than helpful to high-toned people, eager about
right living.

The problems of life are too complex and man's
interest in them too intense to permit of our neglect-
ing, much less despising, any serious effort, in whatsoever age and from whatsoever quarter, to cope with
them ; and the issues are too momentous and too far-
reaching, to justify illiberality in any form. Wisdom
is not the monopoly of any century, or of any person,
or of any people, but "is justified of *all* her children."
Moreover, to theists, the notion of a progressive revelation (place and time being essential moments) is so
necessary to the adequate conception of the Divinity,
that it forbids our restricting the divine revelation to
a single age or section of mankind—to a single school
or country. Christian theism is even more emphatic.
For if Christ is "the Light of the world," it would be
a very feeble rendering of that supreme truth to maintain that the Light did not shine in the far past, as in
the near present, nor there, but only here, and that He

who "made of one blood all nations of men," left all nations of men, save a very few, and all individuals, save a miserable minority, to sit in utter darkness and to generate only falsehood and error. The thought is utterly derogatory to our idea of God, and more especially as that is presented to us in Christ, which will not allow our shutting ourselves out from intercourse and sympathy with the great intellectual past and from the noble souls that illuminated former times and alien lands, and put posterity under an undying obligation. We cut ourselves off from history, and we cut ourselves off from the fulness of the Christian conception alike, if we do not appreciate the high teaching of the Stoics, which, as a matter of fact, led up to and served in measure to mould the ethics of the New Testament, and if we cannot include in "the communion of saints" those pure and noble thinkers (pagans, as we grimly call them) who strove so hard for the cause of righteousness on the earth, enriching humanity, and made the advent of the later civilization possible. Here, as strongly as anywhere, comes home to us the sentiment that "truth is catholic, and nature one."

APPENDIX

—◆—

PRAGMATISM AND HUMANISM
(See pp. 9 and 130)

THE prominence of Pragmatism as a philosophical doctrine at the present moment, and its contact with Stoicism at important points, demand, perhaps, that some brief account of it be here offered and some estimate made of its value.

I

Pragmatism (from the Greek πρᾶγμα, signifying act or deed) is the name that has been given to the recent movement in philosophy which lays the stress on doing or the practical activities of human nature in the interpretation of truth and reality. It originated some time ago with Mr. Charles S. Peirce in America, but has come to Great Britain (name and thing) mainly through Professor William James of Harvard University, who, taking it from Mr. Peirce, reproduced it a few years since in his *Will to Believe*, and, later on, in his *Philosophical Conceptions and Practical Results*, and who is at present actively engaged in defending it against all comers in philosophical magazines—British and other. It has been further developed by Mr. F. C. S. Schiller, of Corpus Christi College, Oxford, who, unmindful of the august associations of the old literary term, has rechristened it "Humanism"—with reference, presumably, to the fact that it makes "man the measure" (*homo mensura*), or bases itself in human nature and human experience.[1]

Of course, it is not a new thing in philosophy to have the practical side of man's nature calling for recognition. Indeed, every philosophy that is supremely and in the first instance *ethical* (such as that of the Stoics), may be termed "pragmatical"; and Kant himself may be designated a pragmatist, if you look merely at the fact that his Ethics gives us his highest teaching, supplementing and transcending that of the Pure Reason. But what is new is the attempt to base cognition as well as ethics on practice—to lay theory of knowledge, as well as morality and æsthetics, on this foundation.

According to Pragmatism, it is not man's intellect or reason (as has been so long maintained) that determines reality and truth, but his will and his feelings—action with a purpose or for an end, action in response to human needs ; and thought itself springs from the same practical root—as Professor James puts it "concepts are teleological instruments." That is true which serves an end or works out a purpose—in other words, which is useful, which produces beneficial consequences, which satisfies us ; that is false which fails to do this. Says the pragmatist, "If it can make no practical difference which of two statements be true, then they are really one statement in two verbal forms ; if it can make no practical difference whether a given statement be true or false, then the statement has no real meaning." Again, "The ultimate test for us of what a truth means is indeed the conduct it dictates or inspires." And again, "To attain perfect clearness in our thoughts of an object, we need only consider what effects of a

---

[1] For a keen controversy regarding it, see *Mind* for the years 1904-1906.

conceivably practical kind the object may involve—
what sensations we are to expect from it and what
reactions we must prepare. *Our conception of these
results*, then, is for us *the whole of our conception of the
object*, so far as that conception has positive significance
at all." [1] Still further, as Mr. Schiller maintains, [2]
" The truth of a thing is to be found in its validity—
which, however, must be *connected* rather than *contrasted*
with its origin. 'What a thing really is' appears from
what it *does*, and so we must study its whole career.
We study its past to forecast its future, and to find out
what it is really 'driving at.' Any complete explanation, therefore, is by final causes, and implies a knowledge of ends and aims which we can often only
imperfectly detect." Hence, Mr. Schiller holds that all
Axioms were originally *Postulates*: you begin by assuming, guessing, supposing, and then act on your
assumption, guess, or supposition ; and if your action
succeeds, the assumption is justified, and if it goes on
succeeding time after time, then the postulate becomes
an axiom—you regard it as universal and as necessary.

The appeal, then, is to experience and consequences :
truth, in order to be true, must have practical results,
it must work—yea more, in the wider humanism, it
consists in consequences, more especially if these are
good. Our beliefs are determined by practical interest.
We believe what serves our purpose, or what points to
an end which we desire, or what satisfies our needs :
we disbelieve what serves no purpose, or what has
proved to be misleading or inadequate to meet our
wants. So, too, of morality : human needs and their
satisfaction determine between right and wrong, and
give us the ethical notions.

Thus, then, in pragmatism (not least in its developed

---

[1] See *Mind*, as already referred to.
[2] See his chapter in Mr. Sturt's *Personal Idealism*, p. 125.

17

form of humanism), the stress is laid on human nature, and more particularly on the practical needs of it ; and reality, as well as truth, is that which interests us and in which we find satisfaction. Other reality there can be none ; for, until a thing interests us and wins our affection, it is nothing to us, but, when it does so, it cannot be taken as anything apart from the subject— its nature is, in measure, determined by its relation to the subject. Reality and truth alike, therefore, are tested by experience and find their verification therein ; and, in the long run, the two are one.

And so, on its negative side, pragmatism is a protest against *a priorism* and Absolutism ; neither of which submits to experience. Indeed, it owes its existence to reaction against that extreme intellectualism which so long ruled, where man was contemplated simply as a rational being, his emotive and his volitional nature being ignored. It is, consequently, essentially inductive in its method, and breathes the scentific spirit through-out. It will not permit truth to be relegated to a transcendent sphere to which experience has no access, nor will it allow experience to be dictated to by mere unverified and unverifiable *a priori* conceptions. The Absolute, if it is taken in the pure metaphysical sense, —as we find it, say, in Mr. Bradley's *Appearance and Reality*, — is a mere name without a meaning, "a worthless technicality" : it sheds no light on life's problems, it solves no difficulties ; on the contrary, it darkens and confuses. Difficulties disappear only under what *works*, and hypotheses have value only if they be *working* hypotheses.

Thus we are done with the old order of things ; and the advance of science has effected the change. "'God geometrises,' it used to be said ; and it was believed that Euclid's *Elements* (I am quoting Professor James, *Mind*, vol. xiii. p. 459) literally reproduced his

geometrising. There is an eternal and unchangeable
' Reason ' ; and its voice was supposed to reverberate
in *Barbara* and *Celarent*. So also of the ' laws of
Nature,' physical and chemical, so of natural history
classifications—all were supposed to be exact and
exclusive duplicates of pre-human archetypes buried
in the structure of things, to which the spark of divinity
hidden in our intellect enables us to penetrate. The
anatomy of the world is logical, and its logic is that of
a university professor, it was thought. . . . But the
enormously rapid multiplication of theories in these
latter days has well nigh upset the notion of any one of
them being a more literally objective kind of thing than
another. There are so many geometries, so many
logics, so many physical and chemical hypotheses, so
many classifications, each one of them good for so much
and yet not good for everything, that the notion that
even the truest formula may be a human device and
not a literal transcript has dawned upon us. . . . It is
to be doubted whether any theoriser to-day, either in
mathematics, logic, physics, or biology, conceives
himself to be literally re-editing processes of Nature or
thoughts of God. The main forms of our thinking, the
separation of subjects from predicates, the negative,
hypothetic, and disjunctive judgments, are purely human
habits. The ether, as Lord Salisbury said, is only a
noun for the verb to undulate. . . . The suspicion is in
the air nowadays that the superiority of one of our
formulas to another may not consist so much in its
literal ' objectivity,' as in subjective qualities like its
usefulness, its ' elegance,' or its congruity with residual
beliefs. Yielding to these suspicions, and generalising,
we fall into something like the humanistic state of
mind. Truth we conceive to mean anywhere, not
duplication, but addition ; not the constructing of inner
copies of already complete realities, but rather the

reacting on imperfect realities so as to bring about a clearer result." Consequently, truth is synthetic in its nature, and not merely analytic.

Such, then, is Pragmatisn or Humanism in brief summary. Let us note—also briefly—its merits and its defects.

II

One great merit is its insistence on or recourse to Experience (widely interpreted), and the necessity of recognizing the emotional and volitional sides of human nature, no less than its rational or intellectual side. That we attend only to what interests us, and that what interests us serves some end or purpose, is a commonplace of modern psychology. We think with a view to an end ; and we believe, in great part, because our belief works out in practice. Human needs do certainly lie at the root of cognition and of belief, no less than of conduct ; and we think and believe in a particular way so long as that way satisfies us or ministers to our desires—only, in estimating our desires, we must take the whole man into account and not merely a part of him ; we must view him *totus, teres atque rotundus*. A belief, for the most part, is not a simple but a complex thing. If it is grounded in the intellect, it is affected also by feeling, association, and interest or conation ; and the strength of it, in the case of any firm conviction, is only partially accounted for by pointing out its rationality : it is the result of many co-operant factors. The forces that play upon us, moulding this way or that, are very diverse, and they all have a practical bearing. Consequently, it is " wisdom " rather than " knowledge " that determines belief, σοφία more than ἐπιστήμη ; and faith enters in, for there is always a *venture* in belief—we trust, where we cannot see.

Pragmatism is thus a wholesome protest against a too narrow or one-sided interpretation of human nature, and against wild speculation divorced from experience. If the primary motive that impels mankind is *to live and to continue living*, then everything must be tested by its bearing on this primordial impulse. To live is to work ; and whatever conserves life, and, still more, whatever conduces to its betterment and fulness, as well as to its conservation, is of primary importance.

Consequently, pragmatism deals with concrete experience, and refuses to be guided by mere abstract thought. " It is the individual concrete experience in all its fulness," says Mr. Schiller (in *Personal Idealism*, p. 127), " which every man worthy of the name wants philosophy to interpret for him ; and a philosophy which fails to do this is for him false."

In this way, in its theory of knowledge, pragmatism refuses to separate subject from object, or to countenance any such unmanageable antithesis between mind and matter as that which Descartes and the Cartesians made. Reality is given in and through our activities ; apart from these, it is a name without a meaning.

So, also, with regard to character and conduct, it insists on concrete experience, and interprets ethical notions in the light of the whole of man's nature, taken, of course, in relation to his environment (social, in particular).

Hence, it protests against mere criticism of incidental points in its doctrine, against mere logic-chopping, which dissects without uniting in a comprehensive view —" confutation by single decisive reasons." It insists that " the one condition of understanding humanism is to become inductive-minded oneself, to drop rigorous definitions, and follow lines of least resistance on the whole.' " [1]

[1] Professor James, in *Mind*, vol. xiv. pp. 190–191.

Lastly, pragmatism has good ground for resisting Absolutism, if by Absolutism is meant the doctrine that demands an Absolute out of all relation to us and incapable of ever being brought into relation ; or if it means a ghostly otiose something, serving no purpose and explanatory of nothing at all. If the Absolute be approached from the side of our activities, an Absolute of the purely intellectual and bloodless type is an impossibility. " ' Pure thought ' which is not tested by action and correlated with experience, means nothing, and in the end turns out mere pseudo-thought." [1]

III

But pragmatism or Humanism, with its virtues, has also its defects ; two of which may here be specialized.

For one thing, *it over-emphasizes action or the will.* In its eagerness to avoid the lop-sidedness of in-tellectualism, it is prone to fall into the opposite extreme of pure voluntarism. It objects to intellect-ualism (an objection perfectly relevant to intellectual monism, Spinozistic or other) that, while the intellect-ualist explicitly admits that man is not merely intellect, but has also feelings and conative impulses which must be reckoned with by the philosopher, he has no sooner made the admission than he proceeds to ignore it, going on his way henceforth unimpeded by it and building up his system on the sole assumption that man is an intellectual being, and that everything must be explained and interpreted solely in the light of reason. But the intellectualist may very well turn round on the pragmatist and say, "You too are very explicit in your enunciation that man's personality consists of feeling, intellect, and will (not of one of

[1] Mr. Schiller, *Personal Idealism*, p. 128.

these alone, but of all three, and all three mutually implicated and interactive); more especially, you insist that there is "no intellection except for practical purposes."[1] But immediately you go on as though will was everything. It suits you, in advocating voluntarism, to associate intellection with volition (and rightly enough); but it is no less convenient for you (and this wrongly) forthwith to forget that, if the theoretical is nothing apart from the practical, 'the practical is always the theoretical in its fulfilment.'"

This, I say, is what the intellectualist may very properly rejoin. For there is no question that pragmatists are disposed to commit two errors.

In the first place, they are apt to forget, and they do forget, that if knowledge and morality, if our ideas and our conduct, are determined by an end or purpose, this very fact of end or purpose, this very fact of a plan being presupposed, implies an intellectual factor. In all conscious actions, intellectual postulates are involved. We must apprehend what we consciously aim at, otherwise our volition would become chance-determined. The true and the right cannot lie in the mere realization of an end or purpose, unless the end or purpose be itself first assumed to be true or right, unless we have some pre-determined or accepted scale of values. There are ends and ends; and even with false or unrighteous ends we may, under certain circumstances, be satisfied: in other words, realizing an end and resting satisfied therewith characterize the true and the right, and the false and the wrong, alike; and if the distinction between these is to be upheld, a criterion must be found outside mere desire and its fulfilment.

But, in the next place, pragmatists deal unfairly with intellect. Sometimes they ignore it, or so sub-

[1] See Professor James, *The Will to Believe*, p. 140.

ordinate it to will and feeling as to disparage it; thereby forgetting their own doctrine that man must be taken in his entire personality, that feeling, intellect, and will are all functions of human nature, and each is of co-ordinate value with the others, and that they are, moreover, mutually implicated—where the one is, the others are also. There can be no real harmony or complete development of our being, if any one of these is degraded. But sometimes also they write as though intellect were actually resolved into feeling and volition, were actually created or "originated" by action; thereby confounding things that differ, and dispensing with that mental function which is perhaps the most fundamental of all, and without which there could be no discrimination or apprehension of difference, and, therefore, no consciousness.

The other defect that calls for notice is, that pragmatism, *though strong psychologically, is weak metaphysically.*

Indeed, metaphysics is distasteful to the pragmatist or humanist: he condemns "all noble, clean-cut, fixed, eternal, rational, temple-like systems of philosophy" (so Professor James puts it);[1] and he gives the following in the humanist's defence:—"These contradict the temperament of Nature, as our dealings with Nature and our habits of thinking have so far brought us to conceive it. They seem oddly personal and artificial, even when not bureaucratic and professional in an absurd degree. We turn from them to the great unpent and unstayed wilderness of Truth as we feel it to be constituted, with as good a conscience as rationalists are moved by when they turn from our wilderness into their neater and cleaner intellectual abodes."

[1] See *Mind*, vol, xiii, p. 467,

This surely is an extreme position. For, although metaphysical systems may not, any one of them, be fully satisfactory—although you may be dissatisfied with Spinoza and Hegel and the Absolutists generally —nevertheless, Nature itself is nothing, even according to the humanists, unless *teleologically* interpreted, and that means metaphysics ; nor is Experience enough to guide us (as even Locke discovered), unless we take along with it its rational implications.

Surely, if human wants are to be the test of truth, as humanists maintain, our *rational* wants must count for something ; and the craving for unity is as natural, and, therefore, as legitimate, as any other. It is misleading to represent Nature as "the great unpent and unstayed wilderness of Truth," and to set it in direct opposition to the rational interpretation of Nature. Nature is only an "unpent and unstayed wilderness" in the sense that our experience is ever widening and ever deepening. But if nature is uniform and our experience is amenable to law, that means that the principles of it are *fixed*, and, in that sense, may be designated "eternal." No metaphysical system need regard Nature as a *known* completed whole ; *stationary*, therefore, for we have exhausted it ; *unprogressive*, for it has nothing further to reveal. Metaphysics is quite compatible with evolution and development, and with a progressive revelation in a progressive experience. But it holds that "evolution," "development," "progress" must proceed upon lines that are already foreshadowed ; and that the process presupposes a *whole*, within which it operates and towards which it tends, and in the light of which, although we may not yet have perfect vision, it finds its interpretation. Have we perfect vision of *any* ideal? And yet ideals are what move us and lead us to higher and ever higher acquisitions. Science, Religion, Morality, Politics,

Education aim at the ideal. Not one of these has full perception of that at which it aims ; and yet the concept is definite enough to be effective. Shall the ideal of the metaphysician alone be incompetent, as being the ideal of a whole interpenetrating and inclusive of all human aspirations and activities (both theoretical and practical), and giving meaning to every other ideal ? At any rate, it is implicitly supposed in science, as in the other provinces, and its ineradicability from human nature, and the satisfaction that it brings to the individual in harmonizing life and experience, should commend it to the pragmatist and humanist, to whom harmony and satisfaction are everything.

INDEX

———

Printed by MORRISON & GIBB LIMITED, *Edinburgh*

MORALS AND LAW IN ANCIENT GREECE

An Arno Press Collection

Apffel, Helmut. **Die Verfassungsdebatte Bei Herodot (3,80-82),** Wuest, Karl, **Politisches Denken Bei Herodot** and Bruns, Ivo, **Frauenemancipation in Athen.** Three vols. in one. 1957/1935/1900

Bevan, Edwyn. **Stoics and Sceptics.** 1913

Bolkestein, Hendrik. **Wohltaetigkeit und Armenpflege im Vorchristlichen Altertum.** 1939

Bolkestein, Johanna Christina. **Hosios En Eusebēs,** and Bolkestein, Hendrik, **Theophrastos' Charakter der Deisidaimonia als Religionsgeschichtliche Urkunde.** Two vols. in one. 1936/1929

Bonner, Robert J. **Evidence in Athenian Courts,** and Harrell, Hansen Carmine, **Public Arbitration in Athenian Law.** Two vols. in one. 1905/1936

Caillemer, Exupère. **Études Sur Les Antiquités Juridiques D'Athènes.** Ten parts in one. 1865-1872

Clerc, Michel. **Les Métèques Athéniens.** 1893

Fustel De Coulanges, [Numa Denis]. **Recherches Sur Le Droit De Propriété Chez Les Grecs** and **Recherches Sur Le Tirage Au Sort Appliqué À La Nomination Des Archontes Athéniens.** 1891

Croissant, Jeanne. **Aristote et Les Mystères.** 1932

Davidson, William L. **The Stoic Creed.** 1907

Demosthenes. **Demosthenes Against Midias.** With Critical and Explanatory Notes and an Appendix by William Watson Goodwin. 1906

Demosthenes. **Demosthenes on the Crown.** With Critical and Explanatory Notes; An Historical Sketch and Essays by William Watson Goodwin. 1901

Demosthenes. **Demosthenes Against Androtion and Against Timocrates.** With Introductions and English Notes by William Wayte. Second Edition. 1893

Demoulin, Hubert. **Épiménide De Crète.** 1901

Diogenes, Laertius. **La Vie De Pythagore De Diogène Laërce.** Édition Critique Avec Introduction et Commentaire par A[rmand] Delatte. 1922

Dyroff, Adolf. **Die Ethik Der Alten Stoa.** 1897

Egermann, Franz. **Vom Attischen Menschenbild** and **Arete und Tragisches Bewusstheit Bei Sophokles und Herodot.** Two vols. in one. [1952]/1957

Erdmann, Walter. **Die Ehe im Alten Griechenland.** 1934

Ferguson, John. **Moral Values in the Ancient World.** 1958

Forman, Ludovico Leaming. **Index Andocideus, Lycurgeus, Dinarcheus** and Preuss, Siegmund, **Index Aeschineus.** Two vols. in one. 1897/1896

Gernet, Louis. **Droit et Société Dans La Grèce Ancienne.** 1955

Gigante, Marcello. **Nomos Basileus.** 1956

Glotz, Gustave. **L'Ordalie Dans La Grèce Primitive.** 1904

Guiraud, Paul. **La Propriété Foncière En Grèce Jusqu'à La Conquête Romaine.** 1893

Haussoullier, B[ernard]. **La Vie Municipale En Attique.** 1883

Hemelrijk, Jacob. **Penia en Ploutos.** 1925

Hirzel, Rudolf. **Agraphos Nomos,** and Marg, Walter, **Der Charakter in Der Sprache Der Fruehgriechischen Dichtung.** Two vols. in one. 1900/1938

Hirzel, Rudolf. **Der Eid:** Ein Beitrag Zu Seiner Geschichte. 1902

Hitzig, Hermann Ferdinand. **Das Griechische Pfandrecht.** 1895

Hruza, Ernst. **Die Ehebegruendung Nach Attischem Rechte** *and* **Polygamie und Pellikat Nach Griechischem Rechte.** Two vols. in one. 1892/1894

Jost, Karl. **Das Beispiel Und Vorbild Der Vorfahren.** 1935

Kohler, Josef and Erich Ziebarth. **Das Stadtrecht Von Gortyn Und Seine Beziehungen Zum Gemeingriechischen Rechte.** 1912

Koestler, Rudolf. **Homerisches Recht** and Vos, Harm, **Themis.** Two vols. in one. 1950/1956

Kunsemueller, Otto. **Die Herkunft Der Platonischen Kardinaltugenden** and Wankel, Hermann, **Kalos Kai Agathos.** Two vols. in one. 1935/1961

Leisi, Ernst. **Der Zeuge Im Attischen Recht** and Schlesinger, Eilhard, **Die Griechische Asylie.** Two vols. in one. 1908/1933

Lotze, Detlef. **Metaxy Eleutherōn Kai Doulōn** and Hampl, Franz, **Die Lakedaemonischen Perioeken.** Two vols. in one. 1959/1937

Lofberg, John Oscar. **Sycophancy in Athens** and Barkan, Irving, **Capital Punishment in Ancient Athens** (Doctoral Dissertation, The University of Chicago, 1935). Two vols. in one. 1917/1935

Martin, Victor. **La Vie Internationale Dans La Grèce Des Cités.** 1940

Maschke, Richard. **Die Willenslehre Im Griechischen Recht.** 1926

Meier, Moritz Hermann Eduard and Georg Friedrich Schoemann. **Der Attische Process.** 1824

Menzel, Adolf. **Hellenika:** Gesammelte Kleine Schriften. 1938

Minar, Edwin L., Jr. **Early Pythagorean Politics in Practice and Theory.** 1942

Oliver, James H.. **Demokratia, The Gods, and The Free World.** 1960

Phillipson, Coleman. **The International Law and Custom of Ancient Greece and Rome.** Volume I. 1911

Pickard-Cambridge, A[rthur] W[allace]. **Demosthenes and the Last Days of Greek Freedom, 384-322 B.C.** 1914

Pringsheim, Fritz. **Der Kauf Mit Fremdem Geld.** 1916

Robinson, David M. and Edward J. Fluck. **A Study of the Greek Love-Names.** 1937

Romilly, Jacqueline De. **Thucydides and Athenian Imperialism.** Translated by Philip Thody. 1963

Schaefer, Arnold. **Demosthenes Und Seine Zeit.** Three vols. 1856/1856/1858

Schodorf, Konrad. **Beitraege Zur Genaueren Kenntnis Der Attischen Gerichtssprache Aus Den Zehn Rednern** and Demisch, Edwin, **Die Schuldenerbfolge Im Attischen Recht.** Two vols. in one. 1904/1910

Schulthess, Otto. **Vormundschaft Nach Attischem Recht.** 1886

[Shellens], Max Salomon. **Der Begriff Der Gerechtigkeit Bei Aristoteles.** 1937

Szanto, Emil. **Das Griechische Buergerrecht.** 1892

Toutain, Jules. **The Economic Life of the Ancient World.** Translated by M. R. Dobie. 1930

Voegelin, Walter. **Die Diabole Bei Lysias.** 1943

Vollgraff, [Carl] W[ilhelm]. **L'Oraison Funèbre De Gorgias.** 1952

188   3901
Dav

THE STOLIC CREED